Rhetorical Knowledge in Legal Practice and Critical Legal Theory

Rhetoric, Culture, and Social Critique

Series Editor
John Louis Lucaites

Rhetorical Knowledge in Legal Practice and Critical Legal Theory

FRANCIS J. MOOTZ III

The University of Alabama Press
Tuscaloosa

Typeface: Perpetua

∞

The paper on which this book is printed meets the minimum requirements of American National Standard for Information Sciences-Permanence of Paper for Printed Library Materials, ANSI Z39.48–1984.

Library of Congress Cataloging-in-Publication Data

Mootz, Francis J., III.
Rhetorical knowledge in legal practice and critical legal theory / Francis J. Mootz III.
p. cm. — (Rhetoric, culture, and social critique)
Includes bibliographical references and index.
ISBN-13: 978-0-8173-1536-8 (cloth : alk. paper)
ISBN-10: 0-8173-1536-5 (alk. paper)
1. Law—Philosophy. 2. Rhetoric. 3. Critical legal studies. 4. Rhetoric. I. Title. II. Series.
K230.M662R48 2006
340′.1—dc22

2006008278

For Caren

for showing me—in ways that books cannot—the vital importance of being a conversation partner

And for Catherine and Daniel

to whom I dedicate this book with love and with confidence in the future that they will help to shape

Contents

Acknowledgments

At this point, this book is a mystery to me; nevertheless, I want to attempt to acknowledge some of the important contributions to my project. This book grew out of an article that originally appeared as Francis J. Mootz III, "Rhetorical Knowledge in Legal Practice and Theory," *Southern California Interdisciplinary Law Journal* 6.3 (1998), and also borrows from material that originally appeared as part of Francis J. Mootz III, "Nietzschean Critique and Philosophical Hermeneutics," *Cardozo Law Review* 24.3 (2003). Although the material has been revised and updated, I remain deeply indebted to those persons and organizations identified in the articles for helping me get this project under way, and I gratefully acknowledge the permission of the *Cardozo Law Review* to use that article as a substantial basis for the book.

Several people read earlier versions of this manuscript in whole or in part, and they provided excellent suggestions as I revised the text for publication. I especially wish to thank Gene Garver, George Taylor, and John Valauri for their careful attention to the manuscript and for their many helpful conversations about hermeneutics, rhetoric, and law over the years. Carlos Ball reviewed my assessment of the *Lawrence* case and offered suggestions and comments that aided my revision of the manuscript. Rob Melick (Dickinson Law School 2007) carefully read the manuscript to identify infelicities and citation problems.

Finally, the series editor, John Lucaites, the acquisitions editor, Dan Waterman, and all of the other professionals at the University of Alabama Press have made navigating this project through the shoals of modern publishing enjoyable. The anonymous reviewers provided very helpful suggestions and critiques, and I thank them for approaching the work seriously and carefully. My copy editor, Lady Vowell Smith, did a superb job as well.

I recall the inspiration provided by two of my professors with gratitude and admiration, and hope that my efforts come close to meeting the standards set by Fred Dallmayr of the University of Notre Dame and William Poteat of Duke University. It is impossible to say more without implicating all of the numerous teachers, colleagues, students, and friends who have helped me to see the world in a certain way, and to seek to understand it in a more productive manner. That my prejudices are embedded in this text is not cause for regret nor are they in any sense "my" prejudices alone; my hope is that they will prove to be productive prejudices for the reader.

Without the interest, love, and support of Caren, Catherine, and Daniel, this book might have been written but I wouldn't have had much fun slogging through. Thanks for understanding why I sometimes keep my nose buried in a book instead of smelling the roses along the way; thanks even more for dragging me away from the books. I dedicate this book to the three of you.

Introduction
Seeking Justice in a Fragmented Legal Culture

It seems that since our globe, as is said, has shrunk, we have acquired more problems regarding justice than we had in previous generations when nations, countries, and continents were isolated. . . . Today more than ever, the questions of justice are global.

If the golden rule or Kant's Imperatives are the most generally accepted precepts concerning individual justice, then Perelman's question re-emerges: how can the general be translated into the concrete and individual?

We must realize that we will be required repeatedly to return to the starting point of every discussion and re-argue what had been previously determined.

Mieczyslaw Maneli
Perelman's New Rhetoric as Philosophy and Methodology for the Next Century

Gadamerian hermeneutics is not just a parochial ingredient of Continental thought, but an important building stone in the emerging global city and in a dialogically construed cultural ecumenicism.

For Gadamer it is chiefly the multiplicity (or multiculturalism) of Europe which harbors the continent's legacy and promise for the world.

> In a world rent by the competing pulls of Western-style universalism and bellicose modes of ethnocentrism, his accent on cross-cultural engagement opens a vista pointing beyond the dystopias of "melting pot" synthesis and radical fragmentation.
>
> ----------
>
> Hermeneutics from this angle is not a synonym for subjectivism and willful appropriation, but for a sustained, dialogical learning process.
>
> Fred Dallmayr
> "Self and Other: Gadamer and the Hermeneutics of Difference"

> Nietzsche is not interested in providing a theory of truth . . . because truth is not something that admits of final determination by a fixed set of criteria. Truth is the fleeting calm between battles within a war that has no preordained or final victor. What *does* interest Nietzsche, however, is ensuring that the struggle continue and that inquiry not come to an end with the enforced peace of dogmatism.
>
> ----------
>
> The new philosopher's goal, then, is not the discovery of absolute truth but the cultivation of a broad-based and flexible understanding through the incorporation and integration of a number of natural drives, some of them "scientific," others "aesthetic."
>
> Christoph Cox
> *Nietzsche: Naturalism and Interpretation*

The longstanding goal of linking a rigorous, philosophical conception of justice to concrete political action appears infinitely more problematic in a world comprised of competing, incommensurable visions of justice rooted in distinct and rich social traditions of political understanding. Globalization—construed broadly as a social, economic, religious, and political development—raises the specter of relativism, not in the form of a conceptual critique, but as a lived reality. The clash today between Islam and the Judeo-Christian West stands as only one stark reminder of the limits of our ability to theorize justice in a politically effective manner.

The global age threatens to devolve into one of two equally unsatisfactory trajectories: either the concept of justice will be a convenient tool for justifying the triumph of a particular worldview through the exercise of military, economic, and political power, or the vacuity of the concept will be invoked to absolve us of responsibility for the nihilistic chaos resulting from the refusal to permit any one worldview to hold sway. More succinctly stated, the belief that "justice" can serve as a productive point of discussion in a multicultural world rent with deep divisions appears extremely naive and deeply problematic.

There is little need to rehearse the disintegration of the ideal of justice in contemporary philosophical discourse. The current aporia is best revealed by recalling the most ambitious recent efforts to escape its grip. In a flurry of exciting work during the past several decades, John Rawls and Robert Nozick captivated philosophers and political theorists by reviving the question of justice through competing visions of the liberal tradition, Jürgen Habermas held open the possibility of rationally critiquing the justice of social relations within the framework of contemporary Continental philosophy, and Alasdair MacIntyre revived Aristotelian virtue ethics as an antidote to the excessive rationalism that he found in the contemporary alternatives. These impressive projects are part of a vigorous and broad-based effort to rescue justice from the disabling quiescence of modern skepticism. Nevertheless, justice remains a bitterly disputed concept, and these philosophical projects have failed to end the disputations. Reminiscent of the collapse of Greek virtue ethics when exposed to different cultures, the Western quest to articulate the principles of justice appears to have exhausted itself in the face of the challenges of globalization.

Against this broad and overarching backdrop, an equally troubling development has occurred in a much more local venue. Theorists have come to recognize that there is no fixed starting point from which to elaborate the requirements of justice even within the parochial confines of American legal theory. Disarray in the political philosophy of justice is mirrored in contemporary American legal theory, where the mythical halcyon days of objectivism and formalism have receded into vague and wistful memories. The "linguistic turn" in legal theory—comprised of a wide variety of approaches that include ordinary language philosophy, deconstruction, and philosophical hermeneutics—has indelibly shaped jurisprudential inquiry by establishing the indeterminate and political character of legal practice. In its most recent manifestations, however, the linguistic turn threatens to bring legal theory beyond the bounds of reasoned inquiry altogether. Radically deconstructive, postmodern theorists begin with the insight that legal relations are linguistically mediated, but they press this point by arguing that language—inveterately heterogeneous and unstable—precludes the possibility that reason might inform the exercise of power. This critique of legal practice parallels the pessimistic assessment that "discourse" in contemporary global politics is always conducted in the shadow of gunboats (economic as well as military). In short, the linguistic turn in legal theory suggests that the well-recognized problem of defining justice in the age of globalization has always been present, although vigorously suppressed, within the familiar confines of American legal thought. The dread lurking behind much contemporary legal theory might be summarized thus: "We have met the Balkans, and they are us."

The intemperate "debate" over affirmative action exemplifies this seeming breakdown in reasoned discourse about the requirements of justice. There would appear to be little hope of resolving pressing questions of social and political justice posed by globalization—problems that include allocating scarce resources and plentiful waste, identifying and defining human rights on a global scale, and preserving the cultural integrity of different peoples—when a wealthy country that enjoys relatively stable political, economic, and social institutions is unable to come to grips with the presence and legacy of racial oppression. For a brief period there appeared to be an emerging political consensus that members of disadvantaged groups are entitled to the benefits of affirmative action by employers and educational institutions who can provide them with the opportunities that would enable them to overcome the pervasive effects of discrimination. However, affirmative action has become the subject of intense and heated debate, figuring largely in political elections and political maneuvering at all levels of government.

Confronted by this political controversy, legal practice appears weak and ineffectual. The debate over affirmative action simply cannot be resolved by articulating positive legal rights that derive neatly and logically from the self-evident requirements of justice. Consequently, judicial resolution of the issue too often is regarded as strategic political action, where victory is achieved rather than consensus being formed. Affirmative action has become part of the aptly named "culture wars," inasmuch as the debate appears to be as intractable as a political dispute arising between two countries that have no cultural commonality. The Supreme Court's recent cases reaffirming the constitutionality of some form of affirmative action in higher education are read by many as revealing that there can be no reasoned resolution of this issue, given the all-too-obvious fissures evident in the competing opinions. The announcement of the decision in the cases was met almost immediately by interest groups declaring their intentions to ensure that future nominees for the high court line up on their side of this battlefield, regardless of their jurisprudential bona fides.[1] For many political actors, the question is one of victory, not reasoning toward a just result.

Radical deconstructionists argue that law is politics, politics is power, and power is ideologically structured. In the controversy over affirmative action, this philosophical skepticism is married to political cynicism, undermining the belief that the justice of affirmative action can be assessed reasonably as a question of law or as a matter of principled political action. Affirmative action is handled by the legal system, critics may charge, but it is handled through the exertion of power rather than through the exercise of reason. If the culture wars in America between the proponents and detractors of affirmative action foreshadow political discourse in the emerging global village, there is cause for serious alarm.

In this book I respond to the radically deconstructive approach by arguing that we can reason about justice, notwithstanding the multicultural challenges that are exemplified by globalization, but that are equally present within American legal practice. Drawing from the complementary philosophical projects undertaken by Hans-Georg Gadamer and Chaim Perelman, I contend that justice is a product of rhetorical knowledge. Rhetorical knowledge is a social activity—a dynamic ground-without-foundation upon which justice may be constructed—rather than the result of a purely contemplative undertaking. Under this view, justice is not a pristine concept requiring philosophical clarification; instead, it is a practical engagement in politics that is historically conditioned and subject to the limitations of human finitude. Rhetorical knowledge is not thwarted by multicultural diversity. On the contrary, rhetorical knowledge is stimulated by cross-cultural engagements. This is not to say, however, that rhetorical knowledge emerges only from the clash of incommensurable traditions. Even within a relatively homogeneous and unified society, members of society draw upon rhetorical knowledge to regenerate their shared lifeworld.

My claim that rhetorical knowledge plays a constitutive role in society is a theoretical argument about certain practices, but my thesis should not be the concern solely of philosophers, political theorists, and sociologists. The American legal system plays an increasingly important role in structuring social relationships and defining shared meanings, and so legal scholars are particularly well suited for exploring the role of rhetorical knowledge. The legal system all too often is marred by a variety of undesirable strategies—including physical force, ideological manipulation, and bureaucratization—but it is precisely the prominent and precarious character of rhetorical knowledge in law that makes the legal system the perfect venue for study. Legal theory suffers by not taking account of philosophical insights into the activity of rhetorical knowledge, but it is no less true that these philosophical insights can be enriched dramatically by drawing much-needed context from work by legal scholars.

Even at this early stage of the book, some readers will challenge my project on the ground that it concedes too much to ongoing practices, and therefore lacks critical purchase. Assessing the activity of legal practice through a theoretical lens ground with Gadamer's philosophical hermeneutics and Perelman's new rhetoric might suggest a myopic deference to the status quo. But this challenge rests on a profound misunderstanding. Rhetorical knowledge emerges from practical encounters that have critical dimensions, and it is only this practical experience of critique that can, in turn, inform a theoretical project of critical inquiry. Gadamer and Perelman expose the error of equating critique with a special form of theoretical insight that can be divorced from ongoing practices in a significant, stable, and definitive manner. As I hope to make clear, by returning to the pathbreaking work by Gadamer and Perelman we can recover important insights that too often get lost in the contemporary rush to establish a new and ever-more radically critical scholarly approach.

Nevertheless, even after infusing Gadamer's hermeneutics with Perelman's classical rhetorical insights the largely implicit critical dimension of their work remains underdeveloped. I bring additional resources to my account by confronting Gadamer with Nietzsche's more irreverent rhetorical perspective. I argue that Nietzsche's model of cultural critique helps to illuminate the prospects and process of legal critique in accordance with the theory of rhetorical knowledge, and that Gianni Vattimo's "weak thought" helps to extend this line of inquiry. In this light, rhetorical knowledge is properly seen as the site not just for elaboration but also for challenge, not just cultivation but also destruction.

My central themes are that rhetorical knowledge—however imperfectly pursued and attained—is a feature of social life; that rhetorical knowledge plays an important role in legal practice; and that legal critique is appropriately grounded by the normative injunction to maximize the generation of and reliance on rhetorical knowledge in the administration of justice by legal actors. If nothing else, I want to make clear that by recovering and cultivating the classic insights of Gadamer, Perelman, and Nietzsche we can gain substantial perspective on our current situation. By definition, the theory of rhetorical knowledge does not call for a brilliant theoretical reconstruction of legal practice that generates prescriptions; instead, it seeks to draw out resources that can help us understand legal practice and engage critically in this practice. Rhetorical knowledge may only be enacted rhetorically.

This book is organized in three parts. In chapter 1, I provide an overview of Gadamer's philosophical hermeneutics and Perelman's new rhetoric, describing how these philosophies shed light on the activity of understanding by invoking the ancient conception of rhetoric. Rhetorical knowledge is not a "second best" concession to the limitations of genuine knowledge; it is a distinct positive accomplishment. I engage in an extended discussion of the problem of affirmative action to illustrate the operation of rhetorical knowledge in legal practice.

In chapter 2, I engage several contemporary theorists as challenging interlocutors in an effort to address the criticism that Gadamer and Perelman provide overly conservative accounts that preclude an effective critique of existing practices. Acknowledging the inadequacy of my Gadamerian/Perelmanesque approach standing alone, I introduce a Nietzschean model of rhetorical critique that builds on my hermeneutical-rhetorical starting point. Although many commentators construe Nietzsche as having definitively repudiated the later "conservative" thinking by Gadamer and Perelman, I find in Nietzsche a challenging supplement that foregrounds the radical implications of their efforts. I then take up the Supreme Court's "gay rights" jurisprudence, not only to show the operation of critical insight within legal practice, but also to exemplify how a critically informed account of rhetorical knowledge can redirect our investigations of legal practice.

In chapter 3, I demonstrate that rhetorical knowledge subtends legal practice and that the concept of rhetorical knowledge is indispensable for understanding the concrete implications of what it means to achieve "justice" in the legal system. Because rhetorical knowledge also shapes the critique of legal practice, I consider the implications for jurisprudential inquiry and suggest a reconceptualization of how best to relate critical inquiries to the practice of law. I bring my discussion to bear on the multiple criminal prosecutions of Dr. Jack Kevorkian and the difficult issue of assisted suicide, looking to an example of justice in action "on the ground," in the context of trials rather than in appellate opinions.

I close with the plea that we pay far greater attention to the operation of rhetorical knowledge. As I hope to make clear in the pages that follow, my reference to rhetoric does not signal a grudging resignation that we must abandon false hopes of a rigorous philosophy of truth, nor does it suggest a celebration of boundless and playful irrationalism. Rather, rhetorical knowledge is a positive achievement that must be nurtured and protected by ongoing social practices. The rhetorical approach that I draw from Gadamer, Perelman, and Nietzsche is a disciplined encounter with the lived experience of rhetorical knowledge, particularly as it is experienced in legal practice.

By defending the idea that justice is achieved through the cultivation of rhetorical knowledge, I pursue the subject-decentering implications of the deconstructive attack on legal rationality and emphatically reject the temptation to champion a conservative retrenchment to comforting and familiar platitudes. Against the received wisdom that Gadamer and Perelman offer a hopelessly conservative approach that cannot coexist with Nietzsche, I read them together with Nietzsche and argue that rhetorical hermeneutics provides a truly radical critique of contemporary consciousness. One consequence of my approach is that the homage to "the Other," so prevalent in works claiming to fully radicalize deconstructive insights, must be replaced by attentiveness to "others." This should not suggest a lack of theoretical rigor, but rather a recognition that the critique of Western subjectivity must proceed from dialogically lived experience rather than from a carefully constructed theoretical posture. The living ground of critique is found in the social experience of hermeneutical-rhetorical dialogue. We need fewer clever theorists speaking from the heights, and many more scholars carefully attending to the experience of critique in legal practice and reflecting on how this experience can be facilitated. This book is a modest step in that direction.

Rhetorical knowledge is possible, but it is not easily achieved. I recognize that my approach poses a substantial challenge, and I certainly do not reach the happy conclusion that "all is well," after pulling the rhetorical rabbit out of a suspiciously convenient hat. Indeed, in an age that is indelibly marked by the quest to analyze methodologically and to exercise control over an object of study, the decentering activity of rhetorical knowledge presents us with an exceptionally demanding task. This book is premised on my belief that legal practice, and the second-order practice of critical legal theory, are important venues for thinking about how we might meet the daunting but inescapable challenge of cultivating rhetorical knowledge.

Rhetorical Knowledge in Legal Practice and Critical Legal Theory

I

Rhetorical Knowledge and Justice

> We need to concentrate on what we are conflicted about and how we become conflicted about such things. In our view this orientation to "how" is cultivated chiefly by rhetorical and hermeneutic training in interpretation and persuasion; it is stabilized (for the moment) in our varied understandings of our own and others' dynamic traditions. In our time, accordingly, rhetoric and hermeneutics should be understood to range from specific arts whose handbooks articulate rules and strategies of invention, address and application to the broadest possible conceptions of rhetoricality (in Bender and Wellbery's phrase) and rhetoricity (in Charles Altieri's) as dimensions of human existence. . . . Indeed, we believe that only rhetoric and hermeneutics, properly redefined, can show how the principled subject-matter disciplines presuppose the non-expert realm of praxis and practical reasoning and how they must, in the beginning and in the end, be responsible to them.
>
> Walter Jost and Michael J. Hyde
> "Prologue," *Rhetoric and Hermeneutics in Our Time: A Reader*

Hans-Georg Gadamer and Chaim Perelman are important contributors to this century's philosophical effort to identify the deficiencies of the Cartesian tradition and to fashion a new account of understanding and knowledge. It is somewhat surprising to find that neither philosopher engages the other's work in a sustained and detailed manner, although this is explained largely by the fact that they write within different intellectual traditions. Gadamer expressly works within and against the German romantic and humanistic tradition, strongly influenced by the pathbreaking phenomenological approach of his teacher, Martin Heidegger. Perelman taught in Belgium and was a logician by training, although his approach was strongly influenced by the return to the Sophists undertaken by his teacher, Eugène Dupréel. Despite these different orientations and starting points, Gadamer and Perelman share important themes: the dialogic character of understanding, the inadequacy of neo-Kantianism as an account of knowledge, and the overriding ethical imperative of holding oneself open to questioning and challenges rather than proceeding as if one possesses apodictic truth. In this chapter, I provide a close reading of their complementary approaches, returning to the origins of contemporary hermeneutical and rhetorical theory. I argue that reading Gadamer and Perelman together reveals the relationship between justice and what I will call "rhetorical knowledge."

Philosophical Hermeneutics: Justice as Conversation

Hans-Georg Gadamer develops his hermeneutical philosophy in a Kantian manner, analyzing how we in fact know rather than presuming that philosophy has the authority to dictate how we should acquire knowledge.[1] Philosophers traditionally regarded hermeneutics as a technical inquiry into methods for understanding different kinds of texts; consequently, theological, legal, and literary hermeneutics developed as separate disciplines that shared, at most, general characteristics. Under the weight of Enlightenment ideology, however, hermeneutics slowly was transformed into a unified scientific methodology of meaning that was grounded in theory and divorced from the practical aims of various disciplines. Textual meaning was equated with the subjective intentions of the author, a historical fact that in principle was subject to philological reconstruction. Gadamer regards Wilhelm Dilthey's attempt to overcome historicism and to preserve the objectivity of the human sciences as the culmination of the Enlightenment approach to hermeneutics, and he champions Martin Heidegger's hermeneutic phenomenology as a momentous break that Gadamer seeks to develop.[2]

After Heidegger, the "problem of hermeneutics becomes universal in scope," and Gadamer argues that all knowledge is subtended by a unitary "hermeneutical situation" that was never captured by the narrow methodological focus of Enlightenment thinking.[3] Although hermeneutical understanding has been devalued because it stands outside the empiricist and rationalist accounts of knowledge, he argues that the hermeneutical dimension of understanding is a primordial experience that enables scientific thought.

Gadamer provides a phenomenological account of the activity of understanding in all of its manifestations—including deciphering, translation, reflection, and critique—without limiting his inquiries to any particular venue of understanding, and without heeding artificial disciplinary borders.[4] Gadamer's principal philosophical claim is that our truthful relation to the world subtends but is not exhausted by modern technical-empirical science. He places in question the Enlightenment paradigm of a monadic, prejudice-free subject decoding the world of objects, and he challenges the belief that we cast interpretations (whether scientific, aesthetic, or political) over the objects comprising the world. Following Heidegger's analysis of being-in-the-world, Gadamer breaks from the metaphysical foundations of the Enlightenment that regard the individual subject as a self-directing center of knowledge, and he uncovers the intersubjective relations that make possible later assertions of epistemological integrity by the subject. His focus is the dynamic web of truth and meaning that we constantly renew simply in the course of living, an intersubjective belonging that lies behind the later methodological attempts to repair localized disruptions of understanding by applying rules of exegesis. From this perspective, interpretation is not just an activity designed to bring certain objects into sharper focus; it is our fundamental mode of existing.[5] Drawing from Gadamer's rich and varied philosophical legacy, I reconstruct an account of rhetorical understanding that he never expressly developed.

Conversation and Hermeneutical Understanding

Gadamer captures the ego-decentering thrust of his philosophy with detailed phenomenological investigations of the life experiences of playing a game, experiencing art, and making sense of history. Perhaps Gadamer's most vivid and succinct model of hermeneutical understanding, though, is his analysis of the give-and-take of everyday conversation. Beginning with the observation that "the more genuine a conversation is, the less its conduct lies within the will of either partner," he argues that the understanding emerging from a conversation is "like an event that happens to us."[6] This analysis introduces a central argument of *Truth and Method:* language is the intersubjective medium of hermeneutical experience, and understanding is an interpretive accomplishment within this medium.

> Conversation is a process of coming to an understanding. Thus it belongs to every true conversation that each person opens himself to the other, truly accepts his point of view as valid and transposes himself into the other to such an extent that he understands not the particular individual but what he says.
>
> ----------
>
> Everything we have said characterizing the situation of two people coming to an understanding in conversation has a genuine application to hermeneutics, which is concerned with understanding texts.
>
> ----------
>
> This is not to say, of course, that the hermeneutic situation in regard to texts is exactly the same as that between two people in conversation [since] one partner in the hermeneutical conversation, the text, speaks only through the other partner, the interpreter.
>
> ----------
>
> [When interpreting a text] the interpreter's own horizon is decisive, yet not as a personal standpoint that he maintains or enforces, but more as an opinion and a possibility that one brings into play and puts at risk, and that helps one truly to make one's own what the text says. . . . We can now see that this is what takes place in conversation, in which something is expressed that is not only mine or my author's, but common.[7]

In these passages Gadamer is not just suggesting a provocative analogy; rather, he is making an ontological claim about the hermeneutical nature of understanding. He argues that all understanding is founded on a decentering "fusion of horizons," an experience that is placed in sharp relief when two conversationalists find the path of their dialogue taking on a life of its own.[8] The "fusion" is not a static commonality, but rather is a movement that carries the speakers forward together in an educative experience.

The central features of Gadamer's philosophy are most clearly revealed by working from his claim that the dialogic encounter of hermeneutical understanding is conversational. Gadamer crystallizes his attack on Enlightenment epistemology by rehabilitating "prejudices," which he defines as the pre-understanding that motivates and shapes all later interpretive encounters.[9] Each participant in a conversation comes to the encounter from a history that will shape the evolving discussion. To be a discussant without prejudices would be to exist outside of history, which would preclude a shared basis from which to engage another person in conversation. Prejudices, then, are not rigid limitations that preclude understanding; rather, they form a horizon that continually is in flux as the person moves through life. Understanding involves the fusion of horizons in which a common subject is taken up by two participants in a manner that allows the subject matter to unfold. A conversation yields understanding when two people, working from their own prejudiced starting points, find common ground sufficient to develop a topic that informs both participants.

> The dialogic character of language . . . leaves behind it any starting point in the subjectivity of the subject, and especially in the meaning-directed intentions of the speaker. What we find happening in speaking is not a mere reification of intended meaning, but an endeavor that continually modifies itself, or better: a continually recurring temptation to engage oneself in something or to become involved with someone. But that means to expose oneself and to risk oneself. Genuinely speaking one's mind has little to do with a mere explication and assertion of our prejudices . . . it exposes oneself to one's own doubt as well as to the rejoinder of the other.[10]

This description accords with the common experience of a genuine conversation, inasmuch as it would be considered strange to refer to the bare transmission of data by one person to another as "conversing." Conversation inevitably involves give-and-take.

In the case of textual interpretation, the horizon of the text is comprised of the history of its reception and recirculation within the culture, a dimension that Gadamer characterizes as the "history of its effects" (or the "historical effectiveness" of the text).[11] We can never read a text for the first time, so to speak, because the way in which the text speaks to us already is shaped by the tradition from which it emerges, even if the current reading transforms and carries forward this tradition. Gadamer is quite serious when he claims that interpreting a text involves entering a conversation with the text and seeking a fusion of horizons.[12] The inevitability of the prejudices of the interpreter and the effective-history of the text means that understanding and application can never be fundamentally distinct activities. Understanding occurs only by virtue of application; there is no ahistorical text-in-itself that can be applied, but rather only a horizonal text that meets an interpreter in a dialogical encounter within a particular context that is structured as a question posed to the text.[13]

Conversation as Rhetorical Exchange

Gadamer signals the tremendous importance of the rhetorical tradition to his approach by using the experience of everyday conversation to explain his philosophy, even if his explicit discussions of rhetoric remain peripheral.[14] Gadamer begins *Truth and Method* by recalling Vico's development of the humanist concept of sensus communis as a means of preserving the independent validity of moral-practical wisdom, as distinguished from the logical-empirical truths of science.[15] John Schaeffer has complained that Gadamer appropriated only part of Vico's holistic concept of sensus communis for the purpose of subjugating it to his hermeneutical model.[16] However, there is sufficient indication that Gadamer aligns himself with Vico's full-bodied conception of "*sensus communis* as an epistemological principle which unites imagination, language, and social institutions in a dynamic, holistic relationship analogous to the simultaneity of invention, figurality, and organization that occurs in extemporaneous oral performances,"[17] even if, in Schaeffer's estimation, Gadamer does not credit Vico sufficiently.[18]

Gadamer aligns Vico with the substantive rhetorical goal of saying the right thing well, and applauds his development of the "positive ambiguity of the rhetorical ideal."[19] Concerned with overcoming the effects of nineteenth-century historicism and romanticism in German philosophy, Gadamer recalls Vico's legacy as the last thinker to hold to the ancient truths of the rhetorical tradition.

> Vico's return to the Roman concept of the sensus communis, and his defense of humanist rhetoric against modern science, is of special

> interest to us, for here we are introduced to an element of truth in the human sciences that was no longer recognizable when they conceptualized themselves in the nineteenth century. Vico lived in an unbroken tradition of rhetorical and humanist culture, and had only to reassert anew its ageless claim. Ultimately, it has always been known that the possibilities of rational proof and instruction do not fully exhaust the sphere of knowledge. Hence Vico's appeal to the sensus communis belongs, as we have seen, in a wider context that goes right back to antiquity and whose continued effect into the present day is our theme.[20]

Vico's importance lies in the way he presciently challenges the unitary Cartesian paradigm of knowledge by reasserting "the independent rights of rhetoric . . . the art of finding arguments [which] serves to develop the sense of what is convincing, which works instinctively and ex tempore, and for that very reason cannot be replaced by science."[21] The rhetorical tradition preserved and advanced by Vico concerns a way of understanding no less legitimate or important than the methodological model of the natural sciences. Indeed, Gadamer asserts that rhetoric "is the universal form of human communication, which even today determines our social life in an incomparably more profound fashion than does science."[22]

Gadamer draws connections between ancient rhetoric and his inquiry into our pre-methodological complex of meanings, but he is careful to distinguish substantive rhetoric, as exemplified in Plato's *Phaedrus,* from the "idle speculations of the sophists."[23] It is important not to misinterpret Gadamer's invocation of Plato as an attempt to constrain rhetoric by linking it to certainty and unchanging truth. Gadamer places much greater emphasis on Plato's activity—writing the Socratic dialogues—than on Plato's philosophical self-understanding, insisting that what we learn from the Platonic dialogues is that it "is more important to find the words which convince the other than those which can be demonstrated in their truth, once and for all."[24] Gadamer argues that genuine rhetoric concerns the "discovery and transmission of insight and knowledge," an event that is exemplified in the "art of leading a conversation."[25] The ancient rhetoricians well understood that the cultural "common sense" serving as a background for all understanding is nourished not on methodologically secured truths, but rather on the "probable" as articulated in contingent and historically defined knowledge. At a key juncture in the conclusion to *Truth and Method,* Gadamer reminds us that his book principally has been concerned with recovering and rehabilitating this rhetorical model of knowledge. Acknowledging that his guiding focus on the "event" of understanding is drawn from "an ancient truth that has been able to assert itself against modern scientific methodology," Gadamer concludes that the "eikos, the verisimilar, the 'probable' . . . the 'evident,' belong in a series of things that defend their rightness against the truth and certainty of what is proved and known. Let us recall that we assigned a special importance [in the introductory section of *Truth and Method*] to the sensus communis."[26] In his review of *Truth and Method,* Klaus Dockhorn suggests that Gadamer underestimates the extent to which the rhetorical tradition underwrites his project; nevertheless, Dockhorn declares that the "widespread depreciation or dismissal of rhetoric . . . should be effectively brought to an end by this book."[27] Gary Madison makes this same point more emphatically, concluding that Gadamer is not advocating that we elevate rhetorical study over philosophy as much as he is insisting on the rhetorical nature of all humanistic inquiry, including philosophy.[28]

Gadamer offers Aristotle's practical philosophy as a model of the role that rhetoric plays in hermeneutical understanding. Gadamer borrows from Aristotle's discussion of *phronesis* not just to describe one of the virtues possessed by the good citizen, but rather to describe a type of knowledge that is distinct from that gained by methodological science.[29] *Phronesis* is the capacity to converse with another and to make practical-moral judgments on the basis of a common, historically transmitted tradition, despite the lack of any firm rules guiding these judgments. Gadamer's reliance on Aristotle clearly signals his commitment to a rhetorical model of human understanding, according to which reasons are given and judgment is informed despite the absence of methodological prescriptions.[30] Practical inquiry is rhetorical and conversational in structure because it works from shared, accepted norms in a creative effort to arrive at acceptable concrete decisions about ethics or politics.[31]

Although Gadamer relies heavily, even if often indirectly, on the classical rhetorical tradition to develop his hermeneutical account of understanding, he resists the temptation to counsel a return to mythical conceptions of the bygone era of the Greek polis. Even as he writes of the necessary interdependence of rhetoric and hermeneutics due to their link to the idea of shared understandings and the need to overcome disruptions in this understanding,[32] Gadamer emphasizes that the hermeneutical task is markedly different from the rhetorical task in ancient Greece. Today, social meanings are reproduced and disseminated through texts (all manner of media) rather than with persuasive speeches made in the Assembly or law courts. Ancient rhetoric was transformed irreversibly by the movement from an oral culture to one founded on writing and reading; rhetorical performances now require a hermeneutical recovery by later readers who might be removed from the original event by hundreds of years and wide cultural differences.[33] Despite this profound change, Gadamer contends that the rhetorical tradition can serve as a resource for textual interpreters in our literate culture.[34] By understanding that some forms of knowledge are predicated on persuasion founded on shared assumptions, the interpreter is better able to reanimate the text by cultivating a broader, shared agreement with it.

Gadamer argues that rhetoric's role of nourishing political society in ancient Greece is paralleled today by the sustaining power of hermeneutical appropriation. Acknowledging Chaim Perelman's important contribution in rehabilitating the full-bodied qualities of ancient rhetoric,[35] Gadamer sets as his task the goal of applying the rhetorical idea of political truth grounded on the probable to the hermeneutical experience, noting that "[c]onvincing and persuading, without being able to prove . . . are obviously as much the aim and measure of understanding and interpretation as they are the aim and measure of the art of oration and persuasion."[36] A prominent venue for this hermeneutical experience today is the legal system, which is premised on the production and interpretation of authoritative texts as sources of governing authority rather than on the performance and reception of speeches before all competent citizens of the polis. Rejecting the scientific impulse to reduce law to a disciplined methodology of application, which would create an unbridgeable chasm between the presumed universal and timeless meaning of the text and the demands of the individual case, Gadamer insists that every attempt to understand a legal text is a function of applying the text to the case at hand.

He regards legal reasoning as a particularly vivid model of all hermeneutical understanding. "It accords with the age-old Aristotelian wisdom that the finding of the law always required the enlarging consideration of equity and that the perspective of equity does not stand in contradiction with the law but precisely by relinquishing the letter of the law brings the legal meaning to complete fulfillment for the first time."[37]

The model of conversation clarifies Gadamer's rhetorical focus. An interpreter understands a text when she falls into conversation with it and allows it to speak to the question posed by the case at hand, rather than by charting in advance the line of inquiry. Rather than adopting a subjective attitude of dominance over the text, the interpreter suppresses her subjective aims and attends to "the saying" of the historically effective text as it is revealed in a given context. The hermeneutic experience of the reader parallels the need for a rhetor to conceive a speech only in connection with the particular audience that will be addressed on a particular occasion, in recognition that persuasive speeches do not exist in the abstract, ready to be used indiscriminately at some point in the future.

Given his claim that all meaning is a product of historicity and context, as exemplified by the event of a conversation, it should be no surprise that Gadamer refuses to hypostatize the current experience of textuality as an essential feature of understanding. Just as the decentering character of interpretation became much more apparent after the move from oral culture to written culture, Gadamer hypothesizes that the rapidly developing computer age might engender an equally significant transformation that will undermine once and for all the parochial scientism of the West.[38] Similar to the alphabet, which "demanded an immense achievement of abstraction and introduced an almost nonhuman distance from everything representational into our forms of communication," the computer appears to be truly transcultural, "comprehen[ding] all of humanity and its forms of life."[39] In this environment, Gadamer contends, prejudices might be shattered more easily as contingent forms of life confront radically different cultures made available by means of instantaneous global information technologies, thereby opening the possibility that the world's population might engage in a shared rhetorical exploration of what it means to cultivate one's humanity.[40]

The Critical Dimension of Conversation

To this point, Gadamer's account has reverberated with conservative overtones: positing the wisdom of the Other, especially in the case of a text embedded in tradition; sublimating individual designs to a fusion of horizons; and proposing that everyday hermeneutical experience reveals important lessons for philosophy rather than vice versa. Gadamer accepts this criticism, if by conservative one means only a refusal to chase after the Enlightenment myth of prejudice-free knowledge.[41] Gadamer rejects the pejorative intent behind this characterization by confronting head-on the implicit understanding of critical practice that informs his detractors. Particularly in his response to Habermas's insistence on the need to develop a critical theory to serve the emancipatory interest in human progress, Gadamer reemphasizes his alignment with the rhetorical model of truth as pointing the way to a more accurate and productive understanding of social critique.

> All coming to understanding in language presupposes agreement not just about the meanings of words and the rules of spoken language; much remains undisputed with regard to the "subject matter" as well—i.e., to everything that can be meaningfully discussed. My insistence on this point is taken to demonstrate a conservative tendency and to deter hermeneutical reflection from its proper—critical and emancipatory—task.
>
> ----------
>
> I would like to see more recognition of the fact that this is the realm hermeneutics shares with rhetoric: the realm of arguments that are convincing (which is not the same as logically compelling). It is the realm of practice and humanity in general, and its province is not where the power of "iron-clad conclusions" must be accepted without discussion, nor where emancipatory reflection is certain of its "contrafactual agreements," but rather where controversial issues are decided by reasonable consideration. . . . Vico rightly assigns [rhetoric] a special value: copia, the abundance of viewpoints. I find it frighteningly unreal when people like Habermas ascribe to rhetoric a compulsory quality that one must reject in favor of un-

> constrained, rational dialogue. This is to underestimate not only the danger of the glib manipulation and incapacitation of reason but also the possibility of coming to an understanding through persuasion, on which social life depends. . . .
>
> Only a narrow view of rhetoric sees it as mere technique or even a mere instrument for social manipulation. It is in truth an essential aspect of all reasonable behavior. Aristotle had already called rhetoric not a techne but a dunamis because it belongs so essentially to the general definition of humans as reasonable beings. However extensive their effects and however broad their manipulation, the institutionalized means of forming public opinion which our industrialized society has developed in no way exhaust the realm of reasonable argumentation and critical reflection that social practice occupies.[42]

In this passage from the afterword of *Truth and Method,* Gadamer once again references Perelman's primary works with the acknowledgment that they form "a valuable contribution to philosophical hermeneutics."[43] Gadamer, therefore, answers those who allege that his philosophy lacks a critical bite by restating his central thesis: an emancipatory critique of society is always derivative of our meaningful participation in society, and so critique is always a particular comportment of belonging. Gadamer stresses that the rhetorical dimension of knowledge provides the motivation and resources for social critique, rejecting the urge to develop philosophical constructs that purport to exert critical leverage from outside the rhetorical arena.

The transition from the oral traditions of the ancients to contemporary written traditions proves to be decisive for Gadamer's account. He argues that critical distance is opened by the existence of written texts, since they introduce a temporal gulf between author and interpreter that can be bridged only with a fusion of the two horizons into a shared point of conversational departure. The participatory immediacy of a rhetorical exchange between two persons permits room for critical inventiveness, but the case of textual interpretation invites critical appraisal to an even greater degree.

> Rhetoric as such, however, is tied to the immediacy of its effect. . . . While under the persuasive spell of speech, the listener for the moment cannot and ought not to indulge in critical examination. On the other hand, the reading and interpreting of what is written is so distanced and detached from its author—from his mood, intentions, and unexpressed tendencies—that the grasping of the meaning of the text takes on something of the character of an independent productive act, one that resembles more the art of the orator than the process of mere listening. Thus it is easy to understand why the theoretical tools of the art of interpretation (hermeneutics) have been to a large extent borrowed from rhetoric.[44]

This analysis holds great significance. By expressly equating the textual interpreter with the rhetorical actor rather than with the receptive audience, Gadamer emphasizes the dynamic character of interpretation and the space for critical reappraisal of the tradition that is opened by, not despite, the decentering dialogic structure of understanding.

It might be surprising that Gadamer expressly praises the role of theory in developing this critical engagement. It is easy to misconstrue Gadamer's careful rehabilitation of Aristotelian practical philosophy in response to modern scientific ideology as an abandonment of theory and a return to practice as the source of human understanding. But in a speech delivered when he was eighty years old, Gadamer acknowledged the importance of theory not only to his life's work, but to social life generally.[45] Gadamer revives Aristotle's practical philosophy not to supplant theory, but rather to restore the essential equilibrium of theory and practice that has been disturbed in modernity. This orientation plays a central role in the critical dimension of his hermeneutics, inasmuch as Gadamer regards critique as a juncture of practical engagement and theoretical reflection.

Modern technological consciousness warps social life because it reduces theory to nothing more than applied research, and it reduces practice to nothing more than the implementation of efficient technologies. This leads Gadamer to ask: "Is there perhaps more to theory than what the modern institution of science represents to us? And, is practice, too, perhaps more than the mere application of science? Are theory and practice correctly distinguished at all when they are seen only in opposition to each other?"[46] He concludes that the opposition of practice and theory is mistaken, and that "theory is just as primordial an anthropological datum as is practical and political power. So everything depends on constantly renewing the balance between these two human forces. And I am convinced that human society exists only because and as long as there is a balance of this kind."[47] Gadamer credits Aristotle for recognizing that theory is a relinquishment of immediate and pressing questions within a practice. Theory can never be completely segregated from practical engagement with others because it is a comportment within practice, but theory is an openness to different understandings that can reveal the unproductive nature of prevailing prejudices.[48] Thus, the relationship between theory and practice is central to critical engagement.

By moving beyond the opposition of *episteme* and *techne,* Gadamer argues that Aristotle provides the key to understanding the relationship between theory and practice. Aristotle accomplishes this by recognizing the role of *phronesis* in generating moral-practical knowledge that results from a cultivated disposition of applying general considerations nondeductively to the practical demands for ethical action in a given context. For present purposes, it is fair to recast the efforts of a *phronimos* as facilitating the critical experience of practical engagement by adopting a theoretical comportment. The resulting hermeneutical understanding represents a dynamic fusion of horizons rather than a slavish adherence to tradition, but also is rooted in the practical demands of a contextualized question rather than rising above the world of practice to dictate from the heights of theory.

Gadamer suggests that Aristotle exemplifies the interaction of practice and theory in his activity of composing the *Nicomachean Ethics,* for Aristotle is theorizing about ethical decision making rather than making ethical decisions. Gadamer's philosophical hermeneutics is a theoretical treatment of the practical activity of interpretation in much the same fashion as Aristotle's practical philosophy is a theoretical treatment of ethical decision making. Because he insists that his philosophical hermeneutics "must arise from practice itself and, with all the typical generalizations that it brings to explicit consciousness, be related back to practice,"[49] philosophical hermeneutics represents a genuine theoretic comportment in the manner modeled by Aristotle's practical philosophy.[50] Theory is a distinctive part of dealing with the paradoxical social demands for action that are placed on individuals, but it remains intimately related to practice and cannot be separated entirely. As Gadamer insists, the "myth of the ivory tower where theoretical people live is an unreal fantasy. We all stand in the middle of the social system."[51] Far from disavowing critical theory, then, Gadamer seeks to find a path back to the theoretical comportment that permits critical insight to flourish within practice.

Justice as Conversation

It may not be immediately apparent how Gadamer's philosophical hermeneutics sheds any light on the problem of defining and achieving justice. His discussions of legal practice are descriptive rather than normative; while illuminating, they remain ambiguous in their appeals to the requirements of justice. In light of his antifoundationalist insistence that all understanding is radically situated in the hermeneutical-rhetorical experience of historical beings, it might be surprising that Gadamer raises the subject of justice in the context of a favorable discussion of Aristotle's classical conception of natural law. Gadamer's invocation of natural law appears strange and misguided, however, only because natural law traditionally is presumed to require invariant moral truths.

Gadamer emphasizes that Aristotle's characterization of natural law as a changeable feature of human existence coincides with his hermeneutical philosophy and differs substantially from post-Thomistic natural law accounts:

> For Aristotle, [the fact that natural law is not timeless and unchanging] is wholly compatible with the fact that it is "natural" law. . . . [Unlike, for example, traffic regulations, there are] things that do not admit of regulation by mere human convention because the "nature of the thing" constantly asserts itself. Thus it is quite legitimate to call such things "natural law." In that the nature of the thing still allows some room for play, natural law is still changeable. . . . [Aristotle] quite clearly explains that the best state "is everywhere one and the same," but it is the same in a different way than "fire burns everywhere in the same way, whether in Greece or in Persia."

> . . . [The guiding principles of Aristotle's natural law] are not norms to be found in the stars, nor do they have an unchanging place in a natural moral universe, so that all that would be necessary would be to perceive them. Nor are they mere conventions, but really do correspond to the nature of the thing—except that the latter is always itself determined in each case [contextually].[52]

Gadamer emphasizes that this understanding of a changeable natural law is reflected in the "certain area of free play"[53] that marks legal reasoning. The classical natural law of Aristotle at once serves as a critique of positivism and the post-Thomistic natural law tradition, and it reinforces that an indeterminate realm of "free play" is not merely a tolerated feature but an essential component of the natural law account. Gadamer looks to classical natural law to uncover how legal and moral deliberation work to address practical problems, thereby recuperating an ontological inquiry into the human experience of normativity by rescuing it from natural law accounts that posit timeless moral truths.

In *Justice and Interpretation,* Georgia Warnke carefully elaborates a Gadamerian-inspired conception of justice that accords with his conversational approach to understanding and his endorsement of classical natural law principles. Warnke contends that the failure of modern political theory stems from its inability to ward off the threats of conventionalism and subjectivism that arise from the acknowledgment that principles of justice always are grounded in particular contexts arising within a social tradition. Theorists are nearly uniform in their response by proposing that unanimous consent, either actual or hypothetical, can validate principles of justice that rise above mere preference. In contrast, Warnke places great emphasis on Gadamer's philosophy to argue that an ongoing "fair and equal hermeneutic discussion" ought to be the central political goal of society rather than unanimous consent.[54] This conclusion follows from the recognition that many political discussions involve "disagreements between equally well-justified interpretations" of the requirements of justice, and so consensus rarely will be attainable.[55] Relying on Gadamer's description of everyday conversation as a model of the rationality of hermeneutical events, Warnke does not abandon the ideal of consensus with regret as much as she champions the vitality of a dynamic dialogue that never is pressured into a univocal agreement binding on all members of society. "Once we make the interpretive turn [with Gadamer], the justification of our principles becomes dialogic and the scope of the dialogue becomes unlimited."[56] Framed by Warnke's observations, Gadamer's recent writings on the challenges and opportunities posed by multiculturalism gain added significance.

Warnke explains her hermeneutic conception of justice by taking up the divisive controversy over abortion. Not only are the bitter debates about the constitutionality of statutes that criminalize or hinder abortion unlikely to lead to consensus about the just resolution of this question, but the very manner of the debates appears to be a positive impediment to justice. Warnke insists that justice is embodied in a tolerant and respectful dialogue between persons who never will reach consensus, rather than in a conclusive victory achieved through strategic argumentation. This understanding accords with Gadamer's critique of the Enlightenment model of knowledge, and can be summarized as equating the requirements of justice with the hermeneutical experience of conversation. In the context of legal practice, this would mean engaging in the free play opened by the legal text in order to determine the correct result.

> The important question, then, is no longer which interpretation of our history and experience is correct because none is exhaustively correct. The important question is, rather, how or why our interpretations differ and what new insights into the meaning of our traditions we might glean from the attempt to understand the cogency of interpretations different from our own.
>
> ----------
>
> Both diversity and dialogue, then, are necessary, not because we could be wrong, but because we can never be wholly correct or rather because the issue is no longer as much one of rightness or wrongness as one of continuing revision and reform.[57]

Warnke modifies Gadamer's approach by supplementing it with a subdued version of Habermas's proceduralist critical theory, arguing that Gadamer is insufficiently attentive to the social forces that can warp practical dialogue and hinder the educative function of conversation.[58] Nevertheless, it is fair to say that Warnke credits Gadamer with the insight that justice is realized in a hermeneutic conversation rather than as the cessation of conversation by achieving the (always unattainable) rationally compelled consensus.

Gadamer explored numerous topics during his long career. Admittedly, my discussion selectively focuses on elements of his philosophy that reveal the rhetorical rationality in hermeneutical experience, but this is a core feature of his philosophical hermeneutics. Although Gadamer's efforts along these lines are not fully elaborated, at several junctures he indicates an awareness and appreciation of Perelman's work on the new rhetoric. By turning now to a similarly selective reading of Perelman's work, I will generate a more full-bodied account that provides the basis for a theory of rhetorical knowledge.

The New Rhetoric: Justice as Persuasion

Unlike Gadamer, Chaim Perelman was motivated from the beginning of his philosophical career to elucidate the principles of justice, and the ancient conception of rhetoric plays an explicit and central role in his philosophy. In his first major work, Perelman demonstrated that arguments about the dictates of justice cannot be rational, since the arguments cannot accord with formal logic; this bizarre conclusion led him to seek an informal logic of justice.[59] Perelman begins by recognizing that the progenitive force of Descartes' philosophical thinking committed the Western philosophical tradition to a univocal vision of truth, according to which at least one party to every real disagreement must be wrong if the disagreement involves a proposition having a truth value.[60] Skepticism is a natural and perhaps inevitable outgrowth of this truncated conception of knowledge and truth. "The imperialism of rationalistic dogmatism finds its counterpart in the nihilism of positivistic scepticism. Either each question is resolved by finding the objectively best solution and this is the task of reason, or truth does not exist and every solution depends upon subjective factors: reason can be no guide to action."[61] Finding that Kant's majestic effort to salvage practical reasoning has failed, Perelman argues that political theorists simply abandoned attempts at rational inquiry into matters of justice and conceded that there can be no demonstrable truth about such matters.[62] Unsatisfied with this bleak situation, Perelman set for himself the task of rethinking the roots of the tradition that led inexorably to these conclusions. In his magnum opus, Perelman describes his philosophical project as a break with the Cartesian tradition and a return to studying the means by which it is possible to secure adherence to reasonable claims regarding the requirements of justice.[63]

Persuasion and Reasonable Adherence

To rehabilitate philosophical inquiry into the means of reasonable persuasion, Perelman rejects the search for timeless truths that is exemplified in Plato's philosophy in favor of the model of thinking provided by Aristotle's rhetorical philosophy.[64] Perelman refines Aristotle's distinction between a dialectical demonstration (involving a rational deduction from agreed, although not necessary, premises) and rhetorical persuasion (the art of convincing a public that is not trained in the dialectical method), arguing that this distinction is not fundamental and that rhetorical persuasion can be reasonable.[65] Joining the truth value of dialectic with the performance of rhetorical persuasion, Perelman contends that the practice of reasoning about matters of justice has an epistemological status between formal deduction and fanatical, irrational adherence.

> Since rhetorical proof is never a completely necessary proof, the thinking man who gives his adherence to the conclusions of an argumentation does so by an act that commits him and for which he is responsible. The fanatic accepts the commitment, but as one bowing to an absolute and irrefragable truth; the skeptic refuses the commitment under the pretext that he does not find it sufficiently definitive. He refuses adherence because his idea of adherence is similar to that of the fanatic: both fail to appreciate that argumentation aims at a choice among possible theses; by proposing and justifying the hierarchy of these theses, argumentation seeks to make the decision a rational one. This role of argumentation in decision-making is denied by the skeptic and the fanatic. In the absence of compelling reason, they both are inclined to give violence a free hand, rejecting personal commitment.[66]

Perelman's central claim is that we can reaffirm the reasonableness of claims about justice only by moving beyond the narrow conception of rationality resulting from Cartesian presuppositions and embracing the broader conception of reasonable action that he fashions from Aristotle's discussion of the rhetorical arts.[67] As Dilip Gaonkar summarizes, Perelman offers rhetoric "as an alternative theory of argumentation that can provide grounding for philosophy, jurisprudence, and the human sciences in the wake of that colossal failure of the logicist tradition in philosophy from Descartes to logical positivism."[68] Perelman's goal was not simply to update the inventory of rhetorical techniques for modern time, but rather to initiate a "rhetorical turn" in contemporary thought.[69]

By distinguishing the rational from the reasonable, Perelman argues, we can preserve the proper scope and role of each mode of thinking. The concept of the rational "is associated with self-evident truths and compelling reasoning" and therefore "is valid only in a theoretical domain,"[70] whereas to reason with another person "is not merely to verify and to demonstrate, but also to deliberate, to criticize, and to justify, to give reasons for and against—in a word, to argue."[71] By opening this space for argumentative reasoning, Perelman does not intend to maintain a strict bifurcation of the rational and the reasonable, since each inevitably plays off the other.

> It is the dialectic of the rational and the reasonable, the confrontation of logical coherence with the unreasonable character of conclusions, which is the basis of the progress of thought. . . . The rational in law corresponds to adherence to an immutable divine standard, or to the spirit of the system, to logic and coherence, to conformity with precedents, to purposefulness; whereas the reasonable, on the other hand, characterizes the decision itself, the fact that it is acceptable or not by public opinion, that its consequences are socially useful or harmful, that it is felt to be equitable or biased. . . . Thus, the idea of the reasonable in law corresponds to an equitable solution, in the absence of all precise rules of adjudication. But it can be that recourse to the reasonable only gives a provisional solution, waiting for the elaboration of new legal construction

> which would be more satisfying. The reasonable guides this endeavor toward systematization, toward the rational systematic solution.[72]

Reason acts as a check on the colonizing imperatives of rationality, just as rationality provides the aspirational model for reasoning.

Persuasion and "Confused Notions"

To emphasize the philosophical nature of his project, Perelman asserts that justice is a "confused notion," by which he means that it cannot be clarified according to the test of absolute truth but can only be developed in the course of responding to the practical demands of political action in a manner informed by reasonable belief.[73] Conceiving philosophy in the Cartesian manner as the means of eliminating confusion precludes philosophy from serving as a guide for civic action, since circumstances often demand a reasonable compromise in response to a choice between two or more courses of action that can be defended equally on logical grounds. What holds true for the topic of justice holds true for philosophical inquiry generally: philosophy often is concerned with confused notions and therefore never reaches definitive conclusions except in the most narrowly defined circumstances. Perelman regards his "new rhetoric" as a philosophical claim about how we reason rather than simply as a handbook of certain technical, forensic skills used in public speaking, concluding that if "rhetoric is regarded as complementary to formal logic and argumentation as complementary to demonstrative proof, it becomes of paramount importance in philosophy, since no philosophic discourse can develop without resorting to it."[74] Unfortunately, Perelman never expanded this insight into a more general philosophy of language that emphasizes pragmatics over semantics and rejects the fantasy of developing an ideal, perspicacious language that can resolve all philosophical problems once they are shorn of the ambiguity and illogic of everyday communication.[75]

The new rhetoric is concerned with reasonable action rather than rational contemplation, and thus resumes "the age-old debate between those who stand for truth and those who stand for opinion, between philosophers seeking the absolute and rhetors involved in action."[76] Perelman crystallizes this opposition by distinguishing rational thought—in which the truth of the matter can be known definitively through careful reflection—from acting reasonably in circumstances in which the "truth" of the matter is uncertain and multidimensional. In the face of limited time and information, profound disagreements about the relevant guiding principles, and the inability to reach complete consensus without the use of force, our challenge is to act reasonably rather than coercively. To overcome the philosophical tradition—epitomized by formal logic—which has disabled the ideal of reasonable action, Perelman outlines an informal logic of social action rooted in practical demands and concerns.[77]

Perelman asserts that the existence of competing arguments should not be regarded as a sign that at least one of the participants has engaged in defective thinking or that the matter in question is one that admits only of irrational adherence. Instead, he demonstrates that argumentation has its own logic or reasonableness that can foster reasonable action even in the face of undecidability under Cartesian strictures of rationality. As a prime example, Perelman points to the operation of the legal system in which arguments are made and action is taken despite the inevitable lack of indubitable knowledge about the questions raised by the case at hand.[78] In this venue and others, it is the process of argumentation that gives meaning to human freedom by underscoring judgment as a reasonable choice among several viable alternatives.[79] Perelman's theme is that norms for action can never be justified purely through empirical observation (empiricism/naturalism) nor purely through conceptual analysis (rationalism), but that this situation does not consign normative inquiry to irrationality (intuitionism/emotivism). Argumentation exists as a shared experience of a lived, practical reasoning.

Transforming Aristotelian Rhetoric

Perelman's philosophical reconceptualization of rhetoric is evident in the ways that he transforms familiar rhetorical principles. The concept of the audience played an important role in Aristotle's *Rhetoric,* but Perelman emphasizes the philosophical significance of the notion of audience in order to describe a mode of knowing, rather than simply identifying the group of listeners who require artful convincing due to their inability or unwillingness to follow the philosopher's dialectical demonstrations.[80] Attention to one's audience signals an ethics of humility in light of the speaker's commitment to persuade rather than coerce her adherence.[81] A speaker who truly addresses her audience remains open to the possibility that she may fail in her task if the audience is not persuaded or that she may even be converted to a new view in light of the rhetorical exchange. Perelman insists that we "must not forget that by listening to someone we display a willingness to eventually accept his point of view."[82] Thus, the audience is not simply an empirical fact that the rhetor must take into account and use in the single-minded pursuit of her goals; it is a community that the rhetor seeks to persuade as an engaged and committed participant.

The extent to which Perelman transforms the conception of the audience is underscored by his notion of the "universal audience," seemingly an oxymoron under the Aristotelian reference to the audience as a means of emphasizing attention to context. Perelman regards the universal audience as the touchstone for philosophical argumentation, which is engaged in persuasion rather than logical demonstration, but which seeks to persuade an anonymous audience of all inquiring minds. "To reconcile philosophical claims to rationality with the plurality of philosophical systems, we must recognize that the appeal to reason must be identified not as an appeal to a single truth but instead as an appeal for the adherence of an audience, which can be thought of, after the manner of Kant's categorical imperative, as encompassing all reasonable and competent men."[83] Perelman employs the concept of a universal audience to capture the self-effacing gesture of philosophical thinking, in which a thinker proposes arguments that she deems acceptable to all reasonable persons, rather than to suggest that the philosopher can invoke a privileged human faculty with access to demonstrable universal truth.[84]

At several points, Perelman appears to equate the hypothetical universal audience with a regulative ideal premised on the actual agreement that all reasonable persons would reach under the circumstances. However, he makes clear that the universal audience is "always a more or less systematized construction" by the rhetor, by which he means that it is part of the speaker's activity rather than a claim about how actual, reasonable persons must react to the argumentation.[85] The universal audience serves a function similar to Vico's sensus communis, then, by representing the speaker's construction of an audience from historical, finite, and communal resources.[86] Although the universal audience is therefore grounded and contextual in its construction and representation by the rhetor, James Crosswhite emphasizes that the defining feature of this rhetorical construction is a gesture that looks beyond any existing audience.[87] This accords with one of Perelman's last characterizations of the universal audience, in which he argued that "every philosopher addresses himself to the universal audience as he conceives it, even in the absence of an objectivity which imposes itself upon everyone."[88] The gesture of constructing a universal audience in philosophical discourse is essential, since it makes clear that the philosopher has no access to a disembodied logic of truth. The philosopher engages in actual discussions with fellow citizens who serve as representatives of the hypothetical community of all reasonable persons who remain to be convinced and whose challenges or obtuseness might always, in principle, lead the philosopher to revise her thinking.

Robert Alexy has suggested that Perelman's universal audience serves much the same role that Habermas's ideal speech situation serves in Habermas's critical theory, namely as an idealized form of dialogic interaction that is anticipated in every genuine communicative exchange.[89] James Crosswhite agrees, but persuasively argues that Perelman succeeds in ways that Habermas cannot, since Perelman avoids becoming entangled in transcendental claims.[90] Reinforcing this distinction, Thomas Conley explains that Habermas regards ordinary speech as potentially ideological and irrational, leading him to reject the rhetorical tradition in favor of attempting to define a universal principle of rationality.[91] This reading is supported by Habermas's comments about his book on legal theory, in which he emphasizes that the validity and legitimacy of legal norms depend upon the participation of all persons possibly affected in rational discourse, a situation that he contrasts with the application of norms to practical situations in judicial decision making.[92] Habermas's approach, therefore, stands in sharp contrast to Perelman's suggestion, explored below, that judicial decision making can serve as a model for moral philosophy.[93]

In addition to reworking the Aristotelian conception of audience, Perelman places great emphasis on the central Aristotelian insight that persuasion can be successful only when it proceeds from prior, shared agreements between the speaker and her audience by effecting a community of interests.[94] Presupposed agreement among the parties is a necessary feature of every act of persuasion because there is no recourse to justifications that exist outside the unfolding historical situation in which both speaker and listener are enmeshed, a historical context which alone can provide grounds for deciding between two alternatives.

> Aristotle emphasized that, when it is a question of dialectical reasoning, it is necessary to begin with what is accepted by the listeners, with what constitutes an accepted opinion, a recognized value. In rhetorical and philosophical tradition, this point of departure has been defined as commonplace.
>
> ----------
>
> It is true that the search for universally valid principles which would provide a common context for all criticisms and all justifications has been a millennial aspiration of all philosophy, and especially of all rationalist philosophy. But, in fact, criticism and justification are always found in a historically determined context. For all societies and for all intellects, there exist certain acts, certain agents, certain values and beliefs that at a given moment are approved without reservation and accepted without argument; hence there is no need to justify them. These acts, these persons, these values, and these beliefs furnish precedents, models, convictions, and norms which in turn permit the elaboration of criteria by which to criticize and to justify attitudes, dispositions, and propositions.
>
> ----------
>
> Every effort to convince presupposes the existence of an agreement on certain notions and principles.[95]

Perelman spends the better part of his treatise cataloguing the techniques for employing "commonplaces" as points of departure when seeking adherence through argumentation.[96]

It bears emphasis that Perelman does not regard this exercise as just a matter of elaborating on the argumentative techniques previously discovered by Aristotle; instead, he seeks to express an important philosophical insight. Prior agreement on matters that cannot be deduced by means of formal logic is an unavoidable starting point for any inquiry, even within the natural sciences, for it is precisely this prior agreement that is recuperated and expanded in the course of seeking to persuade another. Perelman does distinguish arguments seeking agreement about the "real" (including facts, truths, and presumptions) and arguments seeking agreement as to the "preferable" (including values, hierarchies of values, and lines of argumentation). In the former case, one is committed to persuading the universal audience, whereas in the latter instance, one seeks only to assert a validity claim with respect to a particular audience. However, Perelman makes clear that there can be no definitive demarcation between the two, since "[v]alues enter, at some stage or other, into every argument," such that "all audiences, of all kinds, have to take loci [commonplaces of argument] into account."[97] The web of preexisting beliefs subtending any discussion is always subject to testing and revision, although it is impossible for discussants to rise above such beliefs in their totality by grounding their discussion on a rationalist Archimedean point.

Perelman believes that the wisdom of the legal system flows from the fact that it institutionalizes this philosophical insight.

> The exigencies of the juridical order, which continues through all kinds of upheavals as long as it has not been entirely or partially replaced by a new order, clearly show us what is unfeasible in the advice of Descartes, asking us to make a tabula rosa of all our opinions. . . . Nobody has ever seriously put in doubt the totality of his opinions, for they test each other reciprocally: One keeps those which, up to the present moment, have best resisted the testing. This, however, does not guarantee them absolutely against all subsequent tests.
>
> ----------
>
> Thus rationality, as it presents itself in law, is always a form of continuity—conformity to previous rules or justification of the new by means of old values. . . . Law teaches us, on the contrary, to abandon existing rules only if good reasons [drawn from other existing rules] justify their replacement.[98]

In Perelman's view, this epistemological reality translates to the normative principle of inertia: adherence to presupposed agreement embodied in precedents should have presumptive force, although challenges should be recognized if the proposed change is defended by reasons, which of course will be derived from the aspects of presupposed agreement that are not brought into question at that time.[99]

By claiming that the shared assumptions from which we reason have presumptive authority because they are unavoidable, even if they remain subject to revision on a relatively localized basis by working from the undisturbed features of shared understandings, Perelman faces strong criticism that his approach favors a naive acceptance of the powerful force of ideology in shaping the prior agreements in a given society.[100] However, like Gadamer, Perelman resists succumbing to the unattainable goal of rising above situatedness in prior agreement by emphasizing that critical insight is made possible by this very situatedness.[101]

Justice, Legal Practice, and Philosophy as Persuasion

Having established his philosophical orientation with specific references to the legal system, Perelman argues that justice can be the subject of reasoned inquiry despite its "confused" nature. The traditional idea that justice is achieved when the natural law is embodied within positive legal institutions must be rejected to the extent that the natural law is presumed to be a universal and timeless set of directives. However, Perelman argues that both Aquinas and Aristotle invoked a more subtle conception of natural law that accepts the ontological pluralism of legal practice without devolving into a relativistic positivism.

> The idea of natural law is also misconceived when it is posed in ontological terms. . . . Natural law is better considered as a body of general principles or loci, consisting of ideas such as "the nature of things," "the rule of law," and of rules such as "No one is expected to perform impossibilities," "Both sides should be heard"—all of which are capable of being applied in different ways. It is the task of the legislator or judge to decide which of the not unreasonable solutions should become a rule of positive law. Such a view, according to Michel Villey, corresponds to the idea of natural law found in Aristotle and St. Thomas Aquinas—what he calls the classical natural law.[102]

Although legal practice can never be reduced to a formal logic, there is a nature of law in the sense that all legal argumentation works from presumed agreement embodied in commonplaces.[103] Perelman goes so far as to suggest that an analysis of the elements of legal reasoning might provide a map of argumentative strategies by which the demands of justice are articulated, challenged, and defended.[104]

The legal system provides a unique setting for reasoning about justice because the advocate and judge must act; they do not have the option to withhold their judgment and to stay action until certainty is established. As a result, legal judgments represent a further articulation of general principles in the course of resolving the case at hand rather than a deductive application of a legal rule that is thoroughly understood prior to resolving the dispute.[105] Rejecting both formalist jurisprudence and the cynical, demystifying hubris of some forms of critical legal theory, Perelman focuses on the reasonableness that is embedded in legal argumentation.[106] He applies the philosophical import of Aristotle's analysis of equity: legal decisions always require a defense of the preferable outcome in the present case to some degree, no matter how clear-cut the abstract general principle appears to be in addressing the case.[107]

Although the demand for action has always prevented lawyers and judges from engaging in an abstract pursuit of universal certainty, legal theorists only now are beginning to emerge from under the oppressive mantle of scientism to rediscover that rhetoric is a central feature of legal practice.[108] For this reason, Perelman believes that the practice of legal argumentation provides a model for philosophical inquiry, and particularly moral philosophy, and that an analysis of legal practice provides a helpful guide to establishing the appropriate role of philosophical thought.

> After having sought, for centuries, to model philosophy on the sciences, and having considered each of its particularities as a sign of inferiority, perhaps the moment has come to consider that philosophy has many traits in common with law. A confrontation with the latter would permit better understanding of the specificity of philosophy, a discipline which is elaborated under the aegis of reason, but a reason which is essentially practical, turned toward rational decision and action.

> [T]he diverse principles which the philosophers have presented as supreme norms in ethics are in reality only commonplaces, in the meaning of classical rhetoric, that they give reasons which are to be considered in each concrete situation rather than as axioms like those of geometry whose consequences can be drawn by simple deduction. Practical reasoning, applicable in morality, must not be inspired by the mathematical model, which is not applicable in changing circumstances, but by a knowledge characterized by reasonableness and by the taking into consideration diverse aspirations and multiple interests, defined by Aristotle as phronesis or prudence, and which is so brilliantly manifested in law, in Roman jurisprudentia.
>
> ----------
>
> If law has suffered much from being too influenced by the sciences, I believe the same reproach can be addressed to philosophy. . . . If the new concept of law spreads, which is basically a very old one, and which has been forgotten for centuries, philosophers will have much to learn from it. They will look to the techniques of the jurist to learn how to reason about values, how to realize an equilibrium, how to bring about a synthesis of values.[109]

Of course, Perelman does not equate the task of the lawyers and the judge in a particular lawsuit to the task of a philosopher writing about the conditions of justice. However, Perelman insists that it is precisely the principles of the new rhetoric which permit a distinction to be drawn between these two different rhetorical exchanges by attending to the different audiences engaged by these different activities of argumentation.[110]

Rhetorical Knowledge

I read Gadamer and Perelman as challenging supplements to each other in order to develop an account of "rhetorical knowledge" that can serve as the point of departure for contemporary legal theory. Rhetorical knowledge is a practical accomplishment that neither achieves apodictic certitude nor collapses into a relativistic irrationalism. Consequently, rhetorical knowledge can sustain legal practice as a reasonable—even if not thoroughly rationalized—social activity. Before proceeding with an analysis of how the theory of rhetorical knowledge can play an important role in understanding and critiquing modern legal practice, though, it is necessary to move beyond the descriptions of the individual projects undertaken by Gadamer and Perelman by sketching the connections between rhetoric and hermeneutics, and noting the distinctive contributions of each tradition. I conclude that Gadamer and Perelman both offer important insights into rhetorical knowledge that must be carefully integrated into a new approach to law and legal theory.

Hermeneutics and Rhetoric

The new rhetoric and philosophical hermeneutics have a number of natural affinities that flow from their participation in the same broad movement in contemporary philosophy away from the Cartesian paradigm of knowledge. As Morny Joy summarizes, contemporary "rhetoric and hermeneutics are both symptomatic of, and at the same time constitutive of, the changed philosophical situation."[111] This is not to suggest that hermeneutics and rhetoric have maintained wholly separate traditions which only now are being read together productively. It is more accurate to say that the problems and goals of hermeneutics and rhetoric have always been mutually implicated, and that it is our contemporary appreciation and elaboration of this situation that is proving to be instructive.[112] Although Perelman did not work explicitly in the Heideggerian tradition, several commentators have noted that the neo-Aristotelian conjunction of hermeneutics and rhetoric is closely related to Heidegger's attack on the Cartesian tradition that arose out of his own careful reading of Aristotle.[113] Philosophical hermeneutics and the new rhetoric unavoidably and inextricably are complicit in the contemporary challenges to Cartesian metaphysics epitomized by Heidegger's critique, and therefore share substantial common ground.[114]

Gadamer and Perelman undoubtedly strike a similar chord by emphasizing that a return to Aristotelian practical philosophy can expose and overcome the deficiencies of modern philosophical thought.[115] However, both thinkers underemphasize the extent to which philosophical hermeneutics and the new rhetoric reinforce each other in the task of recuperating Aristotle to displace the Cartesian tradition. From a rhetorical perspective, philosophical hermeneutics provides guidance in the face of the "Cartesian anxiety" by providing an ontological account of the social nature of understanding. This proves to be critical for avoiding the relativistic implications of abandoning the Cartesian model of knowledge without offering a new account in its stead.[116] From a hermeneutical perspective, the new rhetoric provides guidance in the face of hermeneutical idealism by moving from an ontology of understanding to political engagement. This proves to be critical for improving ongoing rhetorical practices and avoiding the conservative implications of replacing the Cartesian model only with abstract principles of historicity and finitude. Under this reconfigured and integrated approach, the breakdown of the Cartesian paradigm leads to the rediscovery of a better ontological account of communication and understanding rather than an irrational abandonment of objective methodological inquiry.

The new orientation that emerges from the confrontation of hermeneutics with rhetoric is grounded in the activity of social interaction rather than in theorizing the hermeneutical situation in which each individual finds herself. Nevertheless, this reorientation in philosophical perspective not only facilitates a description of reasonable dialogic interaction, it opens the way for effective critique. Philosophical hermeneutics and contemporary rhetorical theory converge in the claim that there is a lived truth beyond the boundaries of Cartesian metaphysics, a truth that is actualized only in rhetorical exchanges but that can be augmented by a theoretical comportment within these practices.

Perelman's rhetoric and Gadamer's hermeneutics do not by any means mirror each other, but the substantial connections between the principal themes of their work are striking. Most broadly summarized, both emphasize that inventiveness and critique emerge from the shared world of traditionary prejudices through hermeneutical understanding and in the course of rhetorical persuasion. When their work is read together it becomes clear that it is difficult to elaborate one activity without implicating the other. Gadamer and Perelman both look to Aristotle generally, and to his notions of natural law and practical wisdom more specifically, to explain the reasonableness of working through confused notions conversationally rather than methodologically, a practice that draws from existing elements of shared agreement to resolve contemporary problems for the moment rather than for all time. Of greatest significance for present purposes, they both argue that legal practice exemplifies their philosophical arguments. Contemporary work in rhetorical theory and hermeneutical philosophy has largely proceeded on separate tracks, failing to capitalize on the congruities in the foundational texts in these areas. My model of rhetorical knowledge derives from an understanding that is built on the fundamental similarities shared by the new rhetoric and philosophical hermeneutics.

A Positive Account of Rhetorical Knowledge

Rhetorical knowledge is coequal with logical and empirical knowledge, but it is a different way of knowing. Although rhetorical knowledge is a social achievement rather than an intellectual elaboration, it is properly characterized as knowledge. We can know the requirements of justice and we can know solutions to mathematical problems; it is just the case that our knowledge of justice is rhetorical rather than logical. Gadamer and Perelman provide the conceptual resources necessary for providing a positive account of rhetorical knowledge, as opposed to defining it as a watered-down version of "true" knowledge. This positive account provides the basis for claiming that legal practice has an epistemic dimension that goes beyond strategic means-ends analysis.

The bias of the modern age is to equate knowledge with the logical foundations of modern science and to characterize nonscientific discourses as "mere" aesthetics, self-expression, or hortatory moralizing. Because rhetorical knowledge arises out of a historical and social situation that remains dynamic and contingent, it cannot be subsumed under the model of rational thinking according to logical dictates. It is counterproductive, though, simply to reverse the Enlightenment prejudice by falsely aggrandizing rhetorical knowledge and suppressing other ways of knowing. In short, "it is important to seek to understand rhetoric as *a* way of knowing not *the* way."[117] The tragic error of the age of science has not been the championing of a certain mode of knowledge as much as the failure to recognize the multiplicity of ways of knowing. It is important to remember that nobody today proposes to revive Aristotelian biology, and that the growth of scientific knowledge has been beneficial to social life in numerous ways.

Giving into the strong temptation to regard all knowledge as rhetorical knowledge ultimately would undermine the usefulness of the term. Seeking the adherence of others in reasonable argumentation is ubiquitous across disciplines and modes of thought; therefore, in an important sense all knowledge is rhetorically defended and propagated.[118] Thomas Kuhn's account of the history of science as a sequence of incommensurable paradigms of thought has been the fountainhead for an expansive body of work describing the social dimension of science. A shift from one scientific paradigm to another does not reflect the orderly advance of thought according to some wider, methodologically secured rationality, Kuhn teaches, but instead represents the success of proponents of the new paradigm in securing the adherence of the relevant scientific community.[119] Kuhn's insight is too easily accommodated to the prevailing scientistic ideology, however, by dismissing the rhetorical strategies of those engaged in battles to redefine paradigms as unfortunate deviations from the rational elaboration that comprises "normal science," deviations made necessary by our limited ability to perceive the structure of the natural world. Grudgingly conceding the social and historical roots of the prevailing scientific paradigm, defenders nevertheless can champion the rational thought enabled by such irrationally secured initial orientations. The result is to maintain the traditional bifurcation of rhetorical commitment and rational knowledge, even if the dividing line is drawn a little tighter around the citadel of reason, thereby obscuring the positive status of the activity of rhetorical knowledge.

It makes sense to follow Gadamer's somewhat conservative tendency to accord natural science its own (limited) epistemic space so as to avoid developing an account of rhetorical knowledge that is so capacious and abstract as to be unhelpful. Although scientists are able to generate very reliable knowledge that has far-reaching ramifications for social life, their work can never render superfluous the rhetorical knowledge embedded in traditional belief systems that sustain their research agendas. Using "rhetorical knowledge" to refer to this shared, dynamic belief system founded on the probable—as distinguished from the specific field of scientific rationality—permits greater clarity in the discussion. Thus, it is appropriate to speak of two intertwined rationalities and to acknowledge the profound importance of rhetorical knowledge as a dimension of human reason.

> [T]he intrinsic rationality of scientific methods does not imply that scientists themselves, let alone the rest of modern society, use anything resembling these methods to arrive at the beliefs on which they base their everyday behavior. The content of "common sense" gradually changes to reflect the findings of science—often with a "lag" of a century or more—but the process of thinking remains the same. If we identify rationality with scientific method, this would mean that people are still as irrational as ever. But it is much less misleading to conclude that most people have been rational all along in the more relevant sense: namely, they reason from assumptions believed to be true in their community, and which they have no reason to doubt.[120]

In Perelman's terms, science involves claims about the "real" that are directed to a "universal audience," rather than claims about the "preferable" course of action that are directed to a "particular audience" with the goal of inducing the audience's commitment to act. It is now commonplace to recognize that rhetorical principles clarify the different status of scientific rationality and suggest that a measure of caution against the tendency to overgeneralize is appropriate. As Aristotle observed with succinct clarity, it is "a mark of an educated person to look in each area for only that degree of accuracy that the nature of the subject permits. Accepting from a mathematician claims that are mere probabilities seems rather like demanding logical proofs from a rhetorician."[121] Respecting this distinction implies respecting (for present purposes) the disciplinary boundaries of science and humanistic inquiry as demarcating two rhetorical practices that can be usefully distinguished in terms of their goals: scientific knowledge and rhetorical knowledge.

Given that there are different ways of knowing, it follows that it would be a profound mistake to believe that they are equally suited for all purposes. Scientific knowledge and reasoning play only a small, subsidiary role in the establishment and enforcement of legal norms, despite their appealing rigor and consistency. Very few legal questions can be resolved by means of a scientific demonstration. Adjudicating a paternity dispute generally is thought to be a straightforward question of biology, but even in this situation the scientific determination of biological relationships is bounded by legal norms that are not grounded in, nor applied with, scientific reasoning. For example, a putative father who years ago legally acknowledged paternity of a child born to his mistress in order to hide the (groundless) allegations of paternity from his wife might find that his current effort to prove scientifically that he in fact is not the biological father of the child is utterly beside the point for legal purposes.[122] On the other hand, the biological father of a child born to a woman who was then married to another man may find that he has no legal standing as the father even if he offers nearly conclusive scientific proof of his paternity.[123] With respect to most legal questions, of course, claims of scientific knowledge provide support for only one line of argumentation among many pursued by a lawyer, as when a prosecutor introduces DNA evidence demonstrating that the defendant's blood was found at the scene of a murder as part of a much broader case consisting of arguments concerning the defendant's motive, opportunity, and capability to commit the crime. Consequently, not only does it make sense to distinguish scientific claims supported by expert testimony from rhetorical claims about the demands of justice in a given case, it also seems clear that rhetorical knowledge figures far more prominently in legal practice. For example, while it might make sense to admit expert testimony from a linguist as to how an average competent speaker of the English language might understand a certain term in a contract, it would be wholly inappropriate to suppose that linguistic science could be imported to the legal system to settle definitively the normative question about how contract provisions should be interpreted and enforced in specific cases.[124]

Defending the reality of rhetorical knowledge means more than highlighting the limitations of the rationalist account of knowledge. Gadamer and Perelman complement each other because they provide different insights into the activity of rhetorical knowledge as a positive and distinct accomplishment. Each thinker stresses that rhetorical knowledge is knowledge rather than a skill that remains subordinate to rational inquiry.

Gadamer's early writings suggest that he embraced the romantic notion of two cultures of knowing and that he viewed his role as reasserting the legitimacy of humanistic knowing in the face of scientific hegemony. More recently, even as he acknowledged Kuhn's legacy and the undeniable hermeneutical grounding of scientific rationality, Gadamer has avoided the temptation to collapse science into hermeneutics and thereby simply to reverse the hierarchy.[125] Following this lead, I delineate a positive account of rhetorical knowledge that is not beholden to either philosopher's particular project, but that holds true to the central argument propelling both thinkers by seeking to uncover the activity of rhetorical exchange as a vital element of human reasonableness. I begin with a working definition of rhetorical knowledge as the accomplishment of two or more persons working together creatively to refashion the linguistically structured symbols of social cohesion that serve as the resources for intersubjective experience. For the remainder of the book, I explore this paradoxical, self-reflexive definition and then chart the role of rhetorical knowledge in the practice and theory of law.

At the outset, it is important to recall that the positive account of rhetorical knowledge has ancient lineage and is not just a fancy reworking of Aristotelian philosophy by contemporary thinkers. Treating rhetoric as logos is a forgotten part of the legacy of the Greek Sophists, a shrouded inheritance that has been transmitted to us largely through Plato's vitriolic attacks against it and Aristotle's begrudging acceptance of some of its elements.[126] Recovering a conception of rhetoric as the study of logos from the discredited Sophist tradition is a helpful first step toward developing a positive conception of rhetorical knowledge.

Perelman's new rhetoric does not revise Aristotle so much as expand upon Aristotle's concessions to the rhetorical conception of logos promoted by Isocrates in opposition to Plato's philosophy of truth. Although Aristotle chastised the Sophists as boastful pretenders to knowledge, he agreed that "rhetoric is a certain kind of offshoot of dialectic and of ethical studies."[127] In the commentary to his translation of *On Rhetoric,* George Kennedy suggests Aristotle was attempting to recognize the full dimensions of rhetoric without conceding too much to his philosophical adversary, Isocrates.[128] However one interprets Aristotle's equivocations, it appears clear that Aristotle—and even Plato—owes much to the Sophist tradition that emerged with Protagoras and blossomed with Isocrates.[129] Despite this lasting influence, important differences between the older Sophists, as traveling provocateurs, and the rhetorical philosophy of Plato, Aristotle, and even Isocrates remain. "While the rhetoric of the sophists has no end-point, those of Plato, Isocrates, and Aristotle do. . . . [T]he philosophers articulated positions while the sophists provided only op-positions."[130]

A strong argument can be made that the rhetorical tradition stretching from the Sophist Protagoras to Isocrates and then to their Roman successors Cicero and Quintilian provides the most suitable intellectual resources for Perelman's efforts to define a positive account of rhetorical knowledge, given that Aristotle's more limited account never displaces the centrality of formal reason.[131] The Sophists emerged as itinerant teachers when Greece made the transition from an unreflective "mythical-poetic" culture to a literate, critical, and reflective culture of logos. In the face of proliferating opinions about the social and political order, the Sophists set for themselves the task of discerning what constituted good opinions through argumentative assessments of prevailing wisdom.[132] Sophistic irreverence functionally served a growing middle class in an emerging democracy. "Contrary to what some of their critics have said, the sophists' motto was not the survival of the fittest but fitting as many as possible for survival [in the post-aristocratic world]. . . . Insofar as the sophists enabled more people to enter the contests and spectacles of public life, the rhetoric they taught created at least two new possibilities: first, the possibility of the weaker challenging the stronger; and second, the possibility of revitalizing calcified discursive practices."[133] As unreflective custom was replaced by energetic and unceasing disputation, conflicts between plural reasonable social arrangements and political activities became unavoidable.

In a judicious and meticulous book, Edward Schiappa pieces together the teaching of Protagoras to uncover the rhetorical conception of logos that emerged in Periclean Athens.[134] Protagoras was "the most famous and influential" of the older Sophists because he was able "to provide a theoretical justification for the practice of Periclean democracy," which was premised on his democratic conception of knowledge as a product of communal efforts.[135]

> The purpose of Protagoras' theory and practice of logos was to change people for the better. The objective was understood as literally analogous to the art of medicine. The thesis that people can be made more excellent marked a departure from the traditional belief that arete [excellence in civic virtues] was a function of wealth or noble birth.[136]
>
> ----------
>
> Protagoras' rhetorical theory, therefore, can be described as an early formulation or anticipation of just such a relationship between logos and collective judgment.
>
> Far from entailing solipsism or absolute subjectivism, Protagoras' logos is an instrument aimed at intersubjectivity. . . . For Protagoras, a consensus induced through logos was the means of reaching good judgment.[137]

Protagoras regarded this educative function of discourse to be a guiding principle, reasoning that studying the art of discourse is of utmost importance if civic virtue is developed in discourse.

Schiappa stresses that this mission is often misunderstood, as in the case of traditional interpretations of Protagoras's famous "two logoi" fragment. Reading the fragment to mean that the Sophists prided themselves on being able to make the weaker argument appear stronger by force of their rhetorical skills—a common pejorative reading by those who dismiss the Sophists—misses the positive account of knowledge advocated by Protagoras. Schiappa demonstrates that the best reading "understands 'making the weaker account [logos] the stronger' as advocating the substitution of a preferred (but weaker) logos for a less preferable (but temporarily dominant) logos of the same experience."[138] Critics charge the Sophists with relativism because they rejected the idea that any argument could prove itself to be "the stronger" for all time. But, by embracing the "dissoi logoi—human linguistic creations in unceasing contest with one another," the Sophists did not reject the possibility that one argument could emerge from the contest as the better argument at a given time and in a given context.[139] In short, Protagoras champions the process of persuasion by which what was once deemed the better argument is rejected in favor of the (truly, but only for present purposes) better argument.

Michael Gagarin takes issue with the standard interpretation of Protagoras's fragment in a different manner, but his reading also reinforces my working definition of rhetorical knowledge. Gagarin argues that it is only in parodies by Aristophanes and others that Protagoras is reported to claim that sophistic technique could make the weaker argument the stronger argument, with the implication being that the less just and appropriate argument could be made to prevail in debate.

> But there is no evidence that Protagoras or the other Sophists intended "weaker" to mean only "morally inferior." Nor did they necessarily wish to make the weaker *logos* prevail. Only Aristophanes speaks of the weaker *logos* winning, and this outcome is clearly motivated by his plot. Other citations of the expression do not give an article to the second adjective: one should make the weaker *logos* "stronger," not "the stronger." It can be a useful exercise to make the weaker *logos* as strong as possible, even though it may still be weaker no matter how much stronger one makes it.[140]

The point in this ambiguity is that Protagoras is challenging the idea that the value of stronger or weaker is fixed (by superior moral content, victory in debate, and so on), and that the lack of fixity does not necessarily invite the moral relativism that Plato alleges. Rephrased in terms of my definition of rhetorical knowledge, Protagoras and other Sophists argued strenuously that knowledge of the correct course of action emerges in the creative refashioning of the linguistically structured symbols of social cohesion by members of the public.

Isocrates famously challenged the Sophists for peddling technique as wisdom, and in so doing he brought their insights into the realm of philosophy. In response, Aristotle conceded the significance of rhetoric but characterized it as an art with the internal end of finding the available means of persuasion in each case, thus avoiding relegating rhetoric to a crude sophistic technique of inducing one's audience to form certain beliefs. Aristotle's concession provides the opening for Gadamer and Perelman to reconceive the role of rhetoric, but Aristotle must be interpreted liberally in this effort. Given the power of rhetoric to prove opposites, Aristotle insisted that rhetoric remained subordinate to politics, ethics, and ultimately philosophy.[141] This contrasts with Isocrates' efforts to delineate a full-bodied rhetoric as a mode of practical reasoning and a habituation to reasoned participation in civic affairs. "Isocrates situated practical wisdom inside and not apart from the process of deliberation, thereby placing prudence and political oratory in interactions with and reciprocal influence of one another."[142] Isocrates does not consider rhetoric to be a self-enclosed technical mode of reasoning to be employed in response to a pre-given audience; rather, he sees rhetoric as the art of civic discourse in which the rhetor "hails the audience into existence" and is an active agent in the creation of social norms and goals.[143]

Following the Protagorean tradition that found a unique voice in Isocrates, I insist that the results of public rhetorical engagement can be "knowledge." Although the starting points for rhetorical knowledge are the flux of lived existence and the pre-understandings embedded in patterns of social discourse and interaction, rhetorical knowledge is distinguished from habit or convention by its inventive representation and reinscription of the "prejudices" of situatedness. Surveying accepted topics, norms, and opinions as resources for confronting the demands of the present, rhetorical actors continually conjoin these constitutive features of themselves and their society in unique ways. Over the past two hundred years, the public claims made on behalf of American "democracy" have varied widely and evolved dramatically as part of the effort of nation building; yet, amid this variation there has always been a deep and strong connection between these various claims and established American political traditions. The robust debate about what democracy means can thus be characterized as an evolving adaptation of a heterogeneous political tradition to the contested issues of the day. Although the inventive dimension of such elaboration can be almost imperceptible at times, such that a rhetorical exchange appears to be invoking only received wisdom, these incremental changes nevertheless prove to be educative in the long run, leading persons to new understandings not only of their society but also of themselves. Momentous rhetorical events do occur, as when a reconfiguration of communal images dramatically challenges received wisdom and impels an audience to see a matter in new light—consider the appeal to American democratic traditions in Martin Luther King Jr.'s "I have a dream" speech—but it is a mistake to regard these exciting experiences as paradigms of rhetorical knowledge. These moments of rhetorical drama represent relatively rare limit cases, and so focusing attention on them can obscure the everyday "ordinary science" of rhetorical knowledge upon which they build.

Using terms such as "invention" and "refashioning" to describe rhetorical activity is potentially deceptive to the extent that it brings to mind an image of a skilled technician adjusting the rhetorical bonds of society as one might adjust a fuel injection system to maximize engine performance. The distinctiveness of rhetorical knowledge, though, is that it does not service pre-given ends. As praxis exhibiting *phronesis* rather than *poiesis* exhibiting *techne,* rhetorical exchanges redefine the criteria for assessing their accomplishments simultaneously with accomplishing rhetorical knowledge. Thus, one must insist that rhetorical knowledge be characterized as an ongoing accomplishment rather than an elaboration of what is given and remains unquestioned. Syllogistic reasoning from accepted major premises is dialectical in nature and can be a matter of individual effort, even if the proof later is publicized with the intent to persuade others of the correctness of one's reasoning. Rhetorical reasoning, on the other hand, is always a reciprocal activity that depends upon the existence of an ethical relationship between the speaker and audience, although neither wholly surrenders to the other due to the dynamic and sometimes abrasive confrontation between them. This ethical relationship does not require a shared criterion of judgment, but rather is a shared space in which multiple criteria may be jointly proposed, tested, and employed.

Isocrates embodies the merging of practical reasoning and rhetorical performance in his emphasis on kairos rather than genre or methodology.[144] The ethical bond is forged in the spontaneous inventiveness of rhetorical knowledge.

> The notion of *kairos,* the right moment, stood for spontaneity and inventiveness in confronting social situations. Because *kairos* appears as an antipode of genre, some scholars have chosen it as an alternative to the traditional Aristotelian matrix. . . . *Kairos* seems inseparable from the sophistic notion of truths in opposition, *dissoi logoi*. . . . Because the truth is multifaceted, the speaker temporarily resolves the tension between the many possible answers by thrusting

> forth the one most suitable for the moment. The radical unfinalizability of any persuasive statement is thus a condition for a continuous renewal, not a mere repetition, of rhetorical answers to situations. . . . By the same token, a rhetorical *technē cannot supply a definitive repertoire of kairoi.*[145]

Inventiveness in this sense is at once epistemic and ethical.

Thus, we can agree with Andrew King that "a political rhetoric makes no sense apart from the idea of a community," without believing that such a community must be as cohesive and insulated as the Greek polis.[146] Indeed, Isocrates' Panhellenic efforts to fashion a wider community posed a contemporary challenge to such parochial rhetoric. Along different lines, Eugene Garver has argued against epistemic readings of the *Rhetoric* precisely to dislocate Aristotle's argument from a natural form of social life embodied in the polis.[147] Garver believes that recuperating Aristotle in this way opens the possibility for reasoned argumentation in the absence of a substantially shared *nomos,* and he regards the technical features of Aristotle's treatise as the most relevant teachings for today's fragmented culture.[148] Although Garver endorses Aristotle's conception of rhetoric as an ethical practice in the service of politics, Garver's detailed argument is easily assimilated to the "epistemic" response to the dilemma of justice in contemporary legal theory, lending substantial support to my analysis of rhetorical knowledge.

> Excessive rationality is unpersuasive because it makes us suspicious rather than trustful of the speaker. . . . When argument fails by being too logical, it fails by being too strong. Such an idea is impossible in logic—validity is the top of the scale, not a mean. Rhetorical arguments can be so strong, though, that they stop being persuasive. They are so strong that they eliminate the speaker and hearer from the decision process. Demonstrations, [Aristotle] says are insufficient for rhetoric, because the object of rhetoric is judgment, and therefore ethos and pathos have to be involved.
>
> ----------
>
> Deliberating well takes character. Arguing persuasively means showing that one is deliberating well and therefore showing character.

> Without character the speaker will not be able to see different weightings, and so he will be consigned to practicing the sophistic art in which all the things that can be otherwise, the things that form the subject of practical reason, are especially probable. . . . Without character, there is no ethical knowledge. Without ethical knowledge, one is left with empty technique.[149]

In this ethical-rational community of those engaged in debate we find the genesis of a society grounded in rhetorical knowledge.

Gadamer and Perelman share a fascination with the multicultural challenges presented by globalization because they agree that these challenges differ in intensity but not in kind from those arising within a particular culture. Rhetorical knowledge is gained in the reworking of criteria as part of the rhetorical motivation of judgment. The capacity for identifying and drawing upon shared commonplaces in order to bridge wide cultural differences is the same capacity that enables members of a society collectively to make sense of their traditional practices in the (not always slightly) different world of the present. The interaction of audience and speaker in an inventive project defines rhetorical knowledge and distinguishes it from ideological insularity on one hand and manipulation through propaganda on the other.

Jeffery Bineham emphasizes that Gadamer's ontological claim—that human finitude is the defining feature of the hermeneutical situation—does not undermine the claim that we can fashion a rhetorical defense of the "better" course of action that can be assessed according to the standard of reasonableness.

> Neither subjectivity nor universal agreement on the criteria for rationality obtains. . . . Rationality itself is a product of the [hermeneutical] medium, of the language and tradition that have established, for the time being, what is considered reasonable and unreasonable. . . . People live within a medium that does exhibit preferred understandings and interpretations, but other often unnoticed possibilities do exist within the medium and can be embraced and cultivated. For Gadamer this condition rescues hermeneutics from a morally and

> intellectually chaotic relativism. Any medium contains a variety of criteria for the comparison of rival interpretations and understandings. But such comparisons do not require belief in a fixed rule by which to measure progress or worth.
>
> The rejection of [Cartesian] objectivity, therefore, does not deny that arguments and interpretations are subject to critique and correction. Any criticisms will appeal to judgmental standards that may be assumed, for the sake of the criticism, to be fixed.[150]

By inquiring into meaning, modern hermeneutics inevitably asks "how a living verbal system works," which means that "we must take language both as an instrument which produces understanding in us and as a form of life in which we make ourselves understood."[151] Meaning and argumentation are not just compatible, they are mutually implicated.

Set against this more general theoretical backdrop, my positive account of rhetorical knowledge draws specifically from several congenial projects undertaken from different perspectives. First, George Dillon draws explicitly from Gadamer and Perelman to characterize the engagement subtending rhetorical knowledge.

> Gadamer argues that actual argumentation articulates values and beliefs for hearers that they may not have known they hold. As [David] Ingram phrases it, "reason-giving appeals intentionally or otherwise to the inchoate values, interests, and needs of the receiver while at the same time molding them. Far from being a dispassionate affair, the argumentative search for the truth invariably engages passions and prejudices at many different levels, and it is precisely the engagement of these prejudices that elicits recognition and agreement." What Gadamer and Ingram are talking about here is very close to what Chaim Perelman and Lucie Olbrechts-Tyteca call presence, the evoking of which they speak of as "magical" and as involving the imagination as much or more than the reason.[152]

The ground of this distinction is the rhetorical remaking of the terms of argumentation in the course of and by means of argumentation.

Although he expresses misgivings about Gadamer's hermeneutics that

I discuss in greater detail below, Thomas Farrell also builds on Gadamer and Perelman in his account of rhetorical practices.

> The argument for rhetoric's ethical propensity thus turns on the mutual regard that speakers and audience must have for one another, given the simultaneous condition of being a witness to the construction of proof and an agent vulnerable to the partisanship of others.
>
> ----------
>
> What remains is to show how the formal technai of rhetoric may be able to generate new dimensions of practical consciousness while working within the received opinions, appearances, and conventions of everyday life. This inventional process, which may be glimpsed within our earlier conversational setting, typically involves an intersection between the rhetorical speaker's suggested interpretive horizon and the audience's received opinions, cultural norms, or encounter conventions and rules. Given the capacity of rhetoric to range over previous utterance episodes for its topics, themes, and proofs, it is possible for a kind of practical wisdom, or phronesis, to emerge in this sudden joining of otherwise distinct perspective and horizons.[153]

Calvin Schrag contributes additional elaboration of the concept of rhetorical knowledge as part of his ambitious project of preventing the post-Cartesian subject from falling victim to the captious challenges of postmodernism. Schrag argues that the "communicative praxis" of everyday life engenders meaning and rationality. Schrag defines communicative praxis as "an amalgam of discursive and nondiscursive practices, in which the meaning-engendering patterns of the spoken and the written word mix and mingle with meaning-laden actions."[154] Although Schrag does not explain communicative praxis solely with hermeneutics and rhetoric, he conjoins hermeneutics and rhetoric in a description of persuasive reasoning that parallels my description of rhetorical knowledge, arguing that it is "an integral and inaugural moment in the life of communicative praxis."[155] Schrag relies on readings of Gadamer's philosophy and on an understanding of rhetoric consistent with the new rhetoric to reconfigure ethics on the basis of the "incarnation of the logos within discourse and action in a hermeneutic of everyday life. Communicative praxis announces and displays reason as discourse. . . . In entering discourse the logos is decentered and situated within the play of speaker and hearer as they seek consensus on that which is talked out."[156] Judgments about the appropriate course of action (the "fitting response" to a particular social situation) can be reasonable and reasoned under Schrag's account because they arise from the "responsibility of an engaged and decentered moral self as it responds to the prior thought and action already inscribed within a historicized polis," rather than being issued from an "interior construct of a centered and sovereign subject" that today we acknowledge is a subjectivist fantasy.[157]

Consistent with these positive accounts of rhetorical engagements leading to understanding, the theory of rhetorical knowledge overcomes postmodern skepticism by describing decentered agents engaged in ongoing communicative exchanges and meaning-laden actions that traverse various discourses and repertoires of behavior in a constant inventive renewal of the shared meanings that underwrite subjectivity. The fears of relativism occasioned by Protagoras's insistence that "man is the measure of all things" can be put to rest by emphasizing that "man" need not be read as the insular subject that rises above all claims to objective truth. Instead, a provocative reading emerges by construing "man" to be a plural noun encompassing all of humanity.[158] Man collectively is the measure of all things, then, because in our rhetorical exchanges with others we gain insight and knowledge by suffering challenges to our horizonal prejudices. The point is that this measure is real, even if culturally defined. Although the Sophists' "travels and inquiries led them to compare political, legal, social, ethical, and religious customs and ideas and to understand that different people had different views on many issues; . . . at the same time, they seem to have agreed that people everywhere shared certain basic principles. . . . The Sophists thus shared a belief in cultural relativism without necessarily denying that there are fundamental norms of human behavior that cut across cultural differences."[159] Postmodern thinking does not necessarily collapse into relativistic chaos if it pursues the sophistic insights into the social construction of the world in which we continually participate.

Rhetorical knowledge is at once hermeneutical and rhetorical, for it involves both discernment and expression, both understanding and proposing. Hermeneutic idealism and rhetorical methodologism, then, are different exaggerations of the same mode of knowing. After quoting Gadamer on this point, Schrag emphasizes the fundamental linkage of hermeneutics and rhetoric in defining communicative praxis.

> Rhetoric and hermeneutics are thus seen to be incommiscibly yoked, complementary and mutually reinforcing—distinct perhaps, but yet indissoluble. They travel with each other, and they travel together all the way down and all the way back. They are both oriented toward an articulation of meaning and an achievement of self-understanding against the backdrop of public concerns.
>
> ----------
>
> The hermeneutical task of articulating and making manifest the configurations of meaning in our social interaction is seen as an intrinsic component of the task of rhetoric. Rhetorical discourse arises because understanding and consent have been placed into question. Mutual understanding has been disrupted by the insinuation of misunderstanding, and the task of hermeneutical rhetoric is to strive for a rectification of this misunderstanding through a collaborative project of making sense together.[160]

The complex means by which social bonds are proposed, negotiated, and maintained draw upon rhetorical knowledge, which is to say that they involve interactions grounded in both understanding and persuasion.

Finally, several rhetorical scholars have reinforced the philosophical significance of rhetorical knowledge. Robert Scott's seminal claim that rhetoric is epistemic provides important clarification of the concept of "rhetorical knowledge."

> Seeing in a situation possibilities that are possibilities for us and deciding to act upon some of these possibilities but not others must be an important constituent of what we mean by human knowledge. The plural pronoun in the foregoing sentence is vital. As social beings, our possibilities and choices must often, perhaps almost always, be joint. . . . The opacity of living is what bids forth rhetoric. A

> remark in passing by Hans-Georg Gadamer seems to me to be an important insight: the "concept of clarity belongs to the tradition of rhetoric." But few terms are more relative than that one nor call forth more strongly a human element. Nothing is clear in and of itself but in some context for some persons.
>
> Rhetoric may be clarifying in these senses: understanding that one's traditions are one's own, that is, are co-substantial with one's own being and that these traditions are formative in one's own living; understanding that these traditions are malleable and that one . . . may act decisively [with others] in ways that continue, extend, or truncate the values inherent in one's culture; and understanding that in acting decisively . . . one participates in fixing forces that will continue after the purposes for which they have been immediately instrumental and will, to some extent, bind others who will inherit the modified traditions. Such understanding is genuinely knowing and is knowing that becomes filled out in some particulars by participating rhetorically.[161]

Rhetorical knowledge thus encompasses Gadamer's conception of a "truth" that is not methodologically secured and also Perelman's conception of reasonable argumentation that is not rigorously rational.

Scott explores the public rhetorical engagements that produce knowledge in a manner that reinforces Gadamer's concern with the ontology of understanding. Rhetorical knowledge arises not only from public debate but from all dialogical engagements concerning the contingent and probable. Gadamer emphasizes that our mode of existence is dialogic all the way down: thinking and reasoning are conversational even when we silently reflect on a question as a seemingly solitary ego exercising ahistorical rational power. This is what Gadamer means when he insists that thinking follows the logic of question and answer: "Knowledge always means, precisely, considering opposites. Its superiority over preconceived opinion consists in the fact that it is able to conceive of possibilities as possibilities. Knowledge is dialectical from the ground up. . . . A person who thinks must ask himself questions. . . . This is the reason why understanding is always more than merely re-creating someone else's meaning."[162] Solitary thinking is conversational, but even more importantly it is always predicated on actual conversations with others that already have occurred and always anticipates potential conversations with others in the future.

> To think is to think something with oneself; and to think something with oneself is to say something to oneself. Plato was, I believe, quite correct to call the essence of thought the interior dialogue of the soul with itself. This dialogue, in doubt and objection, is a constant going beyond oneself and a return to oneself, one's own opinions and one's own points of view. If anything does characterize human thought, it is this infinite dialogue with ourselves which never leads anywhere definitively and which differentiates us from that ideal of an infinite spirit for which all that exists and all truth lies open in a single moment's vision. It is in this experience of language—in our growing up in the midst of this interior conversation with ourselves, which is always simultaneously the anticipation of conversation with others and the introduction of others into the conversation with ourselves—that the world begins to open up and achieve order in all the domains of experience.
>
> ----------
>
> There are no limits to the interior dialogue of the soul with itself.[163]

Rhetorical knowledge developed in the public square is made possible by the hermeneutical openness that constitutes the very power of human reason.

Michael Billig's recent analysis of the cognitive significance of rhetoric reinforces Gadamer's conversational account of thinking. Also working from the example provided by Plato's dialogues, Billig asserts that "thinking is inherently dialogic . . . not merely the silent argument of the soul with itself, but, even more frequently, it is the noisier argument of one individual with another."[164] In other words, if thinking is rhetorically constituted, then rhetorical engagements are embodiments of cognition.

> The theoretical point is that cognitive processes are not simply anterior to argumentation, but, as anticipations of arguments, they

> are themselves constituted by socially observable arguments. In this sense, as the social constructivists emphasize, human thinking is socially constituted. . . . The rhetoricians, in teaching their pupils the skills of debate, were also teaching the skills of thinking.
>
> ----------
>
> [D]ialogue, with its immediate interruptions and contradictions, can be seen as the process of thinking. . . . Therefore, thinking can be seen as a social, argumentative process, rather than a monological, individual one.
>
> ----------
>
> For the most part, the Platonic dialogues end in a state of aporia, as the participants realize there is always more to speak about. . . . It is not that they have failed to think, but that as they argue rhetorically so they continue to think noisily.[165]

Schrag reaffirms this point by carefully recounting the communal essence of thinking that is revealed by characterizing thought as a dialogue: "Yet, being alone is itself a peculiar modality of being with others; soliloquy is carried on by a language that belongs to the public; and individual acts have meaning only within the wider context of social practices. One can be alone only because one has already been in communal interaction with others; one can speak 'by' and 'to' oneself only with a grammar that has a social history; and one can act as an individual only as differentiated from others within the body politic. Surrounding all individual manifestations of discourse and action is the space of communicative praxis."[166]

All of these thinkers provide important conceptual resources for understanding the nature and function of rhetorical knowledge. My contribution will be to highlight the positive achievement of rhetorical knowledge as a feature of legal practice, but it bears emphasizing that the full ramifications of rhetorical knowledge point toward a new understanding of human existence as an ongoing effort of understanding and reasoning that extends well beyond the setting of legal practice. The theory of rhetorical knowledge is indebted to a strain of thinking reaching from the Sophists to contemporary rhetorical theorists, but all too often this legacy is presented in overly general terms and thereby loses its force as a motivation for social critique. By reading Gadamer and Perelman together with respect to the problematic of justice and legal practice, we gain clarity about this particular site of rhetorical knowledge in a manner that has wider implications. I turn now to the ongoing debate about affirmative action and the legal interventions in this social debate, with a dual purpose. The theory of rhetorical knowledge is clarified by identifying how rhetorical knowledge emerges in these social and legal practices, but it is also clarified by the circumspect manner in which I critically engage these practices. My goal is to reenact the relationship of theory and practice that Gadamer and Perelman so effectively demonstrate in both the content and manner of their philosophical inquiries.

Reasoning about Affirmative Action

The theory of rhetorical knowledge can best be elaborated by turning to an example from the contemporary public square: the seemingly disabling and dissembling "debate over affirmative action." This political and social contest has figured prominently in public life for some time, but the issue recently has acquired an air of serious urgency and holds substantial social, economic, and political repercussions. Initially, one might regard this debate as the last feature of civic life that could shed light on rhetorical knowledge, since it appears to be masked by self-serving political gamesmanship and clouded by a coded vocabulary as perhaps no other public issue in our day.[167] But it is for this very reason that the example serves an important role: not only does it provide a setting in which rhetorical knowledge emerges, it also reinforces the provisional, halting, and dynamic nature of rhetorical knowledge. Only Pollyanna would regard the contemporary discourse surrounding affirmative action as a source of rationally defensible norms, but it is possible to trace the (often unwitting) structuring of the public sphere that occurs even in such a tangled discourse and to describe how reasonable conclusions emerge even from such a fractious and disjointed social space. Moreover, I intend my discussion to model the kind of theoretical comportment toward practical engagements that will be developed further in the next chapter's defense of a critical legal theory rooted in rhetorical knowledge.

My discussion of affirmative action is artificially divided into two parts. In the first part, I survey the general contours of the public debate over affirmative action and identify some of the rhetorical elements at work.

This discussion explains how rhetorical knowledge is possible even if there is no methodologically directed answer to the problem at hand. In the next part, I review the Supreme Court's recent cases concerning the constitutionality of affirmative action in higher education. These cases are embedded in and participate in the cultural discussion of affirmative action, and thus they similarly exhibit rhetorical knowledge in action. The point of my discussion is schematic and illustrative: the payoff for embracing the theory of rhetorical knowledge is not easier access to definitive answers to cultural and legal problems, but rather a better way of appreciating the dynamic of ongoing practices, so as to determine how we can best work through these problems. Social and legal criticism must be grounded in an accurate picture of how we attain rhetorical knowledge.

Rhetorical Knowledge, Justice, and Affirmative Action

The starting point for analyzing the debate over affirmative action is to acknowledge that the "answer" to this conundrum cannot be derived by a logical explication of the relevant concepts by means of a dialectical demonstration. The obligation of those with economic and social power to take affirmative action to make educational and professional opportunities available to members of disadvantaged and marginalized groups in society is not subject to definitive rational explication, but it is subject to reasoned debate as part of ongoing sociopolitical practices. Rhetorical knowledge makes no claim to ahistorical certitude, but rather involves the discovery of more fitting conceptions to serve present social needs and to facilitate the ongoing revision of these conceptions. The debate over affirmative action shows dramatically that rhetorical knowledge is historically conditioned not because it fails to gain perspective on its subject matter, but because its subject matter is thoroughly historicized. For example, the use of affirmative action in higher education against the backdrop of a steadily growing economy and the continued expansion of higher education presents different questions than the use of affirmative action in a society buffeted by a radically restructured economy and various demographic and financial pressures. One cannot help but be struck by the shifting use of images regarding affirmative action in the past fifty years and the changing combinations of these unstable images produced by the participants in the debate. Moving beyond these relatively short-term changes, it would be almost inconceivable that the terms of the current debate over affirmative action would have had any significance in the American colonies or that they will have the same significance in America two centuries from now. As Perelman emphasizes, although natural science successfully restricts the influence of values to the setting of its initial problematics by addressing the persistent reality of the natural world, humanistic inquiries such as politics and law are infused with value determinations at all stages of deliberation and assertion because they pertain to an active social project of value formation.[168] Gaining the adherence of others in political matters and legal disputes is not just a means of implementing predetermined tenets; instead, rhetorical practices at once generate, apply, and critique such tenets.

The competing slogans of equality ("color-blind" treatment of all citizens in all respects) and fairness ("leveling the playing field" for historically disadvantaged groups) are deployed in rhetorical exchanges that can produce rhetorical knowledge. Although these slogans can be wielded for a variety of strategic, even bad-faith, reasons, even the worst abuse of rhetorical practices proves the case for rhetorical knowledge. Those seeking to segregate and denigrate disadvantaged minorities could use the physical coercion of an apartheid regime to secure their goal, just as those seeking to mitigate the economic power of the majority could incite a violent revolution in furtherance of their aims. However, the debate about affirmative action continues, even if suboptimally, by traversing the many discourses within society in order to align points of shared agreement into new constellations of meaning. These shifts in meaning represent modifications of arguments designed to secure the adherence of the body politic which prove to be enlightening (or not) only in the continued discourse about affirmative action. The reality of rhetorical knowledge is proved not because the participants have found the "answer" to the question posed, but because they continue to develop the public discussion of affirmative action along new and more productive lines of argumentation. And productivity is rhetorically acknowledged and secured, which means that there is no point outside the debate from which to judge any such progress.

The question of affirmative action has called forth a base version of rhetorical exchange in many quarters, but it remains rhetorical in nature.

Advocates seek the adherence of specific audiences (in the faculty meeting, for instance), of hypothetical constructions of specific yet dispersed audiences (in presidential politics, for instance), and of the hypothetical universal audience of all reasonable persons (in political-ethical theories, for instance) in a manner of communication that is derivative of conversational exchange. The ongoing struggle to come to terms with affirmative action does not disprove the ability to have knowledge of such matters, but instead it reaffirms that such knowledge holds only for discrete historical situations and is tested constantly and revised as these situations evolve.

Conservative insistence on color-blind policies invites the rejoinder that many of the "neutral" features of decision making are intimately tied to racially exclusive policies—special admissions criteria for children of alumni or business contacts nurtured at suburban country clubs, for example—and that such decisions are always set within wider cultural practices that have a disparate impact on a variety of groups. Similarly, liberal insistence on leveling the playing field invites the rejoinder that "feel-good" de facto quotas have a corrosive effect by leaving the field undisturbed but inviting additional players to try their luck anyway. Equality and fairness are opposed in debate not as abstract conceptions to be dissected, but rather as topics with relevance in and a connection with the real world.

Warren Sandmann clarifies the referents in social and legal argumentation by using Michael McGee's notion of an "ideograph" to demonstrate that terms such as "liberty" are not purely conceptual tools, but rather emerge from and refer back to the material, lived reality of the community.[169] "When we analyze the law as rhetoric, we need to look beyond the personalities of the Justices, and beyond the quasi-logic that appears to support the decisions. We need to look a little deeper and attempt to see the public arguments that created the material for that original and now disputed law, and created the conditions for the judicial decision."[170] Sandmann's approach to analyzing judicial opinions can be expanded to a broader conception of how successful public debate proceeds. Advocates of affirmative action, then, are best counseled to appeal to "fairness" not in abstract ethical terms but in terms of the lived experience of members of the polity that inform the conception of "fairness" as it is deployed in public debate.[171]

The concepts of equality and fairness are not static but are constantly reconfigured by their application in ongoing public disputes. Even the orienting themes of the debate can change, as claims for equality are deployed against the skewed arena of educational opportunities by proponents of affirmative action and claims of fairness are deployed against programs that treat minority applicants differently in substantial ways. There are no invariable starting points from which the debate proceeds, but only topics and lines of argumentation that evolve and play off each other.

Few ordinary citizens venture into public spaces to engage in dialogue about affirmative action, and contemporary etiquette limits the range of conversational experiences when the topic can be taken up with sustained rigor. Consequently, much of the rhetorical deliberation about affirmative action occurs in "individual" thinking—in the soul's dialogue with itself. For those who think, which means to accept the challenge to their prejudices that is posed by questioning, the relatively rare public occasions at which they deliberate about affirmative action serve only to carry forward the deliberative conversation that constitutes them, which in turn is a development of their earlier conversational exchanges with others. The ontological claim that human existence is rhetorical relates not only to the conscious engagement of others in dialogue, but also more broadly to the manner of our existence as reasoning beings. Put simply, thinking is conversationally structured, and so thinking is a form of the hermeneutical and rhetorical processes that generate rhetorical knowledge. Just as an individual can come to "see" a truth by thinking things through, so too a community might acknowledge a truth as a result of public dialogue.

The fact that rhetorical experience, understood as a feedback loop of public discussion and thinking, is capable of producing knowledge might appear to be beside the point, given that actual public debate seems far removed from a conversation and more like competing lectures or insistent demands that warp rather than facilitate thinking. Critics likely will point to the example of the debate over affirmative action as providing strong evidence that "rhetorical knowledge" simply is empty of practical significance. The "knowledge" gained in the public discourse over affirmative action appears to be nothing more than a knack for clever manipulation of slogans in an ongoing effort to achieve a desired (and fixed) end. From this perspective, rhetorical inventiveness is regarded as a morally neutral skill that can be used in harmful ways as easily as beneficial ways. This line of attack, of course, repeats the indictment issued against the teachers of rhetoric in ancient Greece: by confusing rhetorical technique with true knowledge, the critics alleged, advocates of rhetoric paved the way for social manipulation.[172]

Contemporary expressions of caution toward the potential bad uses to which rhetoric can be put are closely related to the ideology of political correctness that plays such a large role in contemporary academic thought.[173] Many theorists will reject the risk implicit in a rhetorical exchange, arguing that the "wrong" answer may (and perhaps often does) hold sway in these exchanges. Because the public debate over affirmative action is so skewed, because the inventiveness employed by the discussants appears to be oriented toward obfuscation and exciting the passions of a defined segment of the population, and because the shifts in the debate seem unmatched by progress in social relations, critics will conclude that rhetorical "knowledge" (and they likely will concede only "technique" or "style") must be carefully guarded and circumscribed, owing to its dangerous implications.

To appreciate the blind alley that this critique of rhetorical knowledge creates, it is instructive to widen the scope of the critique. Characterizing rhetoric as a dangerous facility that may be put to bad uses and therefore must be cautiously supervised is no more accurate than advocating wariness of intelligence because of the threat of devious cleverness, or advocating wariness of altruism because of the threat of naïveté. Certainly all citizens should be concerned and vigilant with regard to the unproductive aspects of the debate over affirmative action, but such concern and vigilance can be played out only in the rhetorical activity of those citizens rather than as a theoretical move to put limits on rhetorical exchanges. Rhetoric is unavoidable as a means of regenerating and creating social and political bonds, and so the question is not so much the limits that should be placed on rhetoric as it is the character of our rhetorical practices. Put differently, we should not take too lightly the concerns about rhetorical practices precisely because these unavoidable practices have such tremendous significance for social life.

The creative reworking of the Aristotelian rhetorical legacy by Gadamer and Perelman points the way to overcoming the fear of rhetorical exchanges about affirmative action. Although Aristotle rejected Plato's univocal vision of knowledge by conceding that rhetoric holds some (ambiguous) significance as an epistemic, social activity, Aristotle nevertheless appears to champion the necessary role of dialectical reason in politics. In contrast, Aristotle's sophistic competitor, Isocrates, fully embraced the politics of the public square, eschewing both the imperial tradition of the Socratics and the amoral attitudes of some of the Sophists in his defense of vibrant public dialogue in which political questions are rhetorically tested.[174] It is this tradition that shapes my account of the reading of Aristotle by Gadamer and Perelman. Isocrates rejected the exuberant playfulness of the itinerant Sophists, but he took seriously their attention to argumentation as an appropriate comportment in an increasingly cosmopolitan Hellas.[175] Isocrates is most accurately characterized as a philosopher of rhetoric, as one whose teaching and thinking existed at the intersection of philosophy (in other words, Plato) and rhetoric (in other words, the Sophists).

> Isocrates articulates a rhetoric whose announced purpose is neither to win contests nor to perform discursive spectacles but to offer insightful advice on social and political issues.
>
> ----------
>
> . . . While Plato's new rulers would be driven by uncompromised intelligence, Isocrates' would possess sound judgment. . . . In short, where Plato saw the cure for rhetoric in dialectic, Isocrates saw it in rhetoric itself.[176]

The example of affirmative action is designed to emphasize the extent to which the rhetorical turn undertaken by Gadamer and Perelman evidences a rejection of Aristotle's caution in favor of an elaboration of his implicit concessions to the radical message propounded by Isocrates and his predecessor Protagoras. To fear sophistic manipulation in the course of a rhetorical exchange is not only reasonable but necessary. To fear rhetorical exchange as an invitation to sophistic manipulation, however, is to eschew the reasonable in a fruitless quest for the rational.

The debate over affirmative action also illustrates the significance of the efforts by Gadamer and Perelman to recuperate the Aristotelian conception of natural law. The seemingly insoluble conflict of values represented by the controversy undermines any claim that there is an invariant, apodictic truth subject to rational explication. But at the same time, it is the very intensity of the debate that signals a connection with moral claims rooted in the reality of human experience. Lloyd Weinreb's contemporary natural law philosophy makes just this point, in a manner that resonates with my reading of Gadamer and Perelman.

Weinreb argues that natural law is nothing more than "an affirmation of the reality of moral experience,"[177] by which he means that natural law "doesn't provide moral truths, it just rebuts skepticism and existentialism."[178] Morality is a feature of a deep communal *nomos* that is real notwithstanding its heterogeneity and contested character. Under his account, the role of natural law philosophy is to reveal this ontology of the human condition in order to facilitate ongoing social practices, and to reveal the impossibility of attaining a God's-eye view from which to judge such practices from the outside.[179] For example, arguments about justice in modern society inevitably are framed in terms of the seemingly antithetical claims of equality and liberty, but this does not disprove the viability of the concept of justice as much as demonstrate that it participates in a deep, dynamic *nomos* and must constantly be worked out in practical situations.[180] As Perelman argues, justice is a "confused notion" that can gain purchase in everyday life only through reasoning; in Gadamer's terminology, the history of working through confused notions constitutes the horizon of tradition in which we are embedded, and to "be situated within a tradition does not limit the freedom of knowledge but makes it possible."[181] In a similar vein, Weinreb argues that natural law is an ontological inquiry into human finitude, our natural condition, in which ongoing reasoning and argumentation is inescapable.

Weinreb contends that the question of affirmative action challenges our sense of justice more than most public policy questions precisely because it brings sharply into relief the antinomic commonplaces of liberty and equality that are the mainsprings of our *nomos*. "We should not expect that disagreement and confusion about affirmative action will be resolved even over a long period of time. The community may come to regard long-standing practices as an acceptable political solution or simply as 'the law.' But no solution will be incorporated within the community's nomos as just, because the terms of the controversy preclude a consistent understanding of responsibility and rights."[182] Supporters of affirmative action argue that members of underrepresented minorities do not bear responsibility for inequalities arising out of past discrimination, which is to say that they do not deserve their current situation; opponents argue that nonminorities do not bear responsibility for actions of others in the past, which is to say that they do not deserve the effects of contemporary affirmative action policies. Weinreb argues that there can be no definitive resolution of a debate framed in this manner, because it replicates the internal tensions of the lived ideal of justice. Both sides in the debate "make precise claims that leave us right in the paradox of the human condition."[183]

The central lesson of the theory of rhetorical knowledge is that this paradoxical impasse does not mean that the debate over affirmative action is a useless exercise. A prejudiced forestructure of meanings cast in tension with each other is not a regrettable limitation on understanding, but rather provides the ground for the activity of reasoning (rhetoric) and understanding (hermeneutics). The cost of knowledge is the inability to secure complete, absolute knowledge; the cost of objective moral experience is to be situated in a practical context and denied the omniscient view from nowhere. But this also means that rhetorical knowledge about affirmative action is possible, and the matter need not be relegated solely to crude political compromise. Weinreb makes a provocative suggestion along these lines, proposing that a rhetorical reconfiguration of the questions at issue might lead to better policy prescriptions in light of our moral-legal *nomos*. "Substantively, affirmative action programs should shift as much as is practicable from measures that are directly and overtly competitive to ones that are not. Instead of preferential selection of applicants for a limited number of places, [completely distinct social] programs should be designed to enhance the capabilities of members of groups that suffered the effects of past discrimination, who should then compete without preference for the available places."[184] He is not arguing that we can escape the aporia, but only that we can more productively address the competing claims. "Enhancement programs are not without cost, which must be met by the diversion of public funds from elsewhere or by increased taxation of private funds. The increase of power of those who benefit is matched by reduced power of those who are obliged to support the programs. But the right to keep one's property free from taxation is not widely asserted anymore; and the tradeoff of rights of those who benefit from taxation and those who are burdened is much less keenly felt. There are not specific winners and losers, as there are if persons compete directly for positions."[185] The manner in which the debate over affirmative action is framed admits of no just resolution because constitutive elements of our lived experience of justice are thrown into fundamental opposition to each other, but this does not mean that it is impossible to deliberate about the justice of affirmative action. Weinreb demonstrates that a reconceptualization of the problem, which requires a high degree of hermeneutical sensitivity and rhetorical competence, can move a localized debate about justice to a more productive starting point.

The tragedy of the affirmative action debate is not that it admits of no right answer for all time or that the participants often are moved by arguments that they later regard as having manipulated their fears and base prejudices. The real tragedy is that the debate takes place in a socially constructed field that seems to limit unnecessarily the ability to acquire rhetorical knowledge. Rhetorical activity only rarely and temporarily is precluded in public exchanges in this country (images of Bull Connor's fire hoses and Richard Daley's combat-equipped police officers come to mind), but it appears equally true that rhetorical activity all too often is an anemic and embarrassingly ineffectual exercise within the institutionally managed arena of public discussion. The example of the debate over affirmative action reveals the epistemic significance of rhetoric but also reveals its fragile and risky nature. Rhetorical knowledge is not an impossible ideal, but it is not easily achieved in the face of entrenched social forces and institutions. The central question, then, is not whether rhetoric is a good or bad basis for public life, but rather how to invigorate ongoing rhetorical practices. To pursue these questions, I turn now to the judicial resolution of the problem of affirmative action because legal practice is one significant locus of the effort to revitalize rhetorical practices.

Rhetorical Knowledge in Law: The Constitutionality of Affirmative Action in Higher Education

The Supreme Court returned to the contentious issue of affirmative action in higher education twenty-five years after deciding in the *Bakke* case that a racial quota utilized by the University of California to admit a medical school entering class was illegal.[186] *Bakke* laid bare the aporia of affirmative action and ignited an ongoing vigorous public debate, but the Supreme Court subsequently declined several opportunities to clarify the ruling when it did not grant certiorari in high-profile cases decided by the Courts of Appeals.[187] The Court's reluctance to revisit the conundrums of *Bakke* was understandable. The *Bakke* case had produced six opinions, none of which garnered a majority, and the decision rested on a bare majority of five justices voting to declare that racial quotas in admissions are impermissible. The case was made more complex by Justice Powell's celebrated plurality opinion for the Court, in which he not only provided the deciding vote to declare quotas illegal but also provided the fifth vote to reverse the state court's injunction against using race in any manner in admissions. Justice Powell famously suggested that carefully constructed affirmative action programs designed to foster diversity could survive constitutional scrutiny, thereby refusing to endorse a bright line rule against race-conscious admissions. Powell rejected a strict "color-blind" interpretation of the Equal Protection Clause, but also rejected the idea of benign discrimination that can serve socially desirable goals. Instead, he invented a new *topos,* the state interest in "the attainment of a diverse student body,"[188] which nevertheless may be implemented only by not focusing exclusively on race or ethnicity.[189] He concluded: "The diversity that furthers a compelling state interest encompasses a far broader array of qualifications and characteristics of which racial or ethnic origin is but a single though important element. Petitioner's special admission program, focused *solely* on ethnic diversity, would hinder rather than further attainment of genuine diversity."[190] Powell's invention invoked both principles and social reality, but there was no guarantee that his effort to steer between the four votes on either side would have any staying power beyond the *Bakke* case.

When the Court agreed in 2002 to review two cases involving the law school and undergraduate admissions programs at the University of Michigan, it signaled that it would confront the ambiguous legacy of *Bakke* directly. In *Grutter v. Bollinger,* the Court approved the law school's consideration of race as part of a holistic review of each candidate's file, because this consideration was for the purpose of creating a diverse student body for the educational benefit of all students by admitting a critical mass of underrepresented minority students.[191] However, in *Gratz v. Bollinger,* the Court determined that the undergraduate admissions practice of granting 20 points out of a maximum of 150 points to candidates who were members of underrepresented minorities was unconstitutional because the plan did not provide an individualized consideration of each candidate, in effect making a minority candidate's race a decisive factor in the admissions decision.[192]

The constitutional question in these cases was simply put: can a state university make admissions decisions based in part on race or ethnicity without violating the Equal Protection Clause of the Fourteenth Amendment? Justice O'Connor's opinion for the majority in *Grutter* upheld the compelling state interest in building a diverse class at the Michigan Law School and found that the admissions plan was narrowly tailored to achieve this permissible goal. Chief Justice Rehnquist's opinion for the majority in *Gratz* accepted the compelling state interest identified in the *Grutter* decision but found that the undergraduate admissions plan was not narrowly tailored and therefore did not survive the strict scrutiny standard of review.

The Court's competing opinions in the two cases reveal that legal practice is grounded in rhetorical knowledge and is not a matter of providing a dialectical elaboration of fixed principles. In *Grutter,* the Court began by recognizing that the antinomy of fairness and equality marking the *Bakke* precedent was a lived reality rather than a conceptual puzzle. The Sixth Circuit had determined that Justice Powell's opinion in *Bakke* was binding precedent, and that the law school's admission program was legitimate under Powell's recognition that affirmative action could be used to build a diverse student body. Justice O'Connor bypassed the technically interesting question of whether Justice Powell's opinion (which had been joined in its entirety by no other Supreme Court justice) should be accorded deference under stare decisis; instead, she began by noting the degree to which his opinion had become embodied in the institutions of higher education. "Since this Court's splintered decision in Bakke, Justice Powell's opinion announcing the judgment of the Court has served as the touchstone for constitutional analysis of race-conscious admissions policies. Public and private universities across the Nation have modeled their own admissions programs on Justice Powell's views on permissible race-conscious policies. . . . We therefore discuss Justice Powell's opinion in some detail."[193] Ultimately, the majority simply adopted Justice Powell's diversity rationale for affirmative action without determining whether his opinion was binding law.

Justice O'Connor's approach to *Bakke*'s precedential value is revealing. She begins by acknowledging that the Court should examine Justice Powell's opinion in detail because his analysis had been internalized by individuals and institutions struggling through the irreconcilable conflict of fairness and equality. When the Court later endorses his diversity rationale, it is clear that the Court is responding to the social reality that initiated its discussion. The doctrinal debate about the precedential authority of Justice Powell's opinion is openly subordinated to its historical effectiveness. This is not surrendering legal principle to the vicissitudes of ephemeral social convention, but rather is an acknowledgment by the Court that principles of law hold meaning only within social settings. Universities and colleges had found guidance in Justice Powell's opinion as they worked through the problems and conflicts arising in the course of implementing affirmative action plans, and the Court began with this lived reality as the starting point for its analysis.

Justice Powell suggested that race-conscious admissions programs could be constitutional if they represented an exercise of academic freedom designed to create a diverse student body for the educational benefit of all students, but he made clear that racial preferences designed to remedy the systemic effects of past discrimination, in addition to outright racial balancing, violated the constitutional ban on racial discrimination by the state.[194] The unresolved tensions between these guidelines and the indeterminate guidance that schools might derive from them preclude a definitive analysis that resolves all potential future disputes. The reason that underrepresented minorities bring diversity to the classroom is just because of the continuing effects of systemic racial oppression in this country; yet, the diversity rationale does not permit schools to implement affirmative action plans to remedy socially entrenched discrimination. The challenge facing the Court in *Grutter* and *Gratz* was to bring additional guidance to bear on this confused notion of achieving racial equity without treating individuals unfairly on account of their race.

Justice O'Connor's opinion does not pretend to resolve this tension as much as work through it. In finding that states have a compelling interest in obtaining the educational benefits that flow from having a diverse student body, the Court emphasized that the benefits of diversity are real in very concrete ways, citing not only the expert testimony offered at trial, but also the amicus briefs filed by large corporations and former high-ranking officers and civilian leaders of the United States armed services.[195] The military brief was particularly pointed in this regard. Asserting that a diverse officer corps is "essential" to the military's ability to carry out its missions, the brief argued that a lack of diversity among officers during the Vietnam conflict caused racial tensions to reach a point "where there was an inability to fight."[196] Overcoming the inadequate representation of minorities in positions of military leadership is not just compelling, it is "deadly serious" because "people's lives depend on" these affirmative action initiatives.[197] Viewed against the background of this social context, the Court held that principles of academic freedom supported the educational judgment of state schools that a diverse student body is a compelling interest.

But the Court does not rest its decision solely on the general educational benefits obtained by having a diverse student body. Justice O'Connor continues:

> Effective participation by members of all racial and ethnic groups in the civic life of our Nation is essential if the dream of one Nation, indivisible, is to be realized.
>
> ----------
>
> In order to cultivate a set of leaders with legitimacy in the eyes of the citizenry, it is necessary that the path to leadership be visibly open to talented and qualified individuals of every race and ethnicity. . . . Access to legal education (and thus the legal profession) must

> be inclusive . . . so that all members of our heterogeneous society may participate in the educational institutions that provide the training and education necessary to succeed in America.[198]

This sensible recognition of the role of education in the stratification of society is troubling in light of the Court's express refusal to permit states to consider race for the purpose of overcoming the systemic effects of past discrimination. Although the Court provides strong support for the "diversity" rationale for affirmative action, it is difficult not to understand that this argument fits into a larger concern about social justice and the health of our democratic polity. By raising the full breadth of these considerations, Justice O'Connor exposes the contest between equality and fairness that fuels the dispute.

The Court's opinion is not a rhetorical failure because it reflects this conflict; the conflict is unavoidable. The measure of the Court's opinion is whether its rhetorical engagement with the intractable oppositions raised by affirmative action is persuasive and productive of future dialogue. Justice O'Connor's opinion succeeds in openly embracing the role of rhetorical knowledge and rejecting the idea that there is a demonstrable logical solution to the question of affirmative action. Although all racial classifications are subject to strict scrutiny under the Equal Protection Clause, Justice O'Connor insisted that the nature of this review is dependent upon the surrounding circumstances. "Context matters. . . . Not every decision influenced by race is equally objectionable and strict scrutiny is designed to provide a framework for carefully examining the importance and sincerity of the reasons advanced by the governmental decisionmaker for the use of race in that particular context."[199] This suggestion drew a predictable rebuke from Chief Justice Rehnquist in dissent, as he argued the necessity of holding firm to a unitary strict scrutiny analysis that does not purport to identify instances of discrimination that have more legitimacy and are more tolerable under the Constitution.[200] In his majority opinion in *Gratz,* he pointedly articulated the strict scrutiny analysis in context-free terms, eliciting in turn a rejoinder in Justice Ginsburg's dissent in *Gratz* that carried the *Grutter* attention to context even further. Justice Ginsburg argued that it is appropriate for governmental actors implementing the Equal Protection Clause to "distinguish between policies of exclusion and inclusion" in light of our long history of racial oppression, and that the Court should permit considerations of race that are designed to achieve equality.[201]

To claim that the apartheid regulations of Jim Crow and the affirmative action policies adopted by the University of Michigan Law School are equally suspect racial classifications risks being unpersuasive because it champions a stark logical consistency without regard for social reality and common sense. Because there is no possibility of a "color-blind" approach at this point in American history, there is no alternative to weighing the impact of public policies that either address race explicitly or solidify the effect of past racial classifications. In *Grutter,* the Court embraced its rhetorical task by reasoning through the contextual complexities of affirmative action, and it derives substantial authority from undertaking this effort. But this is not to say that the persuasive arguments are obvious and unproblematic once the context is acknowledged, because the context itself is contested.

Justice Thomas, the only African American on the Court, wrote passionately against the idea that some racial classifications are benign. Although framed in terms of his acontextual, color-blind approach to the Constitution, these arguments hold power when recast within a rhetorical approach to the problem. Challenging the majority's belief in beneficial racial discrimination, Justice Thomas notes the effect that this ideology has on minority students who either will be ill prepared for the academic challenge at an elite institution or unfairly will be perceived as such by their classmates and future employers. The silence in the record about the performance of the minority students admitted under the law school's affirmative action plan, Justice Thomas writes,

> is deafening to those of us who view higher education's purpose as imparting knowledge and skills to students, rather than a communal, rubber-stamp, credentialing process. The Law School is not looking for those students who, despite a lower LSAT score or undergraduate grade point average, will succeed in the study of law. The Law School seeks only a facade—it is sufficient that the class looks right, even if it does not perform right. The Law School tantalizes unprepared students with the promise of a University of Michigan degree

> and all of the opportunities that it offers. These overmatched students take the bait, only to find that they cannot succeed in the cauldron of competition.
>
> ----------
>
> The majority of blacks are admitted to the Law School because of discrimination, and because of this policy all are tarred as undeserving. When blacks take positions in the highest places of government, industry, or academia, it is an open question today whether their skin color played a part in their advancement.[202]

By inviting a context-specific understanding of racism and the best means for eliminating its grip on society, the majority invites Justice Thomas's rhetorical rejoinder. There is no easy answer, for both positions are plausible efforts to understand the role and effects of affirmative action in contemporary American society in the absence of logically compelling arguments. The task of legal reasoning is to embrace this uncertainty by working through these arguments without guarantees of correctness or finality.

Another important component of the persuasive power of Justice O'Connor's majority opinion in *Grutter* is her rhetorical framing of the problem to avoid the sharpest conflict between equality and fairness. The Court holds that the State of Michigan is permitted to use race-conscious criteria to admit a diverse law school class because the educational benefit of diversity for all students is deemed substantial. The Court rejects the single-valence meritocracy assumed by Justice Thomas's critique and indirectly recognizes that a legal education is an education into forms of social reasoning and persuasion that are not matters simply of cognitive powers exercised through solitary memorization and dialectical reasoning. Justice O'Connor defers to the law school's characterization of its race-conscious admissions program: it is not a plan to deny seats to more-capable white students in an effort to balance the racial composition of an entering class that otherwise would be warped by the effects of racism; rather, it is a plan designed to maximize the learning experience of all law students by preparing them for the complexities of our multicultural society. The former characterization might be justified politically, but it engenders the fundamental conflict that lies at the root of affirmative action policies and therefore is deemed by a clear majority of the Court to be constitutionally infirm. Justice O'Connor embraces the latter approach, which avoids the starkest manifestation of this conflict and promotes a convergence of the guiding principles of fairness and equality, even if it cannot eliminate the tension entirely.

The indirect manner of this shift in orientation also is reflected in what might be the most noticed feature of the majority opinion—Justice O'Connor's stated expectation "that 25 years from now, the use of racial preferences will no longer be necessary to further the [compelling] interest [in diversity] approved today."[203] The Court makes clear that a compelling interest in providing a superior legal education by ensuring a critical mass of minority students in each class cannot be justified as a state program to remedy general social inequities, and yet the Court implies that progress by minority students in the twenty-five years after *Bakke* might be attributed to the approval of race-conscious admission in Justice Powell's concurring opinion. The argument is subtle: by recognizing the effects of racism and the consequential need for affirmative action to build a diverse entering class necessary for a good legal education, law schools will play a role in the slow recovery from the racism that makes minority students diverse in the first place. The intertwined educational and social goals of diversity in higher education are apparent in the Court's analysis, even if not expressly articulated and justified. This complexity in the articulation of the compelling interest provides the opening for the dissenters to make a plausible case under the second prong of the constitutional analysis that the majority is being disingenuous and in fact is permitting state schools to engage in race-based social engineering.

Under the Court's Equal Protection analysis, racial classifications are subject to strict scrutiny and are constitutionally permissible only if they serve a compelling governmental interest and are narrowly tailored to accomplish that legitimate purpose. Although the *Grutter* majority found a compelling governmental interest in creating a diverse educational experience, the law school admissions program could survive strict scrutiny only if the race-conscious elements were narrowly tailored to serve that interest in diversity. Justice O'Connor again relied on Justice Powell's opinion in *Bakke* in determining that the admissions program "must remain flexible enough to ensure that each applicant is evaluated as an individual and not in a way that makes an applicant's race or ethnicity the defining feature of his or her application. The importance of this individualized consideration in the context is paramount."[204] In other words, the Court concedes that racial balancing of the entering law school class, even if for the purpose of creating a diverse student body for educational reasons, would be unconstitutional. The Court held that the law school admissions process is constitutional because race is only one (nondeterminative) factor in evaluating the diversity that a student would add to the class, and the applications are individually evaluated. Although a racially diverse class could be admitted without race-conscious criteria if the law school adopted a lottery admissions program, for example, the Court found that the compelling interest in diversity was tied to providing a quality educational experience, and therefore the Court did not require the school to abandon its interest in building a student body with "elite" credentials in order to achieve diversity in a race-neutral manner.

The dissenting justices in *Grutter* leveled far more serious challenges against the real effects of the law school program, however. Chief Justice Rehnquist caustically attacked the purported desire for diversity: "Stripped of its 'critical mass' veil, the Law School's program is revealed as a naked effort to achieve racial balancing," and the Law School's diversity program "is simply a sham" that can be exposed by a close examination of the admissions statistics.[205] Justice Kennedy endorsed the Court's determination that diversity in higher education is a compelling interest, but he joined Chief Justice Rehnquist's attack on the Court's finding that the law school narrowly tailored its use of race-conscious admissions criteria by characterizing the stated effort to achieve a critical mass of underrepresented minorities as a "delusion" and a "mask," and concluding that the majority "confuses deference to a university's definition of its educational objective with deference to the implementation of this goal."[206] Chief Justice Rehnquist builds a persuasive circumstantial case that the law school admitted students by race in the same proportions that they applied, and that the law school attempted to conceal its race-based admissions by pointing to the variations in the number of matriculating minorities over the years in question, even though the law school can control only offers of admission and not the decision to matriculate.[207]

The majority opinion by Justice O'Connor addresses these concerns by noting that there was no automatic admission of minority students. Observing that the law school "frequently accepts nonminority applicants with grades and test scores lower than underrepresented minority applicants (and other nonminority applicants) who are rejected," the Court concludes that the law school "actually gives substantial weight to diversity factors besides race."[208] Although that argument may be facially persuasive, Chief Justice Rehnquist argues in response that this simply does not address the fact that the law school operated a de facto program of racially proportionate admissions. More troubling, he concludes, is the system of racial preferences at work within the class of underrepresented minorities. Although sixty-seven underrepresented minority students were denied admission despite having LSAT scores and undergraduate GPAs that were higher than some of the admitted Caucasian and Asian American students, Chief Justice Rehnquist emphasizes that fifty-six of these students were Hispanic. Moreover, in one admissions grid, only two of twelve Hispanics were admitted, but all twelve black applicants were admitted.

> These statistics have a significant bearing on petitioner's case. Respondents have *never* offered any race-specific arguments explaining why significantly more individuals from one underrepresented minority group are needed in order to achieve "critical mass" or further student body diversity. They certainly have not explained why Hispanics, who they have said are among "the groups most isolated by racial barriers in our country," should have their admission capped out in this manner. . . . True, petitioner is neither Hispanic nor Native American. But the Law School's disparate admissions practices with respect to these minority groups demonstrate that its alleged goal of "critical mass" is simply a sham. . . . Surely strict scrutiny cannot permit these sort of disparities without at least some explanation.[209]

In other words, the fact that some underrepresented minorities are denied admission appears to result from de facto caps that ensure that offers of admission are made proportionate to the racial profile of the applicants. This suggests parallels to racist admissions policies of the past, such as efforts to ensure that not "too many" Jews were admitted to schools.[210] This also resonates with one of Justice Powell's important insights, that distinguishing "majority" and "minority" populations is an unprincipled undertaking that cannot on its own justify (reverse) discriminatory treatment.[211]

The dissenters relentlessly attack the notion that the law school's plan permits a meaningful distinction between a quota and a "critical mass" of minority students necessary to achieve diversity, but the suspicion that the law school engaged in racial balancing among the groups designated as underrepresented minorities raises the most serious challenge. Noting that the law school claimed to be seeking a critical mass of each underrepresented minority, Chief Justice Rehnquist contends that this cannot be the case because the law school's "admissions practices with respect to these groups differ dramatically and cannot be defended under any consistent use of the term 'critical mass.'"[212] The unintended effect of attempting to make admission offers proportionate to applications when considered by race is to discriminate between members of underrepresented minorities.

Justice Thomas emphasized this point by suggesting that an effort by schools to move beyond the aesthetics of race-based admissions and to "address the real problems facing 'underrepresented minorities,'" rather than "continuing their social experiments on other people's children," would result in an admissions policy more responsive to social reality.[213] For example, black men are particularly underrepresented at the law school, leading him to ask, "Why does the Law School not also discriminate in favor of black men over black women, given this underrepresentation? The answer is, again, that all the Law School cares about is its own image among know-it-all elites, not solving real problems like the crisis of black male underperformance."[214]

This challenge is ironic, of course. Justice Thomas's point is that genuine attempts to address racial inequity would require far more than the Court could countenance as being constitutional. He concludes that the Court permits racial discrimination in admissions, in ways detrimental to some members of underrepresented minorities, and in ways that will be ineffectual in addressing the problems of race in modern society. Near the end of his opinion, Justice Thomas attempts to ensure that an explicit adoption of such fine-tuned race-conscious admissions is clearly foreclosed.

> First, I note that the issue of unconstitutional racial discrimination among the groups the Law School prefers is not presented in this case. . . . I join the Court's opinion insofar as it confirms that this type of racial discrimination remains unlawful. . . . Under today's decision, it is still the case that racial discrimination that does not help a university to enroll an unspecified number, or "critical mass," of underrepresented minority students is unconstitutional. Thus, the Law School may not discriminate in admissions between similarly situated blacks and Hispanics, or between whites and Asians. This is so because preferring black to Hispanic applicants, for instance, does nothing to further the interest recognized by the majority today. Indeed, the majority describes such racial balancing as "patently unconstitutional."[215]

The conflict between fairness and equality will be sharpened all the more if a school attempts to address the complexities of comparative racial disadvantage.

Gratz v. Bollinger, the companion case to *Grutter* that considered the undergraduate admissions program, appears to present a much easier case than *Grutter.* Automatically granting twenty points out of the one hundred points necessary for admission simply because of an applicant's race would appear to be anything but a narrowly tailored program designed to consider race only to the degree necessary to achieve the compelling interest in diversity and only as part of a holistic assessment of each admissions file. As many observers expected, the Court voted six to three to declare the program unconstitutional. Significantly, Justice O'Connor joined Chief Justice Rehnquist's majority opinion and also concurred separately to emphasize the constitutional infirmity of using an automatic plus system based on race rather than using race as one factor among many that are considered as part of an individualized review.[216] However, a close reading of the opinions in *Gratz* reveals that it is not such an easy case and that it in fact underscores the ambiguities and tensions in *Grutter* by raising the possibility that the admissions program in *Gratz* might be a more honest and appropriate means for dealing with the competing interests implicated by affirmative action.

For example, Justice Thomas authored a concurring opinion to specially note that the twenty-point bonus system had the advantage of not discriminating among the members of underrepresented minority groups, and he took the opportunity to reaffirm his reading of *Grutter* to forbid any such discrimination in the assembling of a critical mass for purposes of diversity.[217] By acknowledging that race is an important consideration in general, at least there was no possibility that the undergraduate admissions program could selectively balance the racial composition of the class to the detriment of both nonminority and minority students.

On the other hand, Justice Souter dissented and concluded that the automatic plus factor was not at odds with the notion of building a diverse class. Implicit in his reasoning is Justice Thomas's explicit fear: that it might make more sense to recognize that the individual review of files for purposes of diversity might obscure the fact that being a member of an underrepresented minority in itself matters substantially. "The very nature of a college's permissible practice of awarding value to racial diversity means that race must be considered in a way that increases some applicants' chances for admission. Since college admission is not left entirely to inarticulate intuition, it is hard to see what is inappropriate in assigning some stated value to a relevant characteristic, whether it be reasoning ability, writing style, running speed, or minority race. Justice Powell's plus factors necessarily are assigned some values. The college simply does by a numbered scale what the law school accomplishes in its 'holistic review.'"[218] Souter concludes that by openly acknowledging that race matters significantly, but not going so far as to reserve a certain number of seats for minority applicants, the University of Michigan is honestly pursuing a diverse class rather than using indirect schemes employed by some states, such as admitting the top 10 percent from every high school in the state.

Justice Souter's opinion sets the stage for Justice Ginsburg's dissent, in which she echoes his interest in permitting schools to honestly describe their admissions programs and to openly implement them, but then takes the analysis even further. "The stain of generations of racial oppression is still visible in our society . . . and the determination to hasten its removal remains vital. One can reasonably anticipate, therefore, that colleges and universities will seek to maintain their minority enrollment—and the networks and opportunities thereby opened to minority graduates—whether or not they can do so in full candor through adoption of affirmative action plans of the kind here at issue. Without recourse to such plans, institutions of higher education may resort to camouflage."[219] This "remarkable" passage inflames the chief justice, inasmuch as it assumes that schools will disregard the constitutionality of their actions and that the Court should conform its reading of the constitution to educational practices,[220] but Ginsburg's point does nothing more than bring the analysis full circle. The law school program in *Grutter* was characterized as a sham by Chief Justice Rehnquist and the dissenters, and Ginsburg essentially pleads that the diversity rationale—artificially divorced from underlying issues of social justice and racial equity—will too often produce disingenuous justifications by schools intent on playing their role in the social quest for justice and equality. With this argumentative move it becomes clear that the two cases, *Grutter* and *Gratz,* cannibalize each other in a swirl of opinions that radiate from the safe but indeterminate center staked out by Justice Powell in *Bakke* out to the ends of the spectrum generated by the unresolvable clash between fairness and equality.

The recent Supreme Court affirmative action cases reaffirm the role of rhetorical knowledge in law because, not despite, the confused nature of the reasoning provides no clear-cut answers. The dream of a legal science, in which problems could be solved by deduction from first principles, is implausible; however, this does not mean that legal reasoning is irrational. *Grutter* and *Gratz* exhibit the dialogical character of legal reasoning in a context of extreme undecidability, in which conflicting values and policies make a satisfactory response elusive. Legal rhetoric too often denies its rhetoricity, but in these cases the justices openly construct their arguments as arguments, not as the self-evident and logical unfolding of unimpeachable principles.

The rhetorical knowledge generated by these cases is revealed in the guidance that they give to universities and colleges. It is clear that schools will reorient their admissions programs to better explain the diversity that they seek in their student body, and to ensure a holistic and individualized review of applications (at least regarding race or ethnicity) to achieve this diversity. In the wake of the *Gratz* decision, the University of Michigan immediately hired additional undergraduate admissions counselors at a cost of millions of dollars to ensure that it could meet the standard established by the law school and approved by *Grutter.* The ambiguities and indeterminacies of the cases are not disabling, then, to the extent that they provide sufficient guidance for schools to carry forward the diversity rationale approved in *Grutter.* In this regard it is clear that a school should develop a transparent mission statement regarding its goal of diversity, should act accordingly, and can recognize the legacy of institutionalized racism in this country even if it cannot expressly address it through racial balancing of its classes. Time doesn't stand still, and additional complications will develop as schools attempt to negotiate these general guidelines. Nevertheless, *Grutter* and *Gratz* have generated knowledge about how to resolve competing interests that is sufficient to provide some guidance to schools charting an uncertain path.

Rhetorical knowledge extends beyond these obvious ways in which individuals and institutions adjust their behavior to a changing legal climate. The University of Michigan did more than just adjust to positive legal rules issued by a sovereign; it engaged in internal discussions and developed an approach responsive to the *Gratz* holding in a manner that can be described as altering its culture. Parties begin to see the world differently in response to such an event, with confused notions such as "diversity," "equality," and "fairness" taking on new casts and presenting new problems. Rhetorical knowledge is not knowledge in the sense of being a definitive answer to a problem as much as it is a developing capacity for resolving problems within a dynamic setting. The discourse of affirmative action changed after *Grutter* and *Gratz,* and this changed discourse both reflects and constitutes a changed reality.

Although these Supreme Court opinions exhibit the development of rhetorical knowledge through vigorous exchange, and provide an example of the effects of this deliberation on social life, it remains the case that legal practice too often is artificially constrained in ways that inhibit its character. The institutionally constrained field of legal practice too often yields arguments and decisions that appear to camouflage the weighing and balancing of interests in application to a problem. As the opinions in *Grutter* and *Gratz* amply demonstrate, legal rhetoric also can devolve into ideological contests and disingenuousness, marring the court's role in providing reasoned elaboration of principles and values in new contexts. It would be foolish not to acknowledge the political gamesmanship that is linked to the argumentative struggle in these cases, but there is no easy response to the inevitably risky character of legal rhetoric. There simply is no technology for ensuring good results, for eliminating the risk of rhetorical conflict. Nevertheless, critical appraisal and intervention hold the promise of invigorating the generation of rhetorical knowledge by identifying unhelpful institutional structures and ideological commitments. The next chapter turns to the critical dimension of rhetorical exchanges and to the potential of critical legal theory to maximize the generation of rhetorical knowledge as part of legal practice.

2

Rhetorical Knowledge and Critique

> Who has not had the experience—especially before the other whom we want to persuade—of how the reasons that one had for one's own view, and even the reasons that speak against one's own view rush into words. The mere presence of the other before whom we stand helps us to break up our own bias and narrowness, even before he opens his mouth to make a reply. That which becomes a dialogical experience for us here is not limited to the sphere of arguments and counterarguments the exchange and unification of which may be the end of meaning of every confrontation. Rather, as the experiences that have been described indicate, there is something else in this experience, namely, a potentiality for being other [Anderssein] that lies beyond every coming to agreement about what is common.
>
> Hans-Georg Gadamer
> "Text and Interpretation"

Rhetorical knowledge plays a vital role in social life, in that it is responsive to, and constitutive of, the bonds of sociality. Under Gadamer's and Perelman's accounts, "rhetorical knowledge" is never a cover for the celebration of the status quo because it continually fuels developments and innovations. But the dynamic character of rhetorical knowledge is not enough to allay the fear that it is insufficiently critical by remaining immune to critical interventions that unseat ideological features of the status quo. Rhetorical knowledge might generate new understandings, but in the absence of teleological guarantees there appears to be no assurance that this dynamism is moving in the "right" direction. Put simply, dynamism is not equivalent to progress. Consequently, it is unclear how critics might effectively harness the dynamic activity of rhetorical knowledge in a manner that improves the rhetorical and hermeneutical practices within society. In this chapter I develop the critical element in my account of rhetorical knowledge.

The move by Gadamer and Perelman to displace Cartesian objectivity with a hermeneutical-rhetorical account retains a critical component by resolutely refusing to abandon the criterion of reasonableness. Neither philosopher champions a free-floating play without direction or consequences, and both attend to questions of ethics and justice. Capturing the critical bite in their accounts is difficult, but it emerges more clearly through an investigation of the tension between their approaches. It is a relatively easy matter to align Gadamer and Perelman by charting their parallel use of concepts at a superficial level.[1] However, a closer examination of their work uncovers an important divergence in their orientations. Gadamer develops an ontological account of understanding to fill the philosophical void in a post-Cartesian world, whereas Perelman outlines a descriptive methodology of informal argumentation to preserve sound rhetorical practices against the theoretical challenges of Cartesianism and the practical challenges of violent suppression. By reading Gadamer's investigation of the hermeneutical situation in a manner that corresponds with Perelman's description of rhetorical practices, I describe the ontological space for critique opened by rhetorical engagements and begin to develop guidelines for the practical enactment of critique.

The first step in this complementary reading is to reconcile Gadamer's seemingly uncompromising rejection of methodologism with Perelman's attention to the mechanics of rhetorical practices. Gary Madison provides substantial guidance in this task by radicalizing the postmodern implications of Gadamer's project while also developing a methodology for assessing competing interpretations.[2] Madison argues that Gadamer's hermeneutics, despite its resolute attack on methodologism, "can provide for norms or criteria for assessing interpretations" and "can allow for a logic of interpretation in the light of which rational decisions can be made" about competing interpretations.[3] Such a "logic of interpretation" is not derived from the model of scientific knowledge but rather from rhetoric, which "throughout its long history, as long as that of science itself, . . .

has always opposed an alternative conception of rationality [and] has taught . . . that while in the realm of human affairs and action we can never be absolutely certain of anything, we can nevertheless have legitimate grounds for believing that some things are clearly better than others."[4] In a similar vein, Paul Fairfield connects Gadamer's ontology with William James's pragmatism to argue that "indicating the limits of methodology does not relieve us of the responsibility of engaging in it, and directing our attention to the historicity of the criteria by which we adjudicate between rival interpretations (as is Gadamer's habit) should not deter us from trying to uncover such standards and norms."[5] My complementary reading of Gadamer and Perelman articulates the role and function of critical legal thought by developing a rhetorical "methodology" in the general sense that Madison and Fairfield employ the term, a "rhetorical methodology" that does not run afoul of Gadamer's hermeneutical insights.

Gadamer and Perelman do not provide the missing pieces to the other's philosophy as much as they develop the same argument with different emphases. Read together, they provide a hermeneutical-rhetorical account that recognizes the role of critique in the activity of understanding and opens the way for critical theoretical interventions. Gadamer's reliance on the rhetorical tradition reaffirms the critical elements of his work and provides the basis for thinking methodologically. Reassessing Gadamer's model of understanding as conversation—which was revealed to be a rhetorical model—in conjunction with Perelman's emphasis on persuasion makes it possible to provide an account of interpretive understanding that includes an explicitly critical element. Similarly, Perelman's consistent attack on Cartesian metaphysics in the course of describing the activity of persuasion reaffirms both the critical element of his new rhetoric and its nonrationalist basis. By reading his new rhetoric as a reflection on social activity within the hermeneutical situation described by Gadamer, we can provide a model of critical rhetoric congenial to the postmodern philosophical situation.

I underscore the need to make these accommodations and to effect these shifts in emphasis by confronting each thinker with his staunch critics, and by revising my reading of their philosophies accordingly. I then test the critical potential of my model of rhetorical knowledge by engaging the challenge posed by Nietzsche's radical and thoroughgoing critique. I argue that rhetorical knowledge can accommodate Nietzschean critique because there are significant connections between rhetorical knowledge and Nietzsche's ontological perspectivism and rhetorical approach. I conclude by using the past twenty years' contentious battles before the Supreme Court over the civil rights of gays and lesbians to illustrate the critical dimension of legal practice and also to begin outlining the role that critical theory can play in facilitating rhetorical knowledge.

Conversation and Persuasion as Critique

Critical legal theory is not a tool that is brought to bear on legal practice, as if legal practice is a hermetic activity that requires an external impetus to overcome its ideological shortsightedness. Critical legal theory arises from, and is always continuous with, legal practice, even in the most disruptive critical moments. I begin my analysis of critical legal theory by returning to the general activity of rhetorical knowledge. Although I argue that Gadamer and Perelman have sufficiently addressed their critics' accusation that they have fostered an overly conservative account, I conclude that Gadamer and Perelman account for critique only in an underdeveloped and indirect manner. Working from this inadequate critical opening, in the next section I confront the model of rhetorical knowledge with Nietzsche's far more explicit and radical critical activity.

Philosophical Hermeneutics and Critical Insight

Charles Altieri has chided Gadamer for glibly incorporating rhetorical themes into his philosophy as a means of fending off Habermas's insistent demand that the emancipatory interest manifested in social critique be accorded a role in hermeneutical understanding.[6] Altieri rejects a hermeneutical abdication to abstract "otherness" and argues in favor of a rhetorical view of the "other" as an active agent with whom the interpreter must negotiate the bonds of social life. "I am . . . interested in the ways rhetorical thinking helps us flesh out what is dark about hermeneutics. For by focusing on wills and orientations towards actions, rhetoric reminds us that the limitations in our understanding extend far beyond our inability to penetrate or contain what is excessive and singular."[7] In short, Altieri faults Gadamer for ignoring the wariness that arises in every social experience, and he emphasizes that maintaining this wariness is essential to the task of diagnosing the power lodged within discursive practices and mitigating the effects of such power on social life.

In similar fashion, Thomas Farrell argues that Gadamer has too quickly conflated the model of everyday conversation with the model of rhetorical interaction.[8] Farrell contends that Gadamer's invocation of conversation as a model of understanding hypostatizes the unguarded encounter with another that occurs in casual conversation and thereby obscures the more judicious attitude that occurs in a deliberative exchange.[9] While agreeing that "the reflective capacity of rhetoric is embedded in the reflective capacities of conversation in general," Farrell emphasizes that rhetoric is partisan (monologic speech aimed at effect), whereas conversation is bipartisan (dialogic speech oriented toward understanding).[10] Arguing that Gadamer's comforting vision of conversational give-and-take obscures the more challenging rhetorical moments of deliberative struggle to define a public ethos, Farrell concludes that it is necessary to move beyond Gadamer's insights by developing an explicitly critical rhetoric.

Farrell argues that contemporary rhetorical theory should translate Aristotle's insights to present concerns via Habermas's critical theory, with the aim being to develop normative criteria of successful dialogue.[11] Rhetoric is more than *techne,* which would only underwrite an inquiry into the "actual rules and techniques of discourse practice"; it also has a "prescriptive mission of invention, discovery, and judgment" within the context of "occasions of urgent practical choice" and therefore includes a critical component.[12] Farrell cautiously embraces Habermas's discourse ethics as a means of introducing this critical element, although only after emphasizing Habermas's grudging concession that critical ideality emerges solely from the messy practical engagements of rhetorical exchanges.[13] Farrell argues that this practical experience of rhetorical critique necessarily extends beyond Gadamer's idealization of conversation.

The criticisms of Gadamer voiced by Altieri and Farrell offer, in essential respects, appropriate emendations of Gadamer's hermeneutics. Altieri proposes a more traditional critical project of demystifying surface meanings to expose the exercise of power, whereas Farrell defines critique as a reflective capacity that simultaneously emerges from and gains perspective on practice. Both emphasize that hermeneutics can ill afford to remain passively quiescent in the face of the skewed rhetorical arena of modern culture. They both reject the conclusion that an ontology of situatedness disables the theorist from identifying and encouraging sound rhetorical practices. Confronting Gadamer with these challenges reveals that, in fact, he does recognize the critical dimension of hermeneutical understanding, but that this aspect of his philosophy is not adequately emphasized and developed.

Gadamer's notion of "unproductive prejudices" that are revealed and overcome in a hermeneutical encounter signals his interest in the critical moment of hermeneutical appropriation, although he provides little in the way of suggestions for facilitating this critical event.[14] Altieri's emphasis on "wariness" is meant as a warning that the hermeneutical "fusion of horizons" championed by Gadamer can often serve to concretize the shared ideological limitations in the text and interpreter, but Gadamer never naively sanctions the comforting practice of reading only reaffirming texts. In his discussion of the authority of classic texts, Gadamer emphasizes that historical distance can transform a text into an unsettling and persistently provocative dialogic partner that challenges interpreters to translate its meaning to contemporary concerns.[15] This interpretive experience generates critical insight when the interpreter is (literally) questioned by the text and finds herself adjusting her preconceived notions; simultaneously, the text acquires a new facet in the history of its appropriation to present concerns and inevitably is different when it serves as the focus of critical engagement for future readers.[16] Likewise, Gadamer's fascination with the demands of translating texts from a foreign language reaffirms his belief that a challenging and discomfiting hermeneutical exchange reveals the epistemic potential embedded within interpretation.[17] Regrettably, not only are these themes sketchy, they are consciously suppressed as part of Gadamer's rebuke of Habermas's critical hubris.[18]

The model of conversation provides a focus for drawing the critical impulses out of Gadamer's work. Gadamer's use of "conversation" should not be confused with superficial banter or social pleasantries. Gadamer specifically calls to mind "true" conversations, in which two or more people join in discussion with the aim of coming to an understanding collaboratively about a subject that evolves from their discussion, even though the conversation lacks formal or institutionally guided criteria. A conversation is a dialogic activity that engages the participants rather than mere idle chatter, and for this reason he equates it with rhetorical exchange.[19] By choosing as his guiding metaphor an image of the interpreter enmeshed in an inventional discourse with another person in real time, Gadamer reaffirms his opposition to the exegetical model of a reader prostrate before a classical text that must be honored with reverent deference.[20] Gadamer insists that textual interpretation provides a more expansive hermeneutical encounter than conversation because the text, removed from the immediacy of a given moment, persistently demands that the reader engage in a dialogic exchange rather than falling back on banalities.[21] Because it suspends the ordinary contextual aids used by conversationalists to come to an understanding, reading is derivative of and highlights the reality of conversation, and so Gadamer means quite literally to found his hermeneutics on the experience of conversation.

Perelman's valuable contribution to Gadamer's hermeneutical insight is that he traces the means by which conversationalists inventively shape their dialogue so as to permit them to move beyond the subjective designs of each individual. By offering conversation as a model of hermeneutical understanding, Gadamer indicates that his references to rhetoric are not simply afterthoughts; rather, he embraces the inescapable activity involved in every communicative event of understanding. This recognition is driven home by Gadamer's radical claim that all textual interpreters exhibit something of the reflective inventiveness required of successful rhetors. This understanding of the hermeneutical event as an active, critical appropriation is the core of his philosophy even though he fails to develop the rhetorical dimension of this experience in great depth.

Gadamer's essay in response to Habermas's extended critique of *Truth and Method* provides one of his most explicit discussions of rhetoric, but Altieri is wrong to construe this as mere defensiveness on Gadamer's part. Gadamer reasserts the primacy of linguisticality as a mode of being, not only for hermeneutics but also for rhetoric and sociology. Just as a rhetor never has language at his disposal merely as a tool to motivate action, Gadamer argues, neither can a sociologist wield sociological theory as a tool able to demystify lived experience entirely. Hermeneutical finitude means that "language is not only an object in our hands, it is the reservoir of tradition and the medium in and through which we exist and perceive our world," and so a theorist never gains complete perspective on linguistically mediated practices.[22] This does not signal Gadamer's desire to subdue rhetoric by absorbing it into a passive hermeneutics. To the contrary, his overarching themes are that persuasion can occur within a rhetorical exchange and that truth may emerge despite the lack of recourse to theoretical assurances of the rational criteria to be employed. Gadamer would agree with Altieri that "wariness" is always a feature of the give-and-take of interpretive practice, but he would reject a theory-driven methodological attitude of "wariness" that purports to get behind one's embeddedness in rhetorical practices.

Farrell provides a convincing correction to Gadamer's one-sidedness, and it is no mistake that he invokes Perelman's philosophy as a moderating influence on Habermas's quasi-transcendental, Enlightenment philosophy.[23] He reformats Habermas's celebrated validity claims from ahistorical universal criteria to expressions that are captured in Perelman's argument that "the practical exercise of judgment [cultivates] our recognition of a sense of the universal within the particular."[24] Farrell persuasively challenges Gadamer to the extent that he uses Perelman's new rhetoric to develop the critical element that is suppressed in Gadamer's philosophy. Perelman's new rhetoric thus provides the methodological key to unlock the hidden critical dimension of Gadamer's ontological account, providing a necessary clarification of the nature and potential of rhetorical knowledge.

The New Rhetoric and Critical Theory

Critical theorists similarly challenge Perelman for his apparent conservative conventionalism. Peter Goodrich applauds Perelman's critique of rationalist accounts of knowledge, but he criticizes Perelman's seemingly narrow methodological inquiry into rhetorical practices. Rather than accepting the apparent givenness of meanings in legal texts, Goodrich insists that theorists must relate these meanings "to institutional and ideological practices" that constitute exercises of social power.[25] This theoretical program requires a transition in legal theory from the model of biblical hermeneutics (exegesis of received truth embodied in a text) to a rhetorical model (uncovering the political exertions of authority through historical and social inquiry), a transition that Perelman anticipates but does not complete.[26]

Goodrich acknowledges that Perelman's work marks the reemergence of rhetoric after an extended period of suppression by structural linguistics and formalist jurisprudence, but he finds Perelman's rehabilitative efforts wanting.[27] In Goodrich's account, Perelman fails primarily because he wrongly supposes that the inability to apply formal logic to legal problems forecloses a critique of the internal logic operative in legal discourse.[28] Perelman's too-easy identification with Aristotelian rhetoric and the resulting bias favoring existing authority are "manifestly absurd" in Goodrich's view, particularly since Aristotelian rhetoric was developed for use in the small, homogeneous city-states of ancient Greece.[29] In opposition to this conventionalism, Goodrich advocates a "materialist rhetoric of law" that can serve as a "political instrument for the analysis of legal relations."[30] Goodrich challenges Perelman with a provocative question: "[I]s the study of law primarily to accept legal relations as 'given' and consensual, or is it to treat the rhetoric of law as a primary datum to be evaluated and appraised against the background of the institutional power and social relations of inequality, of superordination and subordination, that underpin that rhetoric and determine its semantic content?"[31] In the face of this challenge, Perelman's careful catalogue of the commonplaces of argument would appear to be almost beside the point.

Supporting this critical challenge, Goodrich also criticizes Perelman for failing to provide a theoretical basis for his approach after correctly displacing rationalist ideology.[32] Goodrich carefully constructs a multifaceted analysis of legal discourse premised on the critique of law as a specialized and determinant discourse. He identifies three features of a robust critical inquiry: using the psychoanalytic model of critique to expose how the internal logic and syntax of legal practice represses the inventive possibilities of working with unstable textual meanings (critique of "intradiscourse"),[33] drawing the connections between the use of concepts such as "economic" in legal discourse and other arenas of social discourse (critique of "interdiscourse"),[34] and describing the organizationally defined limitations on the acceptable uses of authoritative texts within legal practice (critique of "institutionalism").[35] Goodrich characterizes this complex inquiry as "rhetorical" because it involves a civil and political practice rather than the exposition of pre-given truths. "The rhetorical analysis has its basis in forms of political criticism which endeavored to evaluate the relation and appropriateness of language use to its specific context as well as to evaluate the content of the speech in terms of its value for the immediate historical community. These two criteria of analysis combine in the simple claim that all speech is dialogic in character and consequently is best understood not solely in the normative linguistic terms of the various forms of exegesis but rather in the material terms of its specific context and uses."[36] Perelman's rhetorical inquiry is just too simplistic and conventional under Goodrich's account to provide disruptive, and thereby enlightening, insights into rhetorical practices generally and the workings of the legal system in particular.

The criticism of Perelman voiced by Goodrich suggests the need for appropriate emendations of Perelman's new rhetoric to better articulate the critical elements of rhetorical practice. The primary force of Goodrich's criticism derives from his insistence that it is not enough for the theorist to leave the practice as she finds it, since the purpose of philosophy is to gain perspective in a manner that can guide participants in a practice. By working through this challenge to Perelman's new rhetoric, I demonstrate that Perelman does take account of the need for criticism defined in these broad terms, but concede that he does not emphasize this feature of his rhetorical philosophy sufficiently.

Perelman's catalogue of the commonplaces of argument is not just a description of certain moves in a closed language game, but rather is an integral aspect of a radical critique of rhetorical practices. By characterizing commonplaces as resources that serve both as starting points for, and strategies within, attempts to persuade, Perelman makes clear that he does not abandon rhetorical practices to an assumed preexisting logic. The central importance of "confused notions" in Perelman's philosophy reflects his emphasis on the realm of responsibility in the working out of concrete problems.[37] His goal is to facilitate argumentation by providing a better understanding of the dynamics of gaining the adherence of others. If the fabric of civic and social life is argumentation about reasonable courses of action, reflection on the activity of argumentation is the most important critical intervention available to a theorist.

Perelman's analysis of the precepts of natural law provides an illuminating example of his conception of how rhetorical exchanges working from commonplaces contain a critical bite. Perelman rejects the authoritarianism at the core of modern conceptions of natural law as an expression of overreaching rationalism, but he does not regard the tradition as a "mistake" that should be exorcized from our vocabulary. Arguing that natural law principles are commonplaces of argument, not only does Perelman effectively strip these principles of their inauthentic claim to eternal and universal validity, he also empowers legal theorists and practitioners by emphasizing how the principles serve as vital (indeed, unavoidable) resources for innovation and critique of existing legal relations.[38] Gadamer's ontological argument that prejudices enable understanding girds this description of the practice of argumentation. Both philosophers stress that there simply is no place to begin a critical effort except with commonplaces such as "equality before the law," "the rule of law," and so forth, even if the effort is designed to uncover the many abuses cloaked by these signifiers.[39]

Goodrich's challenge is not met by simply acknowledging the critical element of rhetorical exchange, though, because his attack rests on the broader claim that Perelman lacks a theoretical validation of his project. In this regard, Goodrich certainly is correct, although this lack might be attributed to the fact that Perelman was unable to bring his entire vision to completion. Regardless of the explanation, the new rhetoric remains incomplete without an account of the ontological status of rhetorical practices and critical inquiry. Gadamer's philosophical hermeneutics can perform this vital role by providing the theoretical backdrop for Perelman's methodological inquiry into the practice of argumentation.

Goodrich's reliance on a psychoanalytic model for critiquing the internal logic of legal rhetoric is answered by borrowing Gadamer's response to Habermas's similar theoretical move. Acknowledging the reality and importance of psychoanalytic dialogue in the analyst-patient relationship, Gadamer nevertheless questions Habermas's effort to build a critical theory on this model. Psychoanalytic discourse inherently is strategic because one of the parties to the "conversation" is not accepting the truth of the other's assertions at face value, but instead is seeking to get behind the surface discourse and bring suppressed meanings to speech. Gadamer emphasizes that psychoanalytic therapy is a highly specialized and derivative mode of communication, just as science is a highly specialized and derivative style of rational analysis; consequently, it cannot be universalized as the theoretical foundation of all critical understanding.[40] Gadamer's ontological claim that understanding is a historical event resulting from the fusion of the horizons of a prejudiced interpreter and the cumulative significance of a text, when melded with Perelman's philosophy, provides a theoretical grounding of the practical accomplishment of critique that Goodrich demands. Although Goodrich may ultimately be unsatisfied with this grounding, Gadamer lends a clearly articulated philosophical position otherwise lacking in Perelman's project.

I have emphasized this point by pushing Gadamer's insights beyond his own articulations. Gadamer too readily accepts the psychoanalytic account of the therapeutic relationship, and then works to show how the demystifying hermeneutics of psychoanalysis operates as a limit situation. I have argued elsewhere that Gadamer's later writings display a strong affinity with certain postmodern approaches to psychotherapy, and that Gadamer could have better responded to Habermas by making the affirmative claim that philosophical hermeneutics embraces the critical practice exemplified in these approaches to psychotherapy.[41] Once the critical practice of therapy is properly understood in postmodern—rather than scientistic or rationalistic—terms, it is apparent that Gadamer's philosophical hermeneutics remains open to this critical dimension of understanding. In this way, Gadamer's ontological argument provides a reorientation for the critical insights derived from the rhetorical construction of the therapy relationship.

Goodrich's nuanced model of critique is not limited to demystifying a given field of discourse; he also stresses the need to explore the interdiscursive connections between differentiated rhetorical practices such as law and political economy. Perelman shares this approach, as exemplified by his extended discussion of the use of moral terms in legal practice, a convergence that has engendered the age-old debate over the relationship between positive law and ethical norms. Perelman argues that moral terms interpenetrate and shape legal discourse, but that the two discourses cannot be conflated because they are addressed to different audiences.[42] Buttressed by Gadamer's ontological claim about the universality of the hermeneutical situation, Perelman is best read as arguing that rhetorical inquiry, in some important sense, inevitably is interdiscursive. Tracing connections between the uses of the concept of responsibility by moral philosophers, by citizens making ethical judgments, and by lawyers may prove to be illuminating, but there is need for caution. It is foolhardy to seek to gain purchase on these different practices by developing an understanding of "responsibility" in itself, despite the shared rhetorical nature of these practices, since each rhetorical arena has its own important defining features.

Finally, Goodrich devotes attention to the institutional constraints on rhetorical practices, debunking the mythical view of the legal "system" as a neutral vehicle for an unfolding rationality in legal doctrine. Rendering rhetorical theory "material" in this respect is necessary and acknowledged by Perelman, although certainly with less intensity than Goodrich displays. Perelman agrees that the structure of the legal system has a tremendous effect on legal discourse, leading him to stress the rhetorical significance of institutional features such as the adherence to precedent and the hierarchical structure of the court system. For example, Perelman emphasizes that it is the institutional constraints of the legal system designed to ensure stability that differentiate legal and moral reasoning, and he contends that these constraints bring the nature of all practical reasoning into sharper relief.[43]

One might wish with Goodrich for deeper critical impulses on Perelman's part, just as one might wish with Altieri and Farrell for Gadamer to pay greater attention to bureaucratic and hierarchical impediments to hermeneutical understanding. In this respect, Gadamer and Perelman mutually reinforce weak aspects of the other's philosophy by not providing a more radical account of critique, even if it is clear after confronting each thinker with his critics that each also supplements the other in important ways to open the space for critique. For this reason, a complete account of rhetorical knowledge requires more than reading Gadamer and Perelman together. In the next section I draw out and explicate the openings to critical theory that are present, but obscured, in the account of rhetorical knowledge that I have drawn from Gadamer and Perelman.

The Demand for Radical Critique: Challenging Gadamer and Perelman with Nietzschean Critique

Gadamer provides the philosophical underwriting for rhetorical knowledge, to which Perelman adds both reinforcement and substantial detail about rhetorical argumentation. But by pulling Gadamer's work in the direction of the pragmatics of rhetorical engagement, we risk exacerbating each philosopher's seeming unconcern with the role of critical theory. To add sufficient critical depth to the concept of rhetorical knowledge I now challenge Gadamer from another angle entirely: the radical critique initiated by Nietzsche. I begin with an account of Nietzschean critique that connects with Gadamer's ontological grounding of rhetorical knowledge, thereby drawing out the critical element that is present but underemphasized in both Gadamer and Perelman. I then turn to Gianni Vattimo's celebration of weak thought as a window to this critical dimension of rhetorical knowledge. I conclude by bringing my analysis to bear on a concrete issue, focusing on the recent Supreme Court jurisprudence regarding gay rights. My analysis of this case law illustrates the critical openings that occur in the course of generating rhetorical knowledge in a practical setting, but it also exemplifies the role of critical assessments of practice. By confronting rhetorical knowledge with Nietzschean critique, I set the stage for a full consideration of the role of critical legal theory in chapter 3.

Ontological Perspectivism and Rhetorical Knowledge

Nietzsche is a challenging and enigmatic philosopher who resists easy summarization and who has spawned contradictory interpretations of his work. I do not pretend to adjudicate the many contentious battles among Nietzsche scholars with the goal of definitively characterizing his philosophy. My more modest goal is to adumbrate a model of Nietzschean critique that can credibly be reconciled with his texts and that provides guidance for developing the critical element of rhetorical knowledge. I begin by isolating two of Nietzsche's prominent themes: his naturalistic account of ontological perspectivism, and his enactment of critique as an aesthetic and rhetorical practice.[44]

My method for constructing a model of Nietzschean critique is mediative and meliorative, in that I seek to find some common ground in contemporary Nietzsche scholarship. I draw from two competing interpretations: analytic philosophers have characterized Nietzsche as a naturalist whose principal aim is to overcome the metaphysical nonsense embodied in religion and moral philosophy; in contrast, Continental philosophers have emphasized that Nietzsche regards all knowledge as perspectival rather than the result of a correspondence with an objective natural reality. I argue that naturalism provides Nietzsche with a standard by which to judge the metaphysics of modernity, while perspectivism is the means by which Nietzsche deconstructs the Enlightenment conception of the knowing subject. A complementary reading of these elements of his philosophy generates a model of critical theory that fits comfortably with Gadamer's ontology of understanding.

Nietzsche's virulent attacks on Christianity and metaphysics often are presented in naturalistic terms: he criticizes them for turning away from real life,[45] a life that he characterizes as "will to power."[46] This leads some philosophers to argue that Nietzsche's naturalism undercuts his apparent celebration of radical indeterminacy.[47] In the end, the strictly naturalistic reading of Nietzsche paints him as a harbinger of a relentless scientific consciousness that attends only to the real world—which is to say, a perceptible and empirical world—and ceases useless metaphysical speculation. However, this reading cuts against a significant portion of Nietzsche's writing, and it undermines his significance as a serious philosopher who rejects simpleminded realism but nonetheless finds ample resources for vigorous critique.

Nietzsche's assessment of science is far too ambivalent to compel a strict realist reading of his naturalism. The emergence of natural science coincides with the death of God and the movement away from religious metaphysics, but Nietzsche regards much of modern science as theology by other means.[48] Rather than overcoming the "ascetic ideal" expressed in the religious and metaphysical retreat from nature, science intensifies the denial of nature by reducing the world to that which is subject to perspicacious description.[49] In *The Gay Science,* Nietzsche criticizes the sober realists who believe that the world is arrayed before their detached gaze and who refuse to acknowledge the "secret and inextinguishable drunkenness" of life.[50] He regarded the science of his day as the culmination of the

Western metaphysical tradition that threatens to bring on a "midnight" of nihilism, but he believed that this might set the stage for a new dawn in which humankind can affirm the death of God without seeking a surrogate in science.[51] This new day would be the advent of the gay science that Nietzsche heralded: a joyous affirmation of the human condition as will to power.

Under this reading, Nietzsche grounds his unceasing critique in nature, but he rejects the subject/object dualism that defines the self-understanding of the natural sciences of his day in favor of "will to power"—the view that all of nature is constantly engaged in ongoing, active interpretation.[52] Christoph Cox explains that naturalism and interpretivism coexist in Nietzsche's thought by recognizing that "if will to power is the naturalistic theory par excellence, and if will to power essentially involves interpretation, the naturalist is led to assert the primacy and irreducibility of interpretation. . . . In short, for Nietzsche, the natural world is fundamentally interpretive. There is no world other than the natural and nothing outside the interpretive web that constitutes this natural world."[53] Nietzsche propounds a radically "perspectivist ontology of power,"[54] under which humans are not interpretive animals that "create" the world according to their desires, but rather are the most complex beings in a deeply interpretive play of forces that includes all of nature.[55]

Nietzsche delivers naturalistic critiques of Christianity and metaphysics, then, but he is criticizing their abandonment of a natural reality that is deeply interpretive. The absolute and binary world proposed by these fables is a complete abstraction from human nature, because knowledge is gained because of, not in spite of, perspectivity. "Against all realisms, Nietzsche maintains that every ontology is the construction of an interpretation and that no world would remain over after the subtraction of every interpretation. . . . Nietzsche short-circuits the distinction between idealism and realism by dissolving the poles of subject and object into the unified field of interpretation or will to power."[56] In opposition to the ascetic denial of human nature, Nietzsche encourages philosophers to embrace the interpretive character of nature, in order to usher in a new

> "objectivity" . . . understood not as "disinterested contemplation" (which is a non-concept and a nonsense), but as the capacity to have

> all the arguments for and against *at one's disposal* and to suspend or implement them at will: so that one can exploit that very *diversity* of perspectives and affective interpretations in the interests of knowledge. From now on, my dear philosophers, let us beware of the dangerous old conceptual fable which posited a "pure, will-less, painless, timeless knowing subject", let us beware of the tentacles of such contradictory concepts as "pure reason", "absolute spirituality", knowledge in itself";—for these always ask us to imagine an eye which is impossible to imagine, an eye which supposedly looks out in no particular direction, an eye which supposedly either restrains or altogether lacks the active powers of interpretation which first make seeing into seeing something—for here, then, a nonsense and non-concept is demanded of the eye. Perspectival seeing is the *only* kind of seeing there is, perspectival "knowing" the *only* kind of "knowing"; and the *more* feelings about a matter which we allow to come to expression, the *more* eyes, different eyes through which we are able to view this same matter, the more complete our "conception" of it, our "objectivity", will be.[57]

The falsifications introduced by the ascetic ideal, as it is manifested in religion, philosophy, and even science, can be overcome only by affirming that perspectivism is the nature of reality.

This ontological claim immediately raises a problem: Nietzsche must defend his account as providing an accurate, which is to say a truthful, description of the natural world, or his perspectivism inevitably must cannibalize itself. I have endorsed Hales and Welshon's response to this challenge in some detail.[58] Briefly stated, Nietzsche allows that there may be some statements, admittedly not many, that are true "*in all human perspectives,* statements that are true for all humans no matter what else is true in their perspective,"[59] but this does not change the fact that even absolute truths, such as logic or certain causal relationships, are not validated by direct correspondence to a world-in-itself, but instead are only perspectivally true.[60] Thus, perspectivism provides an ontological account that is true in all human perspectives, just as the principles of logic or the laws of causation are absolutely true, but Nietzsche's ontology is not validated by its correspondence with a perspective-independent world, for no such world exists. In Perelman's terms, Nietzsche readily admits that his philosophical activity is rhetorical rather than demonstrative, but his ontological perspectivism is a claim that is directed toward the hypothetically constructed universal audience. This is echoed in Gianni Vattimo's thesis that will to power is an interpretive construct rather than a natural process that can be demonstratively established in a definitive manner:

> If one may say this, the Will to Power is something hermeneutic, something engaged in interpreting. The struggle between the opposing tendencies of a multiplicity of wills is above all a struggle between competing interpretations, as that fragment concerning European nihilism shows. . . . Yet the Will to Power is also hermeneutic in another sense: because it sees the world as a game of competing appearances and perspectives, it is itself one theory among others, an interpretation and nothing else. Nietzsche concedes this point explicitly at the end of an aphorism in *Beyond Good and Evil:* "Assuming this too is only interpretation [. . .] well, so much the better" (*BGE* §22, 31).[61]

This, of course, is not to say that all interpretations have the same truth status or are equally useful.

Nietzsche's naturalistic ontology of perspectivism provides the ground for his critical activity. Interpretations that conflict with human nature as will to power, itself an interpretation, are derided by Nietzsche for their disabling effects. Nietzsche does not anchor his critique in an invariant nature, but rather within the dynamic hermeneutical-rhetorical practices described by Gadamer and Perelman. Admittedly, this would appear to provide only illusory comfort in the face of the contentious public disputes of our day. When a religious fundamentalist criticizes the emergence of gay rights as a decadent affront to man's heterosexual-reproductive "nature," Nietzsche would be embracing the relativism that he so clearly rejected if he conceded that this "perspective" is no less valid than his own perspectivist ontology. Nietzsche's radical critique would be impotent if his perspectival ontology precluded him from successfully rebutting fundamentally inconsistent naturalistic accounts, including religiously inspired natural law theories.

Nietzsche's solution to this dilemma, and his vital contribution to my theory of rhetorical knowledge, is found in his aesthetic-rhetorical enactment of philosophical thinking. Nietzsche's genealogical critique of human nature is rhetorical rather than demonstrative; he argues about matters that lend themselves only to probabilities rather than to definitive resolution. Nietzsche cannot compel the religious fundamentalist to accept his perspectivist ontology, but this is not worrisome to Nietzsche since he is arguing that things couldn't be otherwise. As he aptly summarizes, we "cannot look around our own corner: it is a hopeless curiosity that [seeks to rise above one's perspective to clearly see perspectivity itself]. But I should think that today we are at least far from the ridiculous immodesty that would be involved in decreeing from our corner that perspectives are permitted only from this corner."[62] His goal is to persuade rather than to dictate, and persuasion is a function of what traditionally would be designated as mere style. By cajoling his readers to take his destabilizing critiques seriously, Nietzsche invites them to risk loosening their metaphysical prejudices. If another philosopher pulls with equal vigor in a different direction, so much the better, for it is in the weighing and consideration of different perspectives that one can genuinely experience the perspectivity of nature.

Nietzsche's perspectival ontology and epistemology lead him to embrace the "dangerous maybe" of rhetorical argumentation.[63] A religious fundamentalist and Nietzsche offer competing interpretations and critiques, but Nietzsche's perspectivist account does not force him to concede that these critiques are equally legitimate. Nietzsche's works represent an extended rhetorical appeal that claims to be a better interpretation, all the while admitting that there can be no final demonstration of truth by an appeal to correspondence with the world-in-itself.[64] Knowledge emerges from rhetorical engagements, even if there can be no determinant methodology for compelling recognition of the victorious argument. As a rhetorician, Nietzsche recognized that his ability to persuade requires an audience prepared to hear his message; this leads him repeatedly to bemoan the "herd mentality" that rendered so many of his contemporaries deaf to his philosophy and consigned him to be a "posthumous" philosopher.[65]

Nietzsche's rhetorical conception of critique comes through most clearly when we recognize that his writings exemplify the rhetorical activity to which he refers, when we recognize that he "rethinks philosophy *through rhetoric*."[66] Although he does not offer a detailed theory of rhetorical critique explicitly,[67] Nietzsche praises art because the artist embodies the rhetorical style that breaks free from tendencies toward absolutism. Not only does art serve as a critique of the pretensions of metaphysics, religion, and science, it makes postmetaphysical life bearable by affirming life and modeling an incipient "gay science."[68] Art locates the experience of truth within illusion, and this affirmation of truth captures human nature in a manner that can never be matched by the metaphysical claims of the theologians.

The artistic critique of culture is accomplished through genealogical critique. Genealogical inquiry is a rhetorical practice because it is an active re-visioning of the significance of the past and the potential for the future rather than an uncovering of timeless verities.

> Genealogy's vision is continually directed in three directions at once, always looking toward past, future, and present in a continuing effort to see how each of the three disrupts the others.
>
> It is this continual redirection of forces that constitutes genealogy as critique. It is also a moment of critique that is continually suspended in the field of possibility. In this sense, it is artistic as well, never speaking to the "it was" but only to the "it will have been." The past, for genealogy, always returns from the future *retroactively*. It is this return, for Nietzsche, that always effects a stylistic moment. Genealogy is never dispassionate or removed: it is always a mode of "expression, intention, and the art of surprise."[69]

Nietzsche exemplifies the art of rhetoric as a creative refashioning of accepted topoi to address contemporary questions by means of a re-visioning, or *dunamis,* rather than through the skillful application of a methodology to fixed data, as *techne.* Nietzsche's genealogy revives the Protagorean formulation, in which man is the measure of all things, and emphasizes man's active and creative role in building a *nomos.* At the individual level, Nietzsche characterizes this creative activity as giving style to one's character by working within topoi and constraints that only appear to be limiting, but that in fact are no more limiting than masonry and wood are limiting to an architect or builder.[70]

By embracing the re-visioning power of rhetoric so thoroughly, Nietzsche risks the danger of an untrammeled subjectivism that dissolves into nihilism; in response, he appeals to the "intellectual conscience" that rises above crude sophistic relativism. Our ontological fate is to be "relentlessly antidogmatic, antireductionist, antifoundationalist, and ever in search of new interpretations," but Nietzsche emphasizes that "such inquiry results in 'truths' that, though never absolute or ultimate, deliver all that we actually need from truth and, in any case, all we can ever have of it."[71] Nietzsche's rhetorically structured genealogy involves the active adoption of different perspectives and the disruption of received wisdom in order to break free of metaphysical calcifications. Intellectual conscience demands an honest appreciation of the "relationships *among* perspectives, namely the constant weighing and measuring of interpretations against one another," which in turn serves a number of critical purposes:

> First, it demonstrates the partiality of any one interpretation or perspective. . . . Second, this procedure calls attention to the rules of formation of interpretations and the different sets of these that govern different interpretations, thus highlighting the decisions in favor of one or more of the many criteria that compete for satisfaction in the composition of any interpretation. Thus, entrenchment is weighed against innovation; habit against novelty; simplicity, coherence, utility, and explanatory power against comprehensiveness and precise description, and so on. Third—and highly important for Nietzsche—a consideration of the dominant interpretations of an individual or group produces a whole symptomatology and genealogy of the dispositions and values that motivate these choices. . . . Last, such recognition of the plurality of interpretations and their irreducibility to a single base reveals what Nietzsche calls "the whole marvelous uncertainty and interpretive multiplicity of existence" and thus affirms the world of becoming, change, and semblance.[72]

The promise of intellectual conscience leads Nietzsche to accept the rhetorical construction of the social world with a joyous affirmation.

Nietzschean critique is a rhetorical activity that acknowledges its rhetoricity. He challenges the cultural understandings of his day through genealogical criticism that simultaneously loosens the encrustation of habitual thinking and refashions a dramatically new understanding of cultural traditions. His naturalistic critique appeals to the emerging interpretations that define social reality, even if they remain repressed and are denied. His famous announcement of the death of God is not a suggestion for change made by an all-knowing critic; rather, it is a commentary on what already has occurred, a rhetorical assessment of shifts that are under way but remain unacknowledged. Nietzsche's critical activity is consistent with his perspectivist ontology because he offers an interpretation of a shared reality that is subject to criticism and refinement rather than an eternally valid description of the human condition. In this way, he confronts existence with joy and openness rather than hiding behind the fables that no longer ring true (Christianity) or the new fables that similarly obscure the human condition (positivist natural science).

Reading Nietzsche and Gadamer Together: Vattimo's Hermeneutical Conception of Radical Critique

Nietzsche's ontological perspectivism fits well with the model of rhetorical knowledge that I have built on Gadamer's philosophical hermeneutics, and it provides a necessary supplement by introducing Nietzsche's vigorous critique to the apparently more conservative themes developed by Gadamer and Perelman. After emphasizing the manner in which Nietzsche exploits the critical project that is incipient in Gadamer's philosophy, I turn to Vattimo's development of a critical hermeneutics drawn from Nietzsche and Gadamer to provide an example of the philosophical role of critique in fostering rhetorical knowledge. Vattimo mediates Nietzsche and Gadamer in a manner that reaffirms that rhetorical knowledge includes a substantial critical element.

Nietzsche's ontological perspectivism immediately lends itself to comparisons with Gadamer's claim that every interpretive event involves a fusion of horizons. Just as Nietzsche argues that the perspectival nature of reality requires us to embrace many different perspectives in pursuit of truth, Gadamer argues that the hermeneutical nature of reality requires a fusion of horizons if we are to understand a traditionary text. But on more careful inspection it soon becomes clear that they use these concepts in very different ways, and it is these differences that prove to be instructive.[73] Nietzsche's perspectivism leads him to be wary of his interlocutors. If other thinkers can have only a partial perspective, then it follows that the critic must constantly be on guard against being co-opted by the limited views of those with whom he interacts. In contrast, Gadamer places great emphasis on learning from others by engaging them in a hermeneutical event of understanding in which one accepts the potential superiority of the other's perspective. Gadamer enjoins critical theorists to abandon their wariness and sense of superiority, and he emphatically rejects monological models of critique. Nietzsche and Gadamer both recognize the partiality of perspectives, then, but they appear to draw contradictory conclusions.

Although Nietzsche disdains the herd and expressly refuses to engage others with the goal of changing them,[74] his posture is perhaps best understood as a plea for self-anointed critics to stop engaging others from a position of presumed superiority, because this posture only reinforces the limited perspective of the critic and thus will almost always reinscribe prevailing morality. Nietzsche continually emphasizes the positive nature of critique, which is the hallmark of his gay science.[75] He desperately wants to move beyond a moralistic reproach that is grounded in a fixed and unyielding perspective by forgoing the urge to chastise others; instead, he wants to critique morality itself. It is not the fruitlessness of the fusion of horizons that worries Nietzsche, then, but rather the inevitable tendency to succumb to the temptation to subjugate others to one's own horizon, thereby reinforcing rather than challenging one's perspective from within a prevailing morality. Nietzsche's life suggests that he could see no alternative to a monological critical project undertaken by the few wanderers who had risen above the fetters of his day, even though it should have been obvious to him that this self-aggrandizement undercut his rhetorical radicalism.

Gadamer's fusion of horizons moves beyond Nietzsche in this regard, showing how the Nietzschean critic can reach beyond his prejudiced perspective. Gadamer uses the metaphor of a fusion of horizons to emphasize the finite and historical nature of all understanding. His point is not that one must respect every perspective to some degree, but rather that the confrontations with other horizons—whether provided by the past, distinct cultures, or other distanced perspectives—can provoke us to overcome our own limitations. Nietzsche bemoaned the limitations of German culture for this very reason: his contemporaries were locked in a horizon that stultified thinking rather than provoked new understandings. Gadamer finds the key to breaking the encrustations of traditional thinking in the experience of confronting another horizon.

The difference between Nietzsche's perspectivism and Gadamer's fusion of horizons is sharpened by the recognition that Nietzsche is wary of the stultifying effects of horizontal relationships within a cultural horizon, whereas Gadamer invites the educative effects of vertical relationships between past horizons and the present. Nietzsche's perspectivism properly leads him to mistrust the contemporary understanding of the herd, which often poses as universal and eternal truth. Gadamer's concept of the fusion of horizons most effectively destabilizes these false claims by resituating understanding in an ongoing dynamic application of the past to present circumstances. Nietzsche's perspectivism cautions us against looking for quick answers from our cultural contemporaries, while Gadamer's hermeneutics encourages us to exploit the continuing and creative application of previous understandings in a new setting as the manner in which parochialism is exposed and (incompletely) overcome. Read together, Nietzsche and Gadamer reveal that it is foolish and counterproductive for a cultural critic to claim to have all the answers and to disparage the prejudiced perspectives of his contemporaries, but also that it is equally foolish for the critic to disable his critical agency in the face of his own prejudiced forestructure of understanding as a participant within a cultural perspective.

This complementary relationship is manifest in their different rhetorical orientations. Nietzsche employs rhetoric by searching for appropriate means of persuasion; he makes claims on an audience with the goal of persuading them rather than approaching them with an openness to reaching mutual understanding. In contrast, Gadamer draws from classical rhetoric primarily for the purpose of investigating the hermeneutical bonds that subtend partisan argumentation, although he does offer subtle and penetrating cultural criticism in a number of essays and addresses. Gadamer contributes to the postmodern destruction of the metaphysics of presence by reviving the rhetorical tradition's lesson that reasonable inquiry is grounded in the hermeneutical situation of limited horizons reaching understanding in a moment of fusion. Nietzsche contributes by bringing the hermeneutics of suspicion to bear on the rhetorical situation: because he is wary of his audience, he is not satisfied to engage in ordinary rhetorical inventiveness. Nietzsche does not escape the commonplaces, of course, but he strives to immerse himself in these engagements as a determined advocate who unsettles traditional discourse. Read together, Nietzsche and Gadamer illuminate the full dimensions of rhetorical engagement as intersubjective situatedness and reasoned argumentation.[76]

Gianni Vattimo's nihilistic hermeneutics draws on these converging yet divergent themes in philosophical hermeneutics and Nietzschean critique,[77] even if at critical junctures he claims to align himself with Nietzsche and against Gadamer. Vattimo advocates a nihilistic philosophy of "weak thought," in which philosophical thinking accepts its rhetorical role as cultural criticism rather than continuing to assert its power to deliver accurate and perspicacious descriptions of reality. In the postmetaphysical age that Nietzsche helped to inaugurate, critique can only be thinking within a cultural horizon as a means of recovering from unproductive prejudices (*Verwindung:* working through a problem, surviving an ordeal) and can never be an intellectual overcoming of a prejudiced horizon altogether (*Überwindung:* overcoming an obstacle, moving on).[78] Vattimo thus embraces and continues philosophical thinking in the spirit of Nietzsche's famous aphorism in section 54 of *The Gay Science:* now that philosophy has "awakened" us to the knowledge that we are still dreaming, all we can do is continue the dream.[79] Vattimo understands that Nietzschean philosophical activity is cultural criticism, a *Verwindung* that necessarily occurs within a plural world from which metaphysical thinking cannot rescue us.

Vattimo's nihilistic philosophy appears to disable critical theory by expressly abandoning any fixed ground for critique, but he addresses this Nietzschean dilemma by avoiding sterile metaphysics and embracing the critical and ethical dimensions of his radically nihilistic hermeneutical philosophy. Once hermeneutical philosophy acknowledges that it cannot rise above its historical circumstances, it can embrace its role in generating a *Verwindung* within our cultural moment:

> Hermeneutics can live up to its ethical inclination in an appropriate fashion only by remaining faithful to the instance of historicality. But how? Principally, by thinking of itself not as an ultimately metaphysical descriptive theory of the hermeneutic constitution of existence, but rather as an event of destiny. Hermeneutics must recognize itself as the thought belonging to the epoch of the end of metaphysics, and nothing more. Hermeneutics is not the adequate description of the human condition, which is finally making headway only at a certain point in history, thanks to a particular thinker or a series of fortuitous circumstances. If it theorizes that the experience of truth is belonging and not reflection, it must also say to which epoch, world or provenance it itself as theory belongs.
>
> If . . . the "trivial" and weak hermeneutic thesis recognizes itself as *belonging,* instead of disguising itself as a metaphysical description, then it will see itself as a destiny (a provenance) and will become capable of choice, that is, of morality. Hermeneutics will recognize its destiny, if it understands the *nihilistic* character of its constitution.[80]

Vattimo's translator, Jon Snyder, crystallizes this development in a succinct but rich passage. "The *Verwindung* of modernity is a fundamentally ironic gesture that rejects any heroic or romantic posture vis-a-vis the Western tradition. The decline of modernity, however, also opens up the opportunity for a new,—but weakly new—beginning for thought, and this is what permits us to consider philosophical nihilism a responsible, rather than a despairing, response to the crisis of the contemporary world."[81] Because philosophy cannot pretend to dictate answers that are logically derived from essential foundations, it now sees itself as a political and ethical activity, undertaking what Vattimo calls an "ontology of actuality."[82] Hermeneutic philosophy, as an interpretation that seeks to be persuasive under conditions of "contingency, freedom and risk,"[83] generates a critical intervention into political and ethical matters.

Vattimo's critique of religion provides the most cogent example of his conception of philosophy as cultural criticism, particularly because he adds layers of nuance to Nietzsche's overly shrill assaults. By demythologizing objectivism, Vattimo observes, nihilistic philosophy lends fresh plausibility to religion at a time when the dissembling forces of globalization generate a longing for something vital as an antidote to the emptiness of modernity. Claiming that the "end of metaphysics and the death of the moral God have liquidated the philosophical basis of atheism," Vattimo argues that belief suddenly is possible again.[84] Weak thought liberates religion from God, which is to say that it liberates religion from the philosophical constructions of God as sovereign deity, metaphysical truth, and so on, thereby rendering the experience of belief plausible once again.

But Vattimo claims an even stronger connection between religion and his philosophy: "Hermeneutics can be what it is—a non-metaphysical philosophy with an essentially interpretive attitude towards truth, and thus a nihilistic ontology—only as heir to the Christian myth of the incarnation of God."[85] This paradoxical and surprising situation, in which religion returns to the forefront of social life, is not an ontological necessity but rather a historical development. "Perhaps, not by its essential nature, but *de facto,* . . . religion comes to be experienced as a return. In religion, something that we had thought irrevocably forgotten is made present again, a dormant trace is reawakened, a wound re-opened, the repressed returns, and what we took to be an *Überwindung* (overcoming, realization and thus a setting aside [of religion by philosophy]) is no more than a *Verwindung,* a long convalescence that has once again come to terms with the indelible trace of its sickness."[86] In *Belief,* Vattimo chronicles the return of religion in the wake of the death of God, arguing that nihilistic hermeneutical philosophy embodies the kenosis of the divine (word made flesh) and opens the possibility for realizing (in a new way) the central Christian principle of charity.

Vattimo enacts this critique of religion in a decidedly Gadamerian and Nietzschean fashion, utilizing the resources of tradition as the fuel for a genealogical critique. Given his scathing critiques of Christianity and moral philosophy, Nietzschean critique would appear to be far removed from Gadamer's hermeneutical cultivation of the resources of tradition. But Nietzsche employs a genealogical method, which by definition is a traditionary inquiry that seeks to understand and reconsider the present by thinking through the (often repressed) past. Vattimo endorses Nietzsche's insight that Christianity cannot be overcome in the way that we might overcome a dream by awakening to find that it is not "real." We continue to live in a tradition that has been shaped indelibly by Christianity, and the crucial task is to interpret where we are in this ongoing tradition. In Gadamerian fashion, Nietzsche repeatedly states that Christianity is not (and cannot be) a complete error, that his target is the bad interpretations of the Christian heritage that prevailed in the nineteenth century.[87] He goes "back like anybody who wants to attempt a big jump,"[88] to tell "the *genuine* history of Christianity,"[89] which means to offer a destabilizing interpretation of traditionary prejudices.

Gadamer's philosophical legacy proves to be important for Vattimo at this point, even if in a subterranean manner. During his long career, Gadamer emphasized that moving beyond the Enlightenment's "prejudice against prejudice" does not mean that one is fated to accept an endless nihilistic confrontation between equally prejudiced beliefs. Instead, as exemplified in the experience of art, hermeneutical engagement shatters the interpreter's prejudiced horizon in a manner that permits her to gain perspective on certain "unproductive prejudices" and to move forward. This contemplative attitude—this good conscience—is an openness to the perspectivity of Being and to relinquishing the certainty of metaphysical schemas. Gadamer believes that this can be achieved only through a willingness to enter a conversation and to learn from the other (person, text, or culture) in a playful dialogic encounter that is not methodologically scripted. It is precisely this social dimension of reason that augments Nietzsche's genealogical critique and highlights the possibility and genesis of *Verwindung* after we have awakened to realize that the dream of a theoretical and monological *Überwindung* is impossible.

Vattimo's philosophy (under my account, which is decidedly more charitable to Gadamer) exemplifies the model of critical hermeneutics that I derived from reading Nietzsche and Gadamer together. Critical theory is engaged within a prejudiced horizon and is not a method for overcoming one's horizon. Gadamer's hermeneutical philosophy is best read not as advocating reverence for traditional understandings, but rather as acknowledging that tradition is a linguistically structured and contested medium through which understanding takes place. Nietzsche's critical philosophy is best read not as claiming to have discovered bedrock natural reality through philosophical analysis, but rather as acknowledging that reality is hermeneutically structured and therefore dynamic rather than stable. Vattimo offers an approach to critical theory that brings together these insights and points the way toward rethinking the role of critical legal theory.

The Gay Science of Critical Legal Theory

To this point, my exegesis of Nietzsche's critical challenge to Gadamerian hermeneutics has been cast in philosophical terms, disconnected from legal practice. At this level of generality it is easy to understand that legal thinkers must reject the urge to engage in modernist "strong" theory, but it is difficult to discern what it might mean to pursue the possibilities of "weak" critical theory within law. I bring my discussion to bear on legal theory by exploring the implications of my Nietzschean-Gadamerian model of critical legal hermeneutics through an analysis of four cases in which the United States Supreme Court has grappled with the constitutional issues that circle around the question of the legal status of gays and lesbians in American society. Due to the high-profile nature of these cases and the relative degree of self-reflection apparent in the judicial opinions, these cases provide strong evidence supporting the model of critical legal hermeneutics on their own terms, and do not require much reading against the grain. My thesis is that a critical legal hermeneutics grounded in the theory of rhetorical knowledge provides not only substantial descriptive clarification of what transpires in these cases, but also guidance for effective critical intervention. Critical insight is possible even if (or, more precisely, because) my model of critical legal hermeneutics does not pretend to offer an interpretive methodology that delivers unimpeachably correct answers to specific legal questions. The insight reflected in the notion of "weak" theory is that theory is inextricably linked with practice, but that this linkage is enabling rather than a hindrance.

In 1986, the Court held in *Bowers v. Hardwick* with a five to four decision that a Georgia statute criminalizing sodomy did not violate the United States Constitution when it was applied to an adult man who engaged in consensual sexual activity with another adult man in his bedroom. The majority made clear that Georgia could choose to criminalize acts that it determined to be immoral.[90] Ten years later, in *Romer v. Evans,* the Court again decided by a five to four margin that a constitutional referendum enacted by the citizens of Colorado to preclude municipal measures designed to prohibit discrimination against gays and lesbians in public accommodations was unconstitutional. The Court found that the referendum was motivated by animus against gays and lesbians and was not rationally related to any legitimate state purpose.[91] Then, just four years after *Romer,* the Court again voted five to four in *Boy Scouts of America v. Dale* to hold that a New Jersey antidiscrimination statute prohibiting discrimination on the basis of sexual orientation was unconstitutionally applied to prohibit the Boy Scouts from refusing to allow a gay man to serve as a scout leader. The Court concluded that the Boy Scouts organization has a First Amendment right of association to exclude homosexuals from its leadership positions.[92] Finally, in a five to one to three decision in 2003, the Court in *Lawrence v. Texas* overruled *Bowers* and held that criminalizing the private, consensual sexual intimacy of adult gays and lesbians was a violation of substantive due process. The majority opinion dramatically acknowledged that the liberty interest in preserving intimate relationships from the reach of government proscription applies to gays and lesbians, again with only a five to four margin supporting this result.[93]

The tangled history of these four cases has received extensive scholarly attention, but I do not intend to offer a detailed analysis of the legal rationales in the various opinions and in the numerous scholarly assessments. My goal is to show that the legal reasoning exhibited in these cases is consistent with my model of rhetorical knowledge. These cases illuminate the emergence of critical insight within legal practice, and my discussion of them models the role that critical legal theory can play as a secondary activity. My discussion is schematic and suggestive, therefore, rather than doctrinal. I purposefully do not write with the tone of inevitability, nor do I proceed from a self-satisfied assumption that the correct answers to these cases are obvious. It is precisely by resisting the urge to declare the truth of the matter, to demarcate methodologically permissible and impermissible legal interpretations, that we enable critical legal hermeneutics to have any purchase beyond the artificial realm of the ivory tower. My discussion of these cases shows the power that critique holds as an interpretation offered within a play of interpretations, and rejects the belief that theorists can or should attempt to rise above interpretive activity to prescribe correct interpretations.

Bowers, Romer, and *Dale:* Legal Precedents as Confused Notions

I begin by describing how the opinions in *Bowers, Romer,* and *Dale* clearly exhibit the rhetorical nature of legal argumentation that is revealed by reading Gadamer and Nietzsche together, and in the next section I describe how *Lawrence* was resolved against this confused and agonistic legal backdrop. The most important feature of the first three cases is that they exemplify the rhetorical lesson that how one frames a question largely determines the answer that one generates.[94] The seemingly mundane and technical observation that adroitly framing the question is an important part of argumentation, often taught to students in advocacy courses as a technique for increasing their ability to be persuasive in pursuit of the predetermined goal of victory for their client, in fact reveals something about the nature of legal argumentation that runs much deeper than superficial rhetorical technique. Nietzsche's dramatic efforts to persuade his readers complement Gadamer's ontological focus on the dialogic nature of human understanding. Framing the question at issue is not a matter of demarcating the perspicacious features of the world-in-itself that can later be investigated, but rather is the activity of rhetorical engagement that provides us with a world in the first instance.

In *Bowers,* Justice White's analysis and conclusion for the majority follow naturally from his starting point that the issue presented was "whether the Federal Constitution confers a fundamental right upon homosexuals to engage in sodomy and hence invalidates the laws of the many States that still make such conduct illegal and have done so for a very long time."[95] Having framed the question in this way, the Court is able to distance itself from the issue of "whether laws against sodomy between consenting adults in general, or between homosexuals in particular, are wise or desirable,"[96] and to proceed by demonstrating the obvious point that the Constitution cannot be fairly read within the American constitutional tradition as conferring an affirmative right to engage in homosexual sodomy. The tenor of the opinion is that of a reluctant political actor who must respect the division of judiciary and legislature, suggesting that although the Court may disagree with the impulses of the Georgia legislature it does not have a legitimate political role to play in such matters. The holding naturally follows: because laws criminalizing sodomy are rooted in ancient moral values, they are the rational products of legislative acts that cannot fairly be said to contravene fundamental liberties that are deeply rooted in American legal and social traditions.[97]

Justice Blackmun's dissenting opinion attacks the majority's formulation of the question directly and caustically:

> A fair reading of the statute and of the complaint clearly reveals that the majority has distorted the question this case presents. . . . The Court claims that its decision today merely refuses to recognize a fundamental right to engage in homosexual sodomy; what the Court really has refused to recognize is the fundamental interest all individuals have in controlling the nature of their intimate associations with others. . . . I can only hope that . . . the Court soon will reconsider its analysis and conclude that depriving individuals of the right to choose for themselves how to conduct their intimate relationships poses a far greater threat to the values most deeply rooted in our Nation's history than tolerance of nonconformity could ever do.[98]

Blackmun's challenge openly embraces the rhetorical character of decision making and expressly reframes the question as whether time-honored moral condemnations of the majority of citizens outweigh dynamic constitutional principles of privacy and individual self-determination. The dissent steps back from the specific facts of the case involving consensual sex between gay men and constructs the issue in terms of the scope of privacy for intimate relations generally. The fact that the question comes to the Court in the context of an arrest of two gay men ostensibly does not figure in this approach.[99]

The *Bowers* case provides a stark reminder of the nature of legal argumentation. It is easy to lampoon the myth that legal conclusions are generated deductively by placing the facts under a conceptual rubric of legal principles, but it is also easy to miss the deep critique that the facts, legal principles, and analytical moves all are rhetorically constructed. The majority and dissent both strive to prevent *Bowers* from being a case about an abstract conception of gay rights, much to the chagrin of several of the justices on each side of the case. The primary opinions on both sides of the decision transparently create the legal disputes that they are prepared to countenance and decide. *Bowers* quite expressly demonstrates that the law is not a resource for making decisions when disputes arise, but rather is the activity of framing disputes and then making judgments. Lawyers do not achieve critical insights and then reframe the legal question in response; critical insight is achieved in the rhetorical activity of formulating the question presented.

The rhetorical reality of legal decision making is no less apparent in the two cases that followed *Bowers.* In *Romer,* Justice Kennedy carefully refused to grant protected class status to gays and lesbians that would support application of a "strict scrutiny" standard of review, finding instead that the constitutional referendum failed—in fact, "defied"—the lesser constitutional requirement that legislation bear a "rational relation" to legitimate state interests.[100] But even by framing the question in this manner, he could not justify the majority's holding without concluding, at a minimum, that legislation having no purpose other than disenfranchising disfavored groups as an expression of the animus of the majority of citizens is irrational and therefore unconstitutional.[101] Justice Scalia's characteristically scathing dissent cut through this circumlocution with a determined logical rigor: given the unchallenged *Bowers* holding that a state may criminalize homosexual activity, he argued that it must be the case that a state may enact laws that merely disfavor homosexual conduct by prohibiting municipalities from conferring favored status on individuals "*because of their homosexual conduct.*"[102] Although Kennedy and Scalia openly spar over the legitimacy of legislatively targeting gays and lesbians, in the end they propose competing general characterizations of the question presented by the case. Kennedy declares the Colorado constitutional amendment unconstitutional because it precludes democratic political activities by a minority group for no reason other than animus against the group. In contrast, Scalia argues that the case questions the limits of judicial power to overturn democratic recognitions of "traditional American moral values," arguing that constitutionally precluding those who engage in morally disfavored activity from gaining "special protections" under municipal antidiscrimination laws reflects political decisions removed from the Court's purview.

The same situation holds true in *Dale,* in which Chief Justice Rehnquist begins his analysis by phrasing the question as whether a state may constitutionally prevent an organization from espousing views about the morality of homosexuality.[103] Rehnquist concludes that requiring the Boy Scouts to retain a gay scout leader is tantamount to interfering with the organization's message that homosexuality is not "morally straight," and that the Court "cannot doubt that the Boy Scouts sincerely holds this view."[104] Justice Stevens begins his dissent by undermining Rehnquist's transparent assumption, asking whether an organization may avoid application of state antidiscrimination statutes simply by declaring that its aversion to having gay scout leaders is part of the organization's shared goal in disapproving of homosexuality.[105] His opinion carefully reviews the facts of record to conclude that the Boy Scouts organization "is simply silent on homosexuality. There is no shared goal or collective effort to foster a belief about homosexuality at all—let alone one that is significantly burdened by admitting homosexuals."[106] Because Justice Stevens quite openly declares that the majority feeds on outmoded prejudices against gays and lesbians to support base prejudice by the Boy Scouts unrelated to any genuine expressive goal,[107] Justice Souter wrote separately for the other three dissenters to insist that the current social acceptability of the message purportedly espoused by the group is irrelevant to the analysis.[108] Once again, the rhetorical framing at work in these opinions shapes the relevant facts, the categorization of the legal issue, the analysis, and the conclusion. It is manifest that in each of these cases there are myriad ways in which these elements could be framed differently.

These three cases illustrate that legal reasoning is rhetorical engagement, and is not an epistemic achievement that only later is rhetorically presented for consumption. Specifically, legal reasoning occurs in the framing of the questions presented, in which perspectives are revealed and horizons are fused. Nietzsche's rhetorical advocacy and Gadamer's investigation of the rhetorically secured bonds of community are both necessary to understand the dynamic of legal reasoning exhibited in these cases. As Gadamer emphasizes, the "priority of the question in knowledge shows how fundamentally the idea of method is limited for knowledge. . . . There is no such thing as a method of learning to ask questions, of learning to see what is questionable."[109] Legal knowledge is rhetorical knowledge.

It takes hardly any effort to point out the argumentative strategies invoked by justices on both sides of each case in their search for the grounds of persuasion. But if law is nothing more than rhetorical activity in this narrow sense, there is reason to fear that the caricatures of Nietzsche's perspectivism might gain purchase and lead to nihilistic resignation. Gadamer's philosophy provides the resources to see the degree to which this rhetorical advocacy necessarily is founded in community, within which the variegated horizons that comprise a tradition might fuse in the never-complete and always-provisional activity of understanding. Gadamer does not endorse a simpleminded idealism, in which vigorous advocates suddenly reach a shared answer that causes their differences to disappear effortlessly. Instead, he recognizes that the activity of persuading is always predicated on understanding one's audience, which means that one's position is prefigured and then altered in the course of persuasive discourse, which is always a search for the appropriate question. In short, the rhetorical character of legal reasoning exemplifies the need for Nietzsche's perspectival wariness and Gadamer's hermeneutical charity.

These themes are particularly vivid in the awkward effort by the justices in *Romer* to accommodate not only the preceding tradition generally but the *Bowers* precedent specifically. Justice Kennedy's majority opinion does not mention *Bowers,*[110] although the case clearly loomed large in the minds of all concerned. He carefully distinguishes singling out insular groups for political disestablishment based on personal characteristics from the criminalization of sodomitic acts. But this merely recalls the initial reluctance of the *Bowers* Court to countenance the fact that a criminal statute facially applicable to sodomy by any two persons in fact was being used by the state as a means for selectively harassing gay men.[111] And Justice Scalia's dissent is too gleeful in equating the cases on the grounds that the legitimation of antigay beliefs in *Bowers* necessarily translates to what he contends is a much less drastic expression of the same antigay beliefs that are under review in *Romer.* Scalia openly describes the context of the dispute as a "Kulturkampf" in which the Court can play no role after *Bowers:*

> If it is constitutionally permissible for a State to make homosexual conduct criminal, surely it is constitutionally permissible for a State to enact other laws merely *disfavoring* homosexual conduct. . . . And *a fortiori* it is constitutionally permissible for a State to adopt a provision *not even* disfavoring homosexual conduct, but merely prohibiting all levels of state government from bestowing *special protections* upon homosexual conduct. . . . If it is rational to criminalize the conduct, surely it is rational to deny special favor and protection to those with a self-avowed tendency or desire to engage in the conduct.[112]

While Justice Kennedy's opinion in *Romer* suggested that there was no rational basis for precluding political activity at the municipal level to prevent discrimination against gays and lesbians, the premise of *Bowers* was that it is entirely rational for a state to enact moral condemnations into law. As Justice White concluded in *Bowers,* the law "is constantly based on notions of morality, and if all laws representing essentially moral choices are to be invalidated under the Due Process Clause, the courts will be very busy indeed."[113] Genuine engagement follows the competing constructions of the questions presented; there can be no easy and logical progression that proceeds from the rhetorically determined starting point for analysis.

In addition to the rhetorical character of legal reasoning in the framing of the problem to be addressed, these cases also reveal that the dynamic and polysemic character of the legal tradition fosters critical insight despite the absence of an invariant criterion of judgment. Although the practice of rhetorical elaboration in legal practice necessarily has continuing effects, these effects simultaneously are stabilizing and destabilizing. Phrased in Gadamerian terms, rhetorical elaboration is always prefigured by history and itself has a history of effects, but rhetorical engagement does not unfold in a teleological or even determinant manner. The law is always in flux, particularly at those moments when judges claim to fix the law by their decision in a particular case.

Returning to the cases under discussion illuminates this dimension of legal reasoning. It would be folly to read these cases in an effort to discern wholly distinct and logically pure analyses of doctrine. The ground keeps shifting—first criminal law, then rights of democratic participation, and finally freedom of speech—and these different contexts determine much about the case analysis in a way that precludes a belief that the Court is addressing the general question of "gay rights." Although several justices disavow what they perceive to be the Court's refusal to address this broad, underlying, "real" question, there simply is no "pure, unadulterated" question lurking in the background to be answered. The shifting doctrinal and historical contexts of these cases open different angles on what may appear to be a singular question, and it is through this dynamic that critical distance becomes possible.

Justice Scalia most effectively criticizes the Court's manner of rhetorically narrowing the issues involved in the cases, and he pleads for the Court to acknowledge what he regards as being the "real" issue. In his dissent in *Romer,* Scalia backs away from the doctrinal question before the Court and claims to describe the case in terms of what is really going on: the citizens of Colorado acted not out of animus (having recently repealed anti-sodomy criminal statutes) but rather to express moral disapproval, "the same sort of moral disapproval that produced the centuries-old criminal laws that we held constitutional in *Bowers.*"[114] In response to political success by gays and lesbians at the local level to enact provisions that reflect an acceptance of their sexual orientation, Scalia argues, Colorado enacted the constitutional amendment to reaffirm the state's rejection of homosexuality.[115] In short, the Court is confronting a political battle to set the moral limits of intimate behavior, a political battle that the Court should not enter under the guise of constitutional adjudication. Scalia concludes: "The Court today . . . employs a constitutional theory heretofore unknown to frustrate Colorado's reasonable effort to preserve traditional American moral values. . . . When the Court takes sides in the culture wars, it tends to be with the knights rather than the villeins—and more specifically with the Templars, reflecting the views and values of the lawyer class from which the Court's members are drawn. . . . Striking [the amendment] down is an act, not of judicial judgment, but of political will."[116] Scalia diagnoses the open questions behind the rhetoric, so to speak, even as he disclaims the Court's competence and authority to speak to these questions.

But Scalia remains blind to the constitutive effects of the judicial discourse that he wishes to insulate from the political matters in issue. When Scalia found himself in the majority a few years later in *Dale,* he did not write separately despite the obvious irony. His deference in *Romer* to the political right of Colorado citizens to instantiate their moral beliefs against gays and lesbians in state law is not similarly extended to the political right of New Jersey citizens to instantiate their moral condemnation of discrimination against gays and lesbians into state antidiscrimination law. To conclude that the latter political activities are subject to overriding constitutional principles of free speech does not effectively distinguish *Romer,* in which the former political activities were held to be subject to equally important constitutional limitations. This is not to say that Scalia's positions in the two cases are nonsensical because they are logically contradictory, but rather to demonstrate that his reductive "Kulturkampf" analysis is insufficient to get at what is "really going on." His simplistic account of these cases as nothing more than political referenda on the social acceptability of homosexuality, with no room for judicial review, simply doesn't ring true on its face. The First Amendment context in which *Dale* was decided has an enormous effect on the reasoning, as the Court labored under the (incredibly fragile) conceptual framework of its free expression jurisprudence generally, and the precedent of *Hurley v. Irish-American Gay, Lesbian and Bisexual Group of Boston, Inc.,* more specifically.[117]

These cases demonstrate that interesting legal disputes require more than simple inferences within a doctrinal conceptual framework, but also that the "real question at issue" can't be abstracted from these doctrinal contexts altogether. Critical insight is possible because legal reasoning is instantiated within, but always reshaping, doctrinal traditions. In their own ways, both Gadamer and Nietzsche emphasize the critical potential of tradition. Legal practice, as exemplified in the cases under discussion, gains critical purchase in the rhetorical developments that are possible only by virtue of the resources of tradition. Justice Scalia offers what might appear at first glance to be a Nietzschean critique, cutting through surface appearances to the clash of political power that subtends the doctrinal squabbles. In fact, though, his approach runs contrary to my model of critical insight. First, he attempts to sharply divide the political battle of wills from reasoned legal argumentation, when no such division is possible. The doctrinal disputes bear within them the many underlying political issues and therefore are no less rhetorical and hermeneutical than political disputes. Seen from the opposite angle, he presumes that political battle is purely a question of brute power, when in fact power is exercised rhetorically and hermeneutically, which is to say that it is exercised in part through the doctrinal traditions that hold their own prejudicial power.

If Justice Scalia does not fit the role of Nietzschean critic (a comforting thought for him, we can be sure), how does one approach these cases with the kind of critical energy that Nietzsche unleashed against Christianity and moral philosophy? When Justice Stevens declares that the Court is reinscribing homophobic beliefs under the pretense of neutral constitutional decision making, is he playing the role of Nietzsche declaring that God is dead? In some respects, the answer is yes, although, like Nietzsche, Justice Stevens is fated to wait to see if his announcement of an event that already has taken place is verified in social life. This critical posture cannot be separated from the rhetorical and hermeneutical elaboration of tradition, which is more closely associated with Gadamer's philosophy, but it works from the tradition in a different manner. Justice Stevens builds on converging doctrinal principles to conclude that we already no longer believe that gays and lesbians can be treated as second-class citizens, even if we have not yet completely acknowledged this fact. The homophobic "God" is dead, but not at the hands of a brilliant critic: we have killed him with our ongoing practices. The Nietzschean claim does not rest on timeless absolutes but rather on a philosophical naturalism that regards human nature as deeply interpretive. Vattimo's weak thought gives voice to this approach to Nietzschean critique: we can only claim to be interpreting our provenance. This means that we must be ready to abandon our current beliefs in favor of a better interpretation, but also that we cannot claim recourse to an invariant standard by which to judge interpretations.[118] Where Justice Scalia sees a seething clash of power-interests that is outside the realm of legal thinking, Justice Stevens finds an event that must be announced: the overcoming of outmoded beliefs through the reworking of traditional beliefs that invariably inform legal categories.[119]

Lawrence v. Texas: The Practical Enactment of Critical Legal Theory

The resolution of the status of gays and lesbians in contemporary American society is not a "yes or no" question that can be answered definitively by legal theorists "in the know," who then patiently prod the less perceptive among them to catch up to their superior insight. The complex legal situation is rhetorically negotiated in myriad ways that only appear to be definitively established in the authoritative opinions of the Supreme Court according to an apparent logic of development. The confused legacy of *Bowers, Romer,* and *Dale* provided the doctrinal setting against which the Court decided *Lawrence v. Texas* with competing opinions that highlight the critical element of rhetorical knowledge. In *Lawrence,* the doctrine is reconstituted and extended in unpredictable ways when viewed through the lens of rational, formal deduction, but *Lawrence* makes perfect sense from a rhetorical perspective.

Because the facts in *Lawrence* are strikingly similar to the facts in *Bowers,* one might assume that *Lawrence* intrinsically represents a reconsideration of *Bowers* and nothing more. In both cases, the police entered a private residence by mistake and discovered two men making love, leading to an arrest and criminal prosecution under a state sodomy statute. But the important differences between the two cases, invisible to most nonlawyers, provide important openings for critical reconstruction of the law. In *Lawrence* the two men pleaded nolo contendere to a criminal charge under Texas's "Homosexual Conduct" law, which proscribes "deviate sexual intercourse" with another person of the same sex.[120] Unlike *Bowers,* in which the State of Georgia had dropped the criminal charges before trial, the defendants in *Lawrence* were convicted of the offense after their constitutional challenges to the statute failed, and each defendant was required to pay a fine and court costs. In the petition for certiorari, the defendants emphasized that they experienced the very real harm of a criminal conviction, including reputational harm, disqualification from practicing certain professions, and having to register as convicted sex offenders under the laws of four states.[121] *Lawrence* represents the natural consequence of the *Bowers* decision, with the hypothetical potential for suffering a criminal conviction now presented as a criminal conviction on appeal.

The doctrinal posture of the case is quite different as well. Because the Texas criminal statute applies to conduct only between members of the same sex, the first question presented on appeal to the Court was framed as a challenge under the Equal Protection Clause. This doctrinal distinction yields a new set of arguments and range of justifications that cast the case in a different light from *Bowers,* which dealt with sodomitic acts generally and addressed same-sex intimacy only in the subsidiary opinions. What was only a subtext in *Bowers,* the constitutionality of a state using sodomy laws selectively to harass gays and lesbians, became the lead argument in *Lawrence.*

Finally, it is of no small consequence that *Lawrence* was decided nearly twenty years after *Bowers.* In that time there had been a dramatic shift by legislatures and state courts away from criminal statutes proscribing sodomy, and only two states had valid statutes that explicitly limited the scope of their sodomy statutes to same-sex couples.[122] The Supreme Court's decision in *Romer* had become an anti-*Bowers,* and the defendants sought to clarify that *Romer* had in fact substantially undermined *Bowers* and should not be read narrowly as applying only to issues involving rights of political participation.[123] The defendants expressly asked the Court to overrule *Bowers* in light of the subsequent development of "a more accurate understanding of gay and lesbian couples and families" by the public, implicitly inviting the justices to acknowledge that they too no longer are working from the same unproductive prejudices that produced *Bowers.*[124]

The appeal in *Lawrence* illustrates the hermeneutical appropriation and rhetorical elaboration of legal practice by emphasizing these changing contexts and the development of knowledge, but also illustrates the Nietzschean critique of seeing through a decadent legal commonplace that no longer rings true. The majority opinion in *Lawrence* took the decisive step of overruling *Bowers* and declaring the Texas statute unconstitutional under the Due Process Clause, reasoning that a decision that was grounded in *Romer*'s equal protection analysis might suggest that the state could prohibit sodomy if it did so indiscriminately.[125] Ironically, this amounts to a breathtaking statement of equality, because it works from the premise that there is no legitimate legal distinction between homosexual and heterosexual couples when analyzing the liberty interest in sexual intimacy.

Four justices joined in Justice Kennedy's majority opinion to overrule

Bowers. His analysis begins by noting that two different jurisprudential threads defining the liberty interest in substantive due process cases converge in *Lawrence:* the spatial interest in one's security from "unwarranted government intrusions into a dwelling or other private places" and the more transcendent interest in preserving the "autonomy of self that includes freedom of thought, belief, expression, and certain intimate conduct."[126] This manner of introducing the analysis might signal that a weak case is being propped up by two supports, each of which is insufficient in itself to gird the arguments, but it quickly becomes clear in the course of the opinion that the Court is embracing the stronger claim that the case in fact is an easy case because it is buttressed by multiple overlapping justifications within the substantive due process precedents.

The Court immediately raises the question of *Bowers*'s continuing validity and begins by noting that *Bowers* mischaracterized the issue presented by the petitioner. The question addressed by the Court "we now conclude, discloses the Court's own failure to appreciate the extent of the liberty at stake. To say that the issue in *Bowers* was simply the right to engage in certain sexual conduct demeans the claim the individual put forward, just as it would demean a married couple were it to be said marriage is simply about the right to have sexual intercourse. . . . [The criminal statutes in question] seek to control a personal relationship that, whether or not entitled to formal recognition in the law, is within the liberty of persons to choose without being punished as criminals."[127] The significance of this change in focus, and the concomitant possibilities for new legal developments, cannot be overstated. Rather than a case about the community's time-honored right to ban certain "deviant" sexual practices, the court initiates an inquiry into the scope of the right of couples to preserve their relationship from unwarranted interference. "It suffices for us to acknowledge that adults may choose to enter upon this relationship in the confines of their homes and their own private lives and still retain their dignity as free persons. When sexuality finds overt expression in intimate conduct with another person, the conduct can be but one element in a personal bond that is more enduring. The liberty protected by the Constitution allows homosexual persons the right to make this choice."[128] It is no overstatement to say that, in light of this framing of the question,

Lawrence is an entirely different case from *Bowers* despite the bare factual similarities.

The Supreme Court does not lightly disregard the principle of stare decisis; consequently, much of the majority opinion is concerned with undermining the rationale of *Bowers* and justifying the extreme action of overruling a case that had been decided only seventeen years earlier. Of course, the rephrasing of the question presented in itself is a significant indictment of the Court's "failure" in *Bowers,* but the Court also criticized the substantive analysis in *Bowers.* The Court first casts serious doubt on the historical claim in *Bowers* that proscriptions against sodomy have ancient roots, and on Chief Justice Burger's infamous claim in his concurring opinion that the government's proscription of homosexuality is equally longstanding and firmly rooted in moral and religious traditions.[129] Emphasizing that the questionable historiography in *Bowers* could not be determinative given that the Court is required to determine what the law means today, the Court concludes: "In all events we think that our laws and traditions in the past half century are of most relevance here. These references show an emerging awareness that liberty gives substantial protection to adult persons in deciding how to conduct their private lives in matters pertaining to sex."[130] Judges are not historians, as Gadamer famously analyzes,[131] and the Court introduces historical arguments only to undermine the false claims of necessity that animated *Bowers* rather than to establish the correct result in the case at hand.

Given the recency of *Bowers,* the Court does not attempt to characterize the changing views toward gays and lesbians during the past few decades as new information that simply was unavailable to the *Bowers* Court. Instead, the Court holds expressly: "*Bowers* was not correct when it was decided, and it is not correct today. It ought not to remain binding precedent. *Bowers v. Hardwick* should be and now is overruled."[132] The Court emphasizes that *Bowers* could have been correctly decided at that time by quoting and reaffirming the rationale in Justice Stevens's dissenting opinion. Nevertheless, the historical record, contested and complex as it may be, lends some support to the claim that states have the power under our constitutional system to proscribe homosexual conduct. Therefore, the Court also emphasizes the dynamic character of constitutional interpretation and notes that the framers drafted a generally worded document because they "knew times can blind us to certain truths and later generations can see that laws once thought necessary and proper in fact serve only to oppress. As the Constitution endures, persons in every generation can invoke its principles in their own search for greater freedom."[133] Legitimacy and plausibility demand that the Court openly declare that the *Bowers* Court simply got the case wrong rather than claiming that some fundamental change in society has recently occurred, but these factors also require the Court to acknowledge that its expanding jurisprudence of substantive due process protections for intimate relationships and personal autonomy is responding to the social realm in which it is embedded. Constitutional adjudication necessarily resides between obeisance to the past and a willful construction of the future.

Justice O'Connor's concurring opinion takes a different tack, revealing the open situation presented by the facts of the case and the precedents. Declining to overrule *Bowers* (having joined the *Bowers* majority), she instead concludes that the Texas statute is unconstitutional on equal protection grounds.[134] Justice O'Connor attempts to preserve both *Bowers* and *Romer,* and to avoid extending substantive due process protection to sexual practices per se, by finding that the *Lawrence* case falls within the *Romer* principle that prevents selectively targeting gays and lesbians. This lawyerly attempt to finesse the matter is only thinly veiled, though. Implicitly acknowledging that her resolution might invite states to proscribe sodomy generally (even if they might be planning to prosecute selectively), Justice O'Connor expresses her confidence that "so long as the Equal Protection Clause requires a sodomy law to apply equally to the private consensual conduct of homosexuals and heterosexuals alike, such a law would not long stand in our democratic society."[135]

Justice O'Connor's analysis provides an equally plausible approach to the problem facing the Court, and in many respects her opinion fills out the majority's analysis. On one hand, O'Connor's equal protection analysis simply ignores the problem that retaining *Bowers* as good law poses: there appears to be no reason why states can't generally treat gays and lesbians differently if the Constitution permits states to determine that gays and lesbians live an immoral lifestyle that may be prohibited with criminal sanctions. In other words, accepting an equal protection argument in *Lawrence* simply exacerbates the sharp tension between *Bowers* and *Romer.* On the other hand, O'Connor's attention to the harms of singling out "one identifiable class of citizens for punishment that does not apply to everyone else, with moral disapproval as the only asserted state interest for the law,"[136] reminds us that these legal disputes are not really about the power of the state to police sexual behavior (an issue not seriously in question with respect to matters such as prostitution), but instead are about the limits on arbitrary and selective enforcement of criminal laws against those segments of the population who are deemed immoral or unfit for full civic life. Although Justice Kennedy's majority opinion does state clearly that there are substantive limitations on government intrusion into intimate lives of gays and lesbians, his frequent recitation of the "liberty" interest at stake in the case is underdeveloped. O'Connor's equal protection analysis is not a half measure that the majority finds unnecessary to the disposition of the case, then, but rather is part of the reasoning to the result. Justice Kennedy's rhetoric from *Romer* rings through in *Lawrence* as well, when he emphasizes that criminalizing sexual conduct by gays and lesbians has the adverse effect of inviting more widespread discrimination against them.[137]

The two opinions that declare the Texas law against "homosexual sodomy" unconstitutional elaborate a web of themes that existed in the preceding case law, but both extend the analysis in ways that provide mutual support to the judicial recognition that a state may not single out the intimate lives of gays and lesbians for criminal prosecution. Justice Kennedy's celebration of liberty joins Justice O'Connor's celebration of equality as the working out of confused notions that are intertwined yet distinct. The critical element of legal practice is manifest in this "resolution" of the tensions produced by *Bowers, Romer,* and *Dale.* Lines of inquiry develop without reaching a terminus; the development is intrinsic and unending rather than merely instrumental. From the abstract, confused notion of "liberty" to the more specific doctrinal features of the Court's "fundamental rights" jurisprudence, the *Lawrence* decision plainly is both a watershed of incredible importance and just the beginning of a new conversation.

Justice Scalia's dissent in *Lawrence* drives these themes home in a particularly vivid fashion. In one sense, he reiterates consistent themes from his opinions in the earlier cases; in another very real sense, however, his arguments fall flat and no longer carry themselves with authority. Rhetorical knowledge is not gained only when all persons capitulate to its dictates; sometimes it is most starkly exposed in the dissenting voices that see only sophistry and crude will to power at work.

Justice Scalia's attack on the decision begins by contrasting the Court's willingness to overrule *Bowers* with its unwillingness to overrule *Roe v. Wade,* concluding that the analysis in these decisions is merely a "result-oriented expedient."[138] Most curiously, Justice Scalia emphasizes that reversing *Roe v. Wade* would not have disrupted patterns of reliance in society because it would have returned the state of the law to its prior situation, whereas reversing *Bowers* amounts to a judicial intrusion into the realm of state legislative action and a consequential "massive disruption of the current social order." Logically equating these lines of cases in an effort to show unprincipled decision making by the Court's "liberal" wing, but then distinguishing them based on the degree of social reliance, constitutes a remarkable flight from lived reality and an utter rhetorical failure. As Gene Garver emphasizes, rhetorical reasoning is unpersuasive when it is too logical and does not involve the character of the proponent or the ethos of the listener.[139] It is shocking that Scalia suggests that there is less social reliance among an entire generation of women who have initiated sexual relationships with the understanding that their right to secure an abortion is constitutionally protected than among the citizenry at large in a minority of states who have "relied" on the continuing validity of state criminal laws that reach into their neighbors' bedrooms (and, in those states where the statute is not just directed at conduct by gays and lesbians, most likely into their own bedroom as well). To emphasize the importance of this point: it is not that Justice Scalia is being illogical or irrational but rather that an excess of logic and rationality betrays normative commitments that might not be persuasive if openly espoused.

Justice Scalia correctly notes that *Lawrence* marks a significant departure from the cramped and convoluted jurisprudence of substantive due process analysis grounded in "fundamental rights," but he does not attempt to justify this doctrinal tradition.[140] Instead, he emphasizes the problem of constraining the result in *Lawrence* and raises the entirely logical point that state bans on gay marriage inevitably must be declared unconstitutional, ridiculing in caustic terms the declarations by Justices Kennedy and O'Connor that no such decision is implicit within their analysis: "This case 'does not involve' the issue of homosexual marriage only if one entertains the belief that principle and logic have nothing to do with the decisions of this Court. Many will hope that, as the Court comfortingly assures us, this is so."[141] In contrast to the necessarily logical reasoning of adjudication, Scalia argues that the advantage of leaving such questions to democratic processes is that legislatures may act (illogically?) by eliminating criminal sodomy laws but preserving same-sex marriage.[142] Legal practice continually disproves precisely this distinction, and it would be tedious to undermine Scalia's pretense to neutral and dispassionate analysis. The difficulty of embarking down the path that *Lawrence* opens cannot be denied; avoiding difficulties in such areas, however, is a fool's errand.

Justice Scalia's opinion bristles with antipathy toward gays and lesbians. At most, he concedes a grudging willingness to permit gays and lesbians to promote their agenda "through normal democratic means" and disavows an interpretation of the Constitution that would require states to criminalize sodomy (a bizarre point for him to make, to be sure).[143] However, he pointedly does not endorse Justice Thomas's sentiment that the statute targeting homosexual sodomy is an uncommonly silly law, one that Justice Thomas declares he would vote to overturn as a legislator even though as a judge he concludes that he is not empowered to override the act of the legislature.[144] The persuasive force of Justice Scalia's opinion is lost, and perhaps consciously conceded, as he unleashes a diatribe against the "law-profession culture, that has largely signed on to the so-called homosexual agenda [to eliminate] the moral opprobrium that has traditionally attached to homosexual conduct."[145] Reverting to his "culture war" motif and declaring that the Court has sided with the minority of Americans, Scalia only confirms his own unstated prejudices and allegiances in what he chooses to regard as an unprincipled, political battle of wills. His seemingly critical insights into the play of power—what's really going on—read in this iteration like a parody of Nietzschean critique that only serves to unmask his own solipsistic agenda.

This is not to say that Justice Scalia is wrong because of his rhetorical constructions, or that his wrongheadedness cannot be reversed under any set of circumstances by rhetorical practices. There is no privileged vantage point from which to issue such verdicts. However, the theory of rhetorical knowledge can identify those points in Justice Scalia's argument at which he betrays strange mixtures of an excess of logic and hyperbole as the means of evading the full complexity and significance of the question before the Court. Rhetorical knowledge permits us to see the deficiencies in his arguments, which is part of the process of coming to know the correct resolution of the case at hand in the thick context in which it arises.

Lawrence was not inevitable, in the sense that it unfolded from legal practice naturally and necessarily. Haltingly working through only three principal cases in this area, the Supreme Court struggled in *Lawrence* to give voice to an understanding of the role of community in the lives of citizens who join together in intimate relationships. The critical element of the legal tradition is obvious when this line of cases is read together. In retrospect, the law appears to move toward a result by means of inventive extrapolations and by recharacterizing the nature of the legal questions presented. The answer is rhetorically secured rather than demonstrated, but it is the openness of the work of rhetorical knowledge that makes room for critical distance.

Moreover, initial conclusions about the role of the critical legal theorist follow from the examination of the critical dimension of legal practice. The critical theorist reads the law inventively in the same fashion as judges, but with more freedom (generally as a result of having the leisure to focus on a problem in-depth for extended periods of time, a luxury that is unavailable to virtually all judges). The model of Nietzschean critique of religion, as carried forward by Vattimo, emphasizes that critical legal theory is a *Verwindung* that seeks to persuade others of what already has happened, thereby helping to effectuate the announced event. This interplay of theory and practice within the legal setting is the focus of chapter 3.

In these four cases we find the rhetorical character of legal reasoning, the critical power of tradition, and the potential for Nietzschean critique as a *Verwindung* within a cultural moment. Legal scholars, removed from the immediate field of play, too often lose sight of this critical dimension of legal practice and fall back on claims grounded in an invariant truth. Whether this "truth" is textual plain meaning, neo-Marxist economics, political liberalism, or psychoanalytic theory is beside the point. Legal scholars can tap into the source of critique by recognizing that the model of critical hermeneutics leads them to an engagement with practice. Nietzsche announced the destruction of Christianity from within; critical legal theorists face the same task. Without a guarantee or even firm guideposts, critical legal theorists can move forward most productively by looking to the examples of Gadamer, Perelman, and Nietzsche. Within the play of their differences lies critique.

3

Rhetorical Knowledge in Law

Practice and Critical Theory

> I still feel my wattles grow red as I recall the shock with which, as a dyed-in-the-wool commercial lawyer, I met property phases of mortgage law which left me gasping. "One system of precedent" we may have, but it works in forty different ways. Some day, some one will help the second year student orient himself. Nor does any one bother to present to him the difference between logic and persuasion, nor what a man facing old courts is to do with a new vocabulary; in a word, the game, in framing an argument, of diagnosing the peculiar presuppositions of the hearers. I think the second year student is entitled to feel himself aggrieved. Meanwhile, while we wait upon the treading of the Angel, there is rushing in that calls for doing. Here is a start.
>
> Karl Llewellyn
> "On Philosophy in American Law"

Rhetorical knowledge is a constitutive feature of legal practice, and so my account of rhetorical knowledge grounds any subsequent theoretical reconstruction and critique of legal practice. Drawing from the philosophical insights of Gadamer and Perelman, I have defined rhetorical knowledge as the outcome of efforts to learn from and to persuade another person by engaging in argumentation. Persuasion through rhetorical engagement is deeply connected to understanding through hermeneutical appropriation: legal practice is neither the neutral reception of preexisting law nor the subjective creation of law as an expression of one's insular will. In the first two chapters I used legal examples as I constructed this argument. In this chapter I reverse the focus and analyze legal practice and critical legal theory against the theoretical backdrop of the first two chapters. Critical legal theory can be approached only through legal practice because critical insight is a feature of the hermeneutical-rhetorical practices that yield rhetorical knowledge. Critical legal theory is possible only as a product of the discursive field shaped by rhetorical knowledge, which means that it is both enabled and constrained by the finitude and historicity of our experience. Nietzsche's critical theory, as hermeneutically carried forward in Vattimo's "weak thought," provides a model of the critical theorist who is aware of the constraints and possibilities of rhetorical knowledge but who nevertheless pursues an aggressive and wide-ranging critical project. Critical insight is not a product of theoretical efforts that police legal practice from the "outside," even if it is appropriate to distinguish critical theory and practice. The concept of rhetorical knowledge is indispensable in explaining how legal practice is critical, how critical legal theory is a rhetorical practice, and how these two practices relate to each other.

Legal Practice as the Cultivation of Rhetorical Knowledge

Due to its ubiquity and pragmatic qualities, legal practice is not just one venue among many that exhibit rhetorical knowledge; it is a paradigmatic venue for investigating rhetorical knowledge in action. Given the heavily legalistic nature of our public realm, legal practice touches upon, and often shapes, many issues that reach beyond the basic structuring of political relations. Because legal practice fundamentally is a series of judgments and resulting actions rather than a discipline or mode of inquiry, rhetorical knowledge is put to the test of real (practical) judgment on a daily basis. It is no coincidence that both Gadamer and Perelman emphatically argue that an analysis of the activities of understanding, persuasion, and judgment suffusing legal practice provides the best elaboration of their philosophies. Legal practice is much more than a useful illustration of the previously determined concept of rhetorical knowledge; it is a practice that exhibits and discloses rhetorical knowledge in particularly vivid ways.

I begin by explicitly bringing my model of rhetorical knowledge to bear on the full range of legal practice. My extended discussions of the legal controversies over affirmative action and the rights of gays and lesbians provided necessary illustrations as I developed my model of rhetorical knowledge, but these examples are skewed because they relate to a particularly rarified feature of legal practice: appellate decision making. I turn now to the role of rhetorical knowledge in legal practice generally. After describing the rhetorical features of legal practice, I explain why Gadamer, Perelman, and (implicitly, at least) Nietzsche all regard law as an important arena for rhetorical knowledge, and then I conclude by sketching a new understanding of justice that follows from this philosophical reconception of legal practice.

A Rhetorical Account of Legal Practice

Explaining the role of rhetorical knowledge in legal practice meets a particularly pressing need. Legal commentators have backed themselves into a corner by using unhelpful oppositions to characterize the nature of legal practice, mirroring one of the prominent splits in the philosophical tradition. On one hand are the crude Platonists, not much in evidence today, who are convinced of the conceptual integrity of legal categories and the rigorous nature of legal reasoning. On the other hand are the irresponsible descendants of Gorgias who skeptically view legal practice as the arena of conflict for "hired guns" acting under conditions of undecidability, which means that lawyering can be strategic but never fully rational. Although few scholars adopt one of these caricatures wholesale, most accounts represent a vacillation between, and uncertain reaction to, these two poles. The philosophical movement to revive the sometimes challenging and subtle views propounded by the pre-Socratics and Sophists provides a model for the effort to recover the pragmatic, epistemic, and ethical dimensions of legal practice. The resurgence of pragmatism in legal theory represents a step in this direction, although contemporary pragmatist theories of law threaten to degenerate into a kind of subjectivist idealism by presenting judges as skilled artisans, thereby indulging an egocentric conception of legal knowledge that seems rather naive today.[1]

Revealing how rhetorical knowledge operates in legal practice is made difficult by the fact that legal practice is marked by a vehement denial of its rhetorical nature. This denial usually is expressed by an insistent claim that legal practice involves only dialectical reasoning about objectively determined concepts. Bringing Gadamer's artful analysis that the Enlightenment embodies the prejudice against prejudice to bear in this setting, one might say that legal practice involves the rhetorical suppression of its rhetoricity.[2] Breaking through this deceptive protective barrier does not reveal that the core of legal practice is irrational, although this fear undoubtedly motivates much of the strident anti-rhetorical rhetoric. Rather, focusing on the exercise of judgment informed by more or less persuasive arguments brings to light the possibility and limits of rhetorical knowledge. More and more frequently, commentators discuss the rhetorical dimension of legal argumentation as a means of gaining purchase on the reasonableness of legal practice, thereby confronting directly the chasm between deductive formalism and postmodern irrationalism.[3] Perhaps surprisingly for traditionalist scholars, viewing law as intrinsically and irredeemably rhetorical reaffirms its integrity and legitimacy as a practice of securing reasonable adherence, even as it rejects, once and for all, conceptualist and formalist approaches to law.

A rhetorical view of legal practice begins by emphasizing that legal practice involves much more than judges and lawyers deciphering prior appellate court opinions. Counseling and negotiation comprise the bulk of lawyering, although these activities often are neglected in theoretical accounts of the law. Lawyers meet with clients, elicit their stories, and deliberate with them about appropriate courses of action, sometimes in conjunction with other professionals and advisers. These meetings involve rhetorical exchanges, inasmuch as the lawyer and client seek to understand the client's situation, define the client's goals, and develop the most prudent means of securing these goals.[4] Similarly, negotiations on behalf of clients proceed rhetorically, which is to say that they involve a process of creating shared conceptions from which the parties can develop the optimal structuring of a deal or resolution of a problem.[5]

The obvious challenge to these characterizations—that negotiating a settlement is far removed from the democratic Assembly in ancient Athens—in fact underscores the necessity of adopting a rhetorical understanding of lawyering, since the differences between these venues are best explained by taking account of the rhetorical significance of the differences between the audiences. Lawyers almost constantly are engaged in rhetorical exchanges that produce knowledge, but the lawyer and client begin by seeking self-knowledge through deliberation and consultation before seeking to promote a shared understanding with a wider audience. In most instances, lawyers work to acquire knowledge of their clients' best interests in each given situation. This knowledge is highly contextual and therefore historical: the best interests of a client change with the progress of the lawsuit or negotiation, developments in the client's life, changes in the community, and so forth. Such knowledge, gained by both the lawyer and the client in the course of their deliberative consultation, is properly characterized as rhetorical knowledge.[6]

The activities of lawyers engaged in litigation are more obviously rhetorical in nature. Writing a memorandum of law involves a skill that is difficult to describe and even harder to teach. Lawyers begin crafting a written argument by surveying the published precedents, analogous cases decided in other jurisdictions, and influential secondary works to determine the legal commonplaces at their disposal. Simultaneously, the lawyer constructs a factual narrative of the events or procedures giving rise to the dispute. Searching for a means of persuasion is often quite straightforward—for example, "when a car proceeds through an intersection in such a manner, the driver will be held liable in tort under the established case law"—but in interesting cases the means of successful persuasion are much more elusive. The presentation of the client's story and the presentation of the legal precedents continue to evolve in the process of brief writing until the argument congeals into an appropriate characterization of the matter in question for the intended audience: the judge.

Ultimately, judicial consideration of the case and issuance of a written opinion mark a distinct rhetorical practice shaped by the judge's effort first to persuade herself and then to persuade the parties in the litigation and the hypothetical "universal" audience of all reasonable lawyers. In some high-profile cases, the judge might even view the audience of her opinion as the citizenry at large.[7] The moment of judgment crystallizes the rhetorical engagements pervading legal practice, which both explains and justifies the fascination that theorists display toward the practice of judicial review. Leigh Greenshaw argues that Chief Justice Marshall's emphatic declaration that it is the province of the courts to "say what the law is" pertains not just to the division of responsibility among coordinate branches of government but also to the very nature of legal practice.[8] This insight sustains Greenshaw's claim that legal writing ought to be recognized as a vital and integrated part of the first-year law school curriculum, since "thinking like a lawyer is inseparable from speaking, acting, and writing like a lawyer."[9] Judges and lawyers alike face the rhetorical challenge of "saying what the law is"; this is a rhetorical activity rather than a contemplative exercise, a question of argumentation rather than dialectical demonstration. Greenshaw's description of legal practice mirrors the description of a rhetorical engagement offered in this book: "Written authorities are not law, but cultural resources for lawyers engaged in the practice of law. Law is the ongoing process of giving written authorities meaning in the context of disputes over what they mean in and for particular situations."[10]

Law is an exercise of rhetorical rationality all the way down to the day-to-day interactions of lawyer and client. Critics might reject a characterization of litigation and judicial decision making as rhetorical exchanges, seeing only a manipulative play of power instead. But this cynicism forgets that most lawyering occurs in the interactions between lawyer and client and between lawyers and other professionals working on the client's behalf. Rhetorical knowledge provides a broad and firm base from which the lawyer might employ rhetorical flourish in a later trial. It would require an incredible degree of suspicion and cynicism to see nothing but power plays throughout the deep and wide scope of legal representation.

The Exemplary Significance of Legal Practice for the Model of Rhetorical Knowledge

The philosophical projects undertaken by Gadamer and Perelman provide the appropriate vocabulary for describing the rhetorical knowledge generated by legal practice. Gadamer argues that all understanding involves a fusion of horizons in which the legal text acquires meaning only in its application to the case at hand. Gadamer characterizes the view that "the meaning of a law [is] both juridically and historically the same" as a "legally untenable fiction," since the judge always determines the law's "normative content in regard to the given case to which it is to be applied."[11] He concludes that the "idea of a perfect legal dogmatics, which would make every judgment a mere act of subsumption, is untenable," because human finitude precludes "first understanding a given universal in itself and then afterward applying it to a concrete case."[12] The intersubjective process of understanding the law that occurs in strategizing, negotiating, arguing, and writing an opinion is conversational, inasmuch as no legal actor discovers or pronounces the law ex nihilo through an act of subjective will.

Perelman's work adds methodological detail to this ontological account of legal interpretation and understanding. Lawyers do not work from undifferentiated "prejudices"; they begin their work with a storehouse of arguments and strategies that generally are deemed acceptable and persuasive by the audiences to whom they speak. In his more ambitious moments, Perelman proposes to catalogue the argumentative commonplaces of legal practice, although certainly with the understanding that the object of such a study is a fluid practice rather than a fixed lexicon. In an essay on the potential for achieving justice through legal reasoning, Perelman emphasizes the significance of judicial decision making being grounded in the rhetorical practice of law. Perelman argues that the reasoning employed by judges when confronted with conflicting legal commonplaces

> can be described as dialectic reasoning, because resort must be had to arguments of all kinds that cannot be reduced either to deductive schemes or to simple induction. They frequently combine analogical reasoning and pragmatic arguments with appeals to the rule of justice requiring the like treatment of like situations.
>
> A systematic analysis of the relations between the rules of positive law, the general principles of law, the rules of morality, and the techniques resorted to by legislators and judges to back their statements and their decisions, makes it possible to enumerate, classify, and systematize the models of argument to which lawyers resort when it is necessary to reason in terms of justice.[13]

Legal practice is rhetoric all the way down, with rhetorical engagements layered upon rhetorical engagements in a dynamic and challenging confluence that cannot be constrained by pretenses of analytical certainty. To deny the existence of rhetorical knowledge would be to deny the existence of legal knowledge. Many first-year law students are troubled by what they perceive to be the wide freedom of judges to decide cases on personal whim and then later to supply adequate legal justification for their decision, but it is no surprise to find that these same students have difficulty formulating a coherent argumentative essay for the final exam. It is easy enough to believe that the law is "just rhetoric" when reading a case, but the tremendous challenge of confronting a specific legal dispute and arguing persuasively on behalf of a client quickly demonstrates to students that a rhetorical exchange can be extremely demanding because it is so decentering. Rhetorical engagement demands an intersubjective relationship if it is to be successful in a close case; crude manipulative tricks simply don't work. Gadamer's "fusion of horizons" and Perelman's "audience" are important concepts for describing the challenge confronting a lawyer because they reinforce the radically intersubjective, epistemic dimension of legal practice.

Rhetoric is not merely stylistics that mask the exercise of power; its efficacy derives from participating in the generation and definition of authority. Rhetoric places the issue of power in play precisely because rhetoric is involved in the exercise of political power (as opposed to physical force) in a fundamental way. Once put in play, the question of the exercise of power is subject to challenge and the force of the better argument. Just because rhetorical knowledge is not the product solely of logical deduction, it remains open to contest and reevaluation, particularly with the passage of time. "Rhetoric is not obviously suspect because it is always ideological if there is no ahistorical, neutral space outside of all ideologies. Charisma and emotional appeal do at times influence an argument's success, but in most rhetorical contexts they are so intimately interwoven with logical rigor, evidentiary support, appeal to precedent, shared paradigms, and so forth that it makes only foundationalist sense to try and separate them out and condemn them as illegitimate."[14] This is the sense in which rhetorical knowledge is based on the probable.

A critic might charge that the philosophical gloss provided by Gadamer and Perelman is unnecessary to explain or support the claim that legal practice involves persuasion about matters that cannot be determined with certainty. In fact, after the Legal Realist movement, such a position appears quite unexceptional. However, a philosophical understanding of rhetorical knowledge helps to ensure that the description of legal practice does not slip into pragmatist banalities that obscure more than they reveal. Several recent rhetorical explanations of legal practice provide examples of how the rhetorical model can be conceived narrowly and then applied in an overly conventional manner. Reviewing these efforts as contrasting touchstones permits a demonstration of the advantages of using the concept of rhetorical knowledge to describe legal practice.

The principal danger of pursuing a rhetorical approach is that a theorist might mistakenly reconstruct the rhetorical exchange as a confrontation between insular subjects. Such an approach is predicated on a diminished sense of rhetoric as a set of techniques or strategies that are taken up after the problem is understood and a judgment has been reached. Ultimately, this approach collapses into relativistic conclusions about the status of legal knowledge. All good lawyers size up their opponents and the judge before whom they will appear, but this strategic positioning hardly exhausts the nature of the rhetorical exchanges between a lawyer and her adversaries and the judge. Consciously pandering to one's audience by fashioning arguments thought to be persuasive to the audience is parasitic on a deeper, nonstrategic responsiveness to the audience in which the speaker understands and represents the situation in which strategic action may be deployed. Gadamer's ontological argument is a necessary addition to Perelman's account of the means of argumentation precisely to emphasize this point.

Jerry Frug's essay "Argument as Character" provides an example of how a rhetorical analysis can fail to take account of the ontological dimension of rhetorical exchanges. Frug properly notes that the audience responds to the character of the rhetor as it is displayed in her argument, but he seems to assume that the speaker and audience have preexisting characters, with persuasion occurring only if the speaker's character is compatible with her audience's character.[15] Absent from his account is the reciprocal character-building effect of a rhetorical exchange, captured by Gadamer's notion of a conversational fusion of horizons. Frug's approach easily slips into a crude Nietzschean perspectivism, with persuasion becoming impossible ("I'm a deconstructionist and you're a microeconomist, so what more can we say") or with rhetoric degenerating into a methodology for projecting an appealing "character" wholly for strategic purposes.

The same narrow conception of the rhetorical dimension of legal practice is evident when theorists reduce judging to formulating an acceptable rhetorical justification for a decision. For example, Gerald Wetlaufer proposes to discuss the rhetorical conventions of legal argumentation and opinion writing while leaving aside for the moment "the process by which judges decide the cases with which they are presented."[16] While it is true that judges may seek to spell out their justificatory reasoning in a relatively self-conscious manner, the decision is itself a product of rhetorical exchange to the extent that it can be characterized as a reasoned decision. Later construction of a syllogistic justification is only the tip of the rhetorical iceberg that has resulted in the decision, and undue attention to this latter phase of judging clouds the nature of the rhetorical process in adjudication. Wetlaufer's provocative thesis is that the rhetorical conventions that require lawyers to invoke clarity, univocity, objectivity, and finality when making arguments have "ontological consequences" by limiting the capacities of lawyers and judges to reason about the uncertain issues they confront daily. This thesis assumes even greater significance, though, when the rhetorical field is expanded beyond mere justification to legal reasoning.[17] Wetlaufer substantially undermines his own thesis when he concedes that the delimited rhetorics practiced by litigators probably do not persuade many judges to reach the desired decision, even though the judges later repeat the formal "proof" in their opinion.[18] Wetlaufer's admission suggests that the rhetorical activity of law exists sub rosa and may be shielded from the counterfactual forms of presentation. Wetlaufer's critique would then be read not as a denial of the dynamism and effectiveness of legal rhetoric but rather as an indictment of its lack of honesty and accessibility to those not initiated into the genuine means of persuasion.

Duncan Kennedy's famous critical phenomenology of the act of judging provides a more sophisticated account of rhetorical engagement, but he too begins with the assumption that a judge having a strong political and moral orientation approaches a case with a desired result that must be rhetorically justified with malleable precedent. Kennedy acknowledges that the normative power of the indeterminate textual field is sometimes strong enough to convince the judge to abandon her first inclinations, but one senses from Kennedy's hypothetical first-person account that he has substantial misgivings about the potential ideological effects of institutionally defined authority.[19] Kennedy concludes that rules sometimes bend to the will of the interpreter but that sometimes they do not and that the interpreter sometimes bends to the rule but that sometimes she does not. The confrontation between interpreter and rule is presented in a subtle and sophisticated manner at many points in the article, but Kennedy appears (in the voice of the hypothetical judge) to regard the interpreter's acceptance of the law as a "counter-ideal" situation in which the law "manipulates" the interpreter.[20] Again, legal reasoning is presented as a rhetorical practice only to the extent that it is a strategy pursued by a judge or a force embedded in the social significance of a text. While each of the forces is fluid and indeterminate in Kennedy's account, they do not deliberate together so much as collide.

In each of these accounts, rhetorical exchanges are presented as more or less successful confrontations between a legal actor and other legal actors. In contrast, the concept of rhetorical knowledge derived from Gadamer's and Perelman's philosophies emphasizes that legal practice is a collective practice of lawmaking. The client's story is almost always preformed by the legal tradition when she enters the lawyer's office for the first time, regardless of the level of her sophistication, but the story nevertheless represents a challenge to the lawyer who seeks to develop its present legal significance. The stories told by adverse parties and their lawyers, whether in negotiation or litigation, represent the pragmatically constructed space in which the abstract ideal of the law once again is pressed into service. The clients, lawyers, and judges who are brought together by a particular dispute construct new accounts of the law by means of the myriad argumentative moves made by all concerned over the life of the case. By engaging in legal practice, lawyers constantly learn and grow, not just in their ability to recite the black letter law, but in their ability to create the law of each case.

Rhetorical Invention as Critique

The concept of rhetorical knowledge not only helps to describe the continuities of legal practice, it also clarifies the critical dimension of this practice. Although Wetlaufer's critique of legal practice works from a narrow conception of rhetoric, it does pose an important challenge: do the rhetorical devices used by practicing lawyers serve as powerful constraints that preclude a robust legal dialogue? My analysis of rhetorical knowledge leads me to answer this question cautiously with a qualified "no." The critical component inherent in rhetorical exchanges is an unavoidable feature, and therefore it is operative to some degree despite the cramped syntax of formal legal argumentation. It is essential to recognize the significance of institutional and social barriers that inhibit realization of this critical element in its full rigor, but it is no less important to avoid overestimating the challenge in a manner that bifurcates critical legal theory and legal practice. It is necessary to explore the critical dimension of legal practice in greater detail because critical legal theory is best characterized as the project of identifying impediments to maximizing this critical dimension.

The mistaken character of formalist accounts of law is now obvious to most lawyers, and so it might seem plausible to conclude that the truncated legal rhetoric employed by lawyers and judges in their formal presentations does not completely suppress the rhetorical nature of law and the operation of rhetorical knowledge. With the advent of Legal Realism, theorists relearned what practicing lawyers have always known: effective lawyers are not obsessed with manipulating the formalistic and deductive conventions of legal argumentation since these devices are insufficient to resolve the indeterminate legal question that they face. Rather, good lawyers concentrate on motivating the judge or opposing party by educating them about the reality of the situation and pointing the way toward a reasonable legal solution, even if convention requires them to do so under cover of highly rationalistic legal dogmatics. After all, when both advocates in every case argue that the precedents are clear and univocal, that the singular rule articulated in the precedents definitively resolves the case at hand, and that all arguments offered by the opponent are entirely specious and without merit, one must conclude that persuasion is being accomplished by some means other than these bare stylistic conventions of litigation advocacy. It is certainly frustrating that a syllogistic veneer is later draped over the full rhetorical encounter because this exercise undoubtedly affects legal practice for the worse, but legal stylistics only obscure and do not preclude the inventive use of commonplaces that defines the rhetorical exchange.

Legal argumentation always invites a critical use of commonplaces, even when the argument is styled in terms of "obedience to the law." Gadamer and Perelman both stress that law is never understood abstractly but only in reference to its application to a specific case, regardless of our pretensions to the contrary. Without a deductive formula or a rationalist algorithm to bridge the hypothetical meaning of the law in itself and the demands of the case at hand, persuasion always involves some measure of invention in the form of re-presenting the relevant law and the facts at issue. Without foundational guarantees of certainty, reasonable means of persuasion and meaningful deliberation emerge as part of the inventive task of developing plausible arguments within the openness of rhetorical exchanges. The activity of invention is the critical element of legal practice, since it represents the disruption of stubborn, habitual manners of thinking.

At this juncture it is helpful to relate this characterization of the critical dimension of legal practice to the philosophical groundwork of the previous chapters. Gadamer makes the same claim forcefully in his response to Habermas's theory of systematically distorted communication. When Habermas insists that hermeneutic understanding must be supplemented by a distinct critical inquiry to avoid the warping effects of ideology, Gadamer regards this extreme suspicion of language as an abstraction from the linguistically structured hermeneutical situation that opens the world to us only by virtue of its prejudiced character.

> The fact that we move in a linguistic world and grow up into the world through an experience pre-formed by language does not at all remove the possibilities of critique. On the contrary, the possibility of going beyond our conventions and beyond all those experiences that are schematized in advance opens up before us once we find ourselves, in our conversation with others, faced with opposed thinkers, with new critical texts, with new experiences.
>
> ----------
>
> To sum up, I would say that the misunderstanding in the question of the linguisticality of our understanding is really one about language—i.e., seeing language as a stock of words and phrases, of concepts, viewpoints and opinions. In fact, language is the single word, whose virtuality opens for us the infinity of discourse, of speaking with one another, of the freedom of "expressing oneself" and "letting oneself be expressed." Language is not its elaborated conventionalism, nor the burden of pre-schematization with which it loads us, but the

> generative and creative power to unceasingly make this whole once again fluent.[21]

An explicit reference to rhetoric at this juncture would add force to his argument, but Gadamer's starting point is central to understanding the potential for critical legal theory: a preexisting legal system is not an ideological trap that precludes justice; it is the condition of the possibility for rhetorical knowledge to illuminate the requirements of justice.[22]

Bernard Jacob defends Perelman's account of legal rhetoric against charges that it is overtly conventional by emphasizing Perelman's celebration of the critical element of legal practice. Legal commonplaces serve as the springboard for invention, meaning that "the opportunity for reconsideration, innovation, rejection, and amendment appears as a moment in the basic structure of every legal problem."[23] Commonplaces do not form a closed ideological mindset but rather provide the "prejudices" from which understanding may proceed. The key insight of the "rhetorical turn" is that the rhetorical field includes a self-reflexive capacity that provides the opening for criticizing the rhetorically configured ideologies of contemporary society.[24] Despite the attempts of many talented systematizers through the years, legal commonplaces have proved to be recalcitrant to the effort to develop an axiological calculus. Rather than congealing as a formal system, commonplaces remain starting points for dynamic rhetorical engagements that cannot be charted in advance.[25] Invention is not only a possibility opened by argumentation; it is a precondition of understanding and persuasion. Even when an advocate claims that the present case is identical to a previously decided case, the lawyers and judge must take up the case at hand and the legal tradition inventively, since no two cases are ever exactly alike in every conceivable sense. Because judgment is never a matter of pure subsumption—meaning that legal practice always requires an interpretive understanding of the situation and a persuasive presentation of this interpretation—it is inevitable that commonplaces are employed inventively to some degree. Critique is a feature of legal practice because legal practice is never a rote repetition of what has preceded, even when the traditional rule is affirmed.

Calvin Schrag provides important philosophical clarification of these issues. Schrag rejects a theoretically secured critique in favor of what he terms "praxial critique," by which he means the critical development of practices that occurs as part of the practices. He proposes

> [a] resituation of critique within the space of our communicative practices and the dynamics of our lifeworld involvements. Rather than a centripetal activity issuing from the subject-centered rationality of an isolated epistemological, moral, or aesthetic subject, we understand critique as a centrifugal deployment of discursive and nondiscursive social practices. Critique, thusly contextualized, falls out as a communicative project, a praxis that finds its resources in the dialogic transactions and institutional forms that make up the fabric of our socio-historical existence. . . . [I]t rests content to discern and assess the play of forms of thought and action against the background of changing and historically conditioned patterns of signification.[26]

Schrag's philosophical point is easily brought to bear in the setting of legal practice; in fact, legal practice appears to exemplify the exercise of critical reason as described by Schrag.

The rhetorical nature of the critical element of legal practice provides the key to a new understanding of justice. The description of legal practice as a series of interconnected rhetorical exchanges that are oriented to rhetorical knowledge stands in sharp contrast to the traditional accounts of the relationship between legal practice and principles of justice. Legal positivism characterizes law as a distinct socially defined practice that stands independent of moral inquiry. Under this view, the substantive justice of a law is properly considered only when the law is enacted—or in the event that a judge must fill a "gap" in the law—since legal reasoning is regarded as a practice that is distinct from speculations about the requirements of justice. Legal positivism represents a reaction to the older natural law tradition which equates justice with the realization of the fixed principles of natural law in the positive legal realm. Adopting the model of rhetorical knowledge entails a rejection of both legal positivism and traditional natural law theory and, therefore, signals a new conception of the relationship of law and legal practice.

Perelman's analysis of justice as a confused notion and Warnke's Gadamer-inspired account of justice as hermeneutical conversation provide the basis for a detailed consideration of the role of critique in securing justice. Justice is not a yardstick with which to define or measure legal practice; it is a "confused notion" that operates in legal discourse on several different levels. On one hand, justice is a topic with well-established lines of argumentation dating back to the Greeks. This topic is particularly confused, however, because it is bound up with the substantive question of how we take up the topic. We must discuss questions of justice only in a just manner, one might say. On the other hand, then, justice refers to the practical situation in which the opportunity for acquiring rhetorical knowledge about the just manner of proceeding is maximized.

Justice is not a fixed state of affairs toward which practice reaches. Instead, it is a normative characterization of the manner in which the practice should regenerate itself: "justice" challenges where discussants now stand as well as impels them forward to a new mode of social interaction. As Perelman skillfully demonstrates, principles of justice do not provide determinate guidance to legal practice; rather, they serve as commonplaces for argumentation within legal practice. Justice is a quality of becoming, rather than a telos or a lost innocence.

Perelman emphasizes that the timeworn question animating the clash between natural law and legal positivism—"Can justice conflict with law?"—no longer makes sense once legal practice is recognized to be a rhetorical engagement. "The question can be put in this way only if no account is taken of the distinction we have established between formal justice [the abstract principle of equal treatment of like cases] and concrete justice [the practical assessment of the criteria of 'equality' in a given case]. Indeed, an attempt to judge law in the name of justice is possible only by means of a confusion. Law will be judged by means, not of formal justice, but of concrete justice, that is of a particular conception of justice which assumes a settled scale of values."[27] The formal conception of justice as a fixed standard leads natural law advocates to import the logical criteria of judgment to law, equating just laws with those that faithfully reflect the requirements of justice. The emptiness of this abstract, strong conception results in the efforts of legal positivists to differentiate morality and justice from legal practice. Perelman contends that the starting point for this false debate must be abandoned. "Our actions and decisions are never 'true'; they are correct, conform to a moral or legal order, are expedient, just, equitable or reasonable. . . . When we discuss fundamental norms we are concerned much less with their truth than with their interpretation."[28]

This practical conception of justice converges with Gadamer's conversational ethic of holding oneself open to the rhetorical claims made by others. Gadamer concludes that the "hermeneutical experience . . . has its own rigor: that of uninterrupted listening."[29] The practical and ethical implication of this conclusion is clear: "[H]ermeneutic philosophy understands itself not as an absolute position but as a way of experience. It insists that there is no higher principle than holding oneself open in a conversation."[30] Justice can be realized when one's prejudices are challenged by a confrontation with the other, even if the "other" is a hypothesized dialogue partner in the soul's conversation with itself. The breaking up of "our own bias and narrowness" through such encounters permits the elaboration of the requirements of concrete justice.[31] In the legal setting, justice is not a matter of manipulating pre-given substantive rules but rather is lodged in the interstices of the practice of re-creating the law through dialogic openness oriented toward taking appropriate action within the context of an individual case.

Justice in Action

The concept of rhetorical knowledge can help us understand how justice can be realized through law. Rather than choosing another dramatic exercise of the Supreme Court's discretionary jurisdiction to serve as the final arbiter of constitutional rights, I describe justice in action at the more mundane level of local prosecutors, judges, and juries.

Dr. Jack Kevorkian was arrested numerous times for violating Michigan criminal law by assisting patients to commit suicide, and his extensive efforts to publicize his activities succeeded in making his name virtually synonymous with this important legal question. Judges first dismissed charges against him, finding that Michigan law did not criminalize this practice. Fearing that people would begin traveling to Michigan to commit suicide, the legislature enacted a law specifically banning assisted suicide. Kevorkian ultimately was arrested and then tried and acquitted twice under the statute, but he was unable to successfully assert a constitutional limit on the state's power to criminalize assisted suicide.[32] Parties in other jurisdictions originally had more success in challenging similar criminal statutes,[33] but the United States Supreme Court eventually rejected the claim that the federal Constitution prohibits states from criminalizing assisted suicide.[34] After the statute lapsed, Kevorkian was tried for the common law crime of assisted suicide, but again he was acquitted. Finally, Kevorkian was charged, convicted, and imprisoned by the State of Michigan for second-degree murder after he injected a man with a fatal dose of drugs to end his suffering.

Familiar and tired responses quickly come to mind in response to the obvious questions: what is the just resolution of these cases, and how can justice be determined in such situations? A natural law advocate might argue that the criminal laws against this practice are fully just, insofar as they represent an appropriate respect for human life that does not permit active termination of life even when requested by a suffering individual. The moral status of the law would be coincident with its characterization as a just law. A positivist might argue that such laws are duly enacted and clearly apply to the cases at hand, subject only to jury nullification (regarded as an extra-legal, extra-rational kind of safety valve) or a constitutional limitation on the power of the legislature to pass the laws in question. Consequently, the justice of the law becomes a matter of social policy properly assessed by legislators who act outside the more constricted dialogue of legal reasoning. In both instances, the justice of the situation is defined external to legal practice, with the debate hinging on the proper relationship of legal practice to this external reality.

In contrast, a rhetorical account of justice insists that such laws are just if they are applied in an open and deliberative process that leads to rhetorical knowledge of the matter at hand. Legislators, judges, and juries all participate in an ongoing, historically shaped rhetorical practice of creating the law that cannot be wholly separated from, nor simply conflated with, ethical deliberation about the matter. Although Aristotle's distinction between judicial rhetoric and deliberative rhetoric may have made sense in his day, in contemporary American society many legal cases move well beyond narrow argumentation about the facts of the case and their significance under the law.[35] Abortion, school desegregation, civil rights, assisted suicide: the list of important social policy questions taken up by legislatures and in the courtrooms of America seems endless. The Kevorkian prosecutions are discrete moments within contemporary social and legal practices that traverse a number of discourses and carry forward the historical trajectories of past confrontations about these important issues. Passage of the statute banning assisted suicide and its subsequent interpretation by Kevorkian, his lawyer, prosecutors, jurors, judges, and even the citizenry represent a series of events in the ongoing effort to determine the justice of permitting assisted suicide. This is not a question that can be abstracted from the facts of the particular case, as Kevorkian's initial success in challenging the law through jury nullification quickly evaporated in the context of his increasingly questionable practices. Justice relates to the character of these rhetorical engagements in working through the questions at hand, and recourse to arguments about justice will continue to be made by all sides of this issue regardless of the path that the law takes. The law is just when these argumentative positions are taken up freely in an arena that grants them a fair hearing, which is not to suggest that "freely" and "fair" can be resolved other than within the ongoing legal consideration of these cases.

The multiple unsuccessful prosecutions of Jack Kevorkian for assisting persons to commit suicide, followed by the successful prosecution of him for second-degree murder, provide a complex example of the rhetorics of legal practice. The Kevorkian trials have faded from memory to some degree, but during the 1990s he was constantly in the news and his name became well known throughout the United States and the world. The facts and circumstances of his activities and prosecutions are sufficiently complex to merit a book-length scholarly treatment, but a schematic overview of this episode in American public life can serve to illuminate the rhetorical and hermeneutical characteristics of legal practice.[36]

Kevorkian began assisting people to commit suicide in the State of Michigan, which did not have a criminal statute that specifically proscribed assisted suicide. In 1990, he provided Janet Adkins with the means to commit suicide and then assisted her in doing so. Adkins was only in the early stages of Alzheimer's disease and had beaten her son in tennis a few days prior to her suicide.[37] She had no physician-patient relationship with Kevorkian until she contacted him for assistance. Consequently, the case did not present a scenario that would predispose a prosecutor to decline prosecution, and Kevorkian was charged with assisted suicide. However, the trial court dismissed the criminal charges, finding that Michigan law did not impose criminal penalties for assisting in a suicide. Nevertheless, the court enjoined Kevorkian not to assist any more persons to commit suicide, leading Kevorkian to appeal the injunction and set into motion one of the threads of legal analysis that arose from his actions. The injunction ultimately was upheld by the Michigan Court of Appeals in 1995, but only after the Michigan Supreme Court decided, in a case stemming from another assisted suicide by Kevorkian, that assisted suicide is a crime under the common law of Michigan.[38]

Kevorkian persisted in his efforts to assist people to commit suicide during the pendency of the litigation surrounding the Adkins case, which had brought incredible media attention to his activities. In 1991, he assisted two women—Marjorie Wantz and Sherry Miller, strangers to each other—to commit suicide together at a remote cabin. Again, the trial judge dismissed the charges for the reason that assisted suicide was not a crime under Michigan law. Kevorkian continued to assist people to commit suicide, and he made it quite clear that he would continue to do so unless he was successfully prosecuted. In no uncertain terms, he dared the State of Michigan to try to stop him in his quest to assist people who had chosen to end their lives.

Kevorkian's highly visible activities intervened in a national debate that had already resulted in legal cases seeking to articulate the contours of a constitutional "right to die." Working from the United States Supreme Court's determination in the traumatic case of Karen Quinlan that a competent person has the constitutional right to refuse lifesaving medical treatment under certain circumstances, doctors and patients had begun campaigns to legalize assisted suicide for some terminally ill patients. Ultimately, at the height of the attention generated by the Kevorkian prosecutions, two high-profile cases were filed in federal district court seeking to establish the constitutional right of a person to seek the assistance of his physician to end his life in the face of a painful terminal illness. These cases posed the heartrending scenarios of terminally ill and suffering individuals seeking to end their lives, compassionate treating physicians who were motivated to alleviate suffering and to maintain the dignity of their patients in their final days, and a political plea that this ultimate and deeply personal decision should not be overridden by state criminal law. These two cases met with success in the courts of appeals, with the Ninth Circuit holding that bans on assisted suicide violate the Due Process Clause[39] and the Second Circuit holding that they violate the Equal Protection Clause.[40] However, in 1997 the Supreme Court refused to extend its decision in the *Cruzan* case[41] and held that there is no constitutional right under equal protection or due process principles that prevents states from making assisted suicide a crime.[42]

Kevorkian was acquitted of assisted suicide by three different juries in 1994 and 1996 but was convicted of second-degree murder in 1999. It is tempting to connect his fate to the fortunes of the simultaneous federal constitutional litigation. However, it is clear that the Kevorkian prosecutions involve far more than a general responsiveness to certain appellate decisions of prominent federal courts. The Kevorkian prosecutions reveal the complex hermeneutical and rhetorical reality behind the more generalized appellate case law, which purports to rise above the crosscutting complications of everyday life. In fact, it would be productive (although speculative) to consider how the increasingly bizarre situation surrounding the prosecutions of Kevorkian in Michigan might have had an effect on the Supreme Court when it adjudicated the constitutionality of state bans on the practice. The Court favorably cited the Michigan cases dealing with Kevorkian for the general legal principle that assisted suicide should be distinguished from refusing life-prolonging medical interventions and that it may properly be criminalized. However, Kevorkian's efforts to push the limits of the willingness of juries to acquit him and the gathering controversy over his practices might well have played a role as a background factor that affected the Court's analysis.

Kevorkian's initial prosecutions were dismissed by the trial judges for the reason that Michigan law did not clearly prohibit assisted suicide; consequently, these cases never reached a jury. In recognition that Kevorkian was accelerating his assisted suicides and had no intention of stopping them, and in response to the resulting intense publicity that threatened to make Michigan a tourist destination for death, on December 15, 1992, the Michigan legislature hurriedly passed a statute criminalizing assisted suicide. Later, in response to an increase in suicides assisted by Kevorkian, the legislature voted to accelerate the effective date of the statute to February 1993. The issue then appeared to be joined: Kevorkian was determined to continue to assist people to commit suicide regardless of a clear legal prohibition, and Michigan had legislated a clear criminal ban precisely to apply to Kevorkian's activities. Kevorkian's battle against the social proscription of assisted suicide was now a battle over the constitutional power of the state to enact a criminal statute that expressly made assisted suicide illegal.

At this point, the drama quickly intensified. First, two different trial judges declared the new statute unconstitutional: one in response to a declaratory judgment action, and one in the course of dismissing criminal charges brought against Kevorkian under the statute. Kevorkian's practices now were inextricably linked to the public debate over assisted suicide: rather than litigating the matter solely as a declaratory judgment about abstract rights, Kevorkian continued to assist with suicides and then challenge the state to try to convict him. A criminal conviction of Kevorkian under the new statute seemingly was no more and no less than an endorsement of the state's right to intervene, whereas an acquittal was portrayed as the jury's manner of rejecting the appropriateness of legal regulation of such matters. Jack Kevorkian literally embodied the debate over assisted suicide through his statements and his actions.[43]

Kevorkian's first prosecution under the new statute involved a case that Kevorkian's attorney, Geoffrey Fieger, had determined was the "right case" with which to challenge the statute, unlike the highly ambiguous situations presented when Kevorkian assisted Janet Adkins, Sherry Miller, and Marjorie Wantz to commit suicide.[44] Thomas Hyde was a thirty-year-old man in the late stages of Lou Gehrig's disease, a horrendous condition under any account. Hyde and his family presented a strong emotional appeal that he should be allowed to end his suffering without intervention by the state. The first person whom Kevorkian assisted after the statute took effect presented an equally compelling case: Ronald Mansur was a fifty-four-year-old man suffering from excruciating bone and lung cancer. Immediately following Mansur's death, Fieger had predicted confidently: "They'll never find a jury that will convict Kevorkian. It's not a crime to be present when someone commits suicide," and legal experts agreed that proving the elements of the crime would be difficult if the only witness to the crime was dead.[45] With the Hyde case, however, Kevorkian directly challenged prosecutors to charge him by admitting that he helped Hyde to kill himself and by providing videotaped statements by Hyde expressing his wish that Kevorkian assist him.

Kevorkian's team of jury selection experts reportedly were satisfied from the outset that the jury seated for the Hyde trial would not convict Kevorkian.[46] At trial, several jurors wiped away tears as they watched a videotape of Hyde describing one month before his death how much he wanted to end his suffering with Kevorkian's help.[47] But later interviews established that the jury did not simply react to the powerful emotional moments of the trial and reflexively acquit Kevorkian. Before adjourning deliberations for the weekend, the jury had voted seven to five to convict; by the following Monday morning the vote had swung to eleven to one to acquit him of violating the statute, and deliberations continued until the acquittal was unanimously endorsed.[48] Reportedly, only five jurors expressed support for assisted suicide and opposition to passage of the statute. As later explained by several jurors, despite their personal misgivings about assisted suicide generally and about Kevorkian's methods specifically, they voted to acquit because they believed that Kevorkian intended only to help Hyde relieve his suffering (intent was an element of the statutory crime), and that Hyde should have the ability to choose for himself whether suicide was the only option.[49]

The highly public trial resulting in a jury acquitting Kevorkian after he had made clear that he assisted Thomas Hyde to commit suicide suggested to many that Kevorkian might be immune from conviction. But contemporaneous reports also suggested that the speed and missionary zeal with which Kevorkian dispatched his clients, and his strange behavior generally, indicated that Kevorkian might not present the best case for legalized assisted suicide. Jack Lessenberry's *Vanity Fair* article "Death Becomes Him," appearing just after Kevorkian's acquittal, described the strange sync achieved by the rather bizarre and erratic Kevorkian wanting to be convicted and martyred for the cause and the flamboyant and attention-hungry Fieger. In response to Kevorkian's earlier cases involving women who appeared to be motivated to commit suicide in order to ease the burden on their families rather than to end painful suffering of the kind being endured by Mansur and Hyde, some commentators already had questioned whether Kevorkian in the end might be hindering the movement to ensure access to assisted suicide for some patients. In response to the dismissal of murder charges for the deaths of Sherry Miller and Marjorie Wantz, Sara Engram wrote:

> Some of the doctor's harshest critics are those who agree that people should be allowed to seek the assistance of a physician when the time comes to die. It's easy to see why.
>
> ----------
>
> None of the deaths would have been approved by the Washington state proposal [to legalize assisted suicide in some circumstances]. Even so, these stories may well have frightened enough Washington state voters to assure defeat of the referendum.
>
> That raises the question: If Dr. Kevorkian believes so strongly in assisted suicide, why does he continue to draw headlines by participating in deaths in ways that no responsible society can condone?
>
> If physician-assisted suicide is justifiable—and there are responsible, conscientious doctors who believe that under certain circumstances it can be—the issue deserves debate. Dr. Kevorkian is providing diversions from the serious questions by continuing to take advantage of Michigan's [pre-statute] legal loopholes.[50]

These misgivings about Kevorkian's earlier activities were not brought to the foreground in the Hyde trial, but it was clear that identifying Kevorkian with the campaign to legalize assisted suicide might prove problematic. The rhetorical complexity of the issue was manifest.

Kevorkian was charged with violating the statute a second time, but the jury again acquitted him, finding that he intended to ease the suffering of the two "victims" rather than to help the individuals kill themselves.[51] Despite the jury's decision, the American Medical Association excoriated Kevorkian, whose license to practice medicine had long ago been revoked, by stating that the jury's refusal to convict him amounted to "a serious blow to quality, compassionate patient care. It sends a message that the dignity and value of human life at its end stages is irrelevant."[52] But this assessment of Kevorkian's actions likely would have rung hollow in the jury's ears. One of the individuals assisted by Kevorkian was Dr. Ali

Khalili, a physician specializing in pain control, who drove to Michigan and sought Kevorkian's assistance to end his suffering from bone cancer. Kevorkian recognized, as the jury must also have recognized, that Khalili had chosen to make a statement by seeking Kevorkian's help, since Khalili had sufficient knowledge and access to drugs to end his own life without assistance.[53]

Although he had carefully selected his test cases and successfully avoided conviction, Kevorkian acknowledged that his practices required wider justification and legitimacy. Immediately following the first acquittal, he welcomed democratic input into the practice and limits of assisted suicide.

> "We need medical input on this now," [Kevorkian] said. "We're going to set guidelines so it's done correctly and the public is going to have input, not legislators, but the public."
>
> Arthur Caplan, director of the Center for Bioethics at the University of Pennsylvania, said Kevorkian's comments show that "he understands that he's been out there so far on the fringe that he will not attract followers unless checks and balances are built in . . . he knows that killing people 24 hours after you meet them, in the back of a van, is not going to make him much of a poster child for the assisted-suicide movement."[54]

Similarly, after his second acquittal Kevorkian promised that he would not abuse what now appeared to be immunity from prosecution, pledging that he would only act "for human benefit."[55]

The dramas of these two criminal prosecutions cannot be overstated. From the bizarre—Kevorkian intently studied a book of Japanese vocabulary during parts of the first trial[56]—to the incredibly poignant—witnessing the emotional videotaped statements made by Kevorkian's clients prior to their deaths—the trials embodied all the diversity and complexity that one might expect this public issue to generate. From all accounts, the jury took its oath of duty seriously, did not react on simplistic or raw emotion, and deliberated about the complex questions presented by the cases. Juror statements consistently recognized that a criminal conviction of Kevorkian would undermine the autonomy and privacy of the persons who chose to end their lives, and they rejected the idea that

Kevorkian could be convicted for attempting to assist in this ultimate exercise of autonomy. As one juror summarized, "Personally, I am against suicide, but I feel each person should be able to make their own choice."[57] As one of two nurses on the jury, and having cared for two family members during their terminal illnesses, one juror strongly supported the right of the suffering patient to make this decision: "I don't believe it's our obligation to choose how much pain and suffering someone else can go through . . . I believe that that's between them and their God."[58] Because the assisted suicide statute distinguished between providing the means for suicide from providing drugs to ease suffering that might have the effect of shortening life, the jury was able to "see" the case as not requiring conviction. In other words, the jury did not cast aside the law but reasoned about the meaning of the law in the case before them.

The Michigan statute against assisted suicide expired before the second trial, and following the acquittal it appeared that Kevorkian had won his battle against an express legislative prohibition. However, the early criminal charges brought against Kevorkian had slowly made their way through the appellate process, resulting in a decision of the Michigan Court of Appeals that a physician could be found guilty under the murder statute for assisting in a suicide.[59] The Michigan Supreme Court disagreed, finding that assisted suicide could only be punished under the "savings clause" of the criminal code, which provided for punishment of up to five years in prison for committing an offense indictable at the common law if no punishment is expressly set forth in the criminal code.[60] As a result, the criminal prosecutions for the 1991 deaths of Sherry Miller and Marjorie Wantz suddenly resumed, but with a crucial difference. Rather than requiring the jury to find Kevorkian guilty of a capital crime, the court's holding opened the way for a more plausible conviction of a crime that could carry a punishment of no more than five years of imprisonment.

It was clear that this trial was not going to be a replay of the previous two trials. First, the basis for the indictment was the common law, which arguably punished persons assisting with a suicide for the crime of murder, but which the Supreme Court had subjected to a "reinterpretation" in order to reduce the applicable penalty to the baseline established in the savings clause. Second, these suicides were among the early, questionable cases that had given even supporters of assisted suicide great pause.[61] This important dimension of the case was foreshadowed in 1995 when the Michigan Court of Appeals affirmed a trial judge's exercise of equity jurisdiction to enjoin Kevorkian permanently from assisting with more suicides, following the judge's dismissal of charges related to Janet Adkins's suicide. The court described the troubling facts surrounding the Adkins case that justified imposing an injunction, despite the trial court's conclusion that Michigan law did not criminalize the behavior clearly enough to support prosecution:

> The court found that defendant was not professionally qualified to evaluate the physical or emotional status of Ms. Adkins. Moreover, the court found that defendant made no attempt to take a comprehensive medical history, conduct a physical examination, order any tests, assess Ms. Adkins' medical status, or consult with experts. The court found that Ms. Adkins, who was fifty-four years old, was neither imminently terminally ill nor suffering from pain. After reviewing the videotaped interview conducted by defendant with Ms. Adkins and her husband, the court found that she was coherent, responsive to verbal communication, and without any obvious physical or mental impairment. The court noted reports that she had played tennis within days of her death. Likewise, the videotape demonstrated that defendant made no real effort to discover whether Ms. Adkins wished to end her life, relying largely on the statements of her husband and a few limited responses from Ms. Adkins. The court found that defendant appeared to be in a hurry during the videotaped interview. The court found that Alzheimer's disease was not within the province of defendant's specialty and that his actions did not conform to accepted medical standards.[62]

Many of these same factors were present to a greater degree in the Wantz case, which involved a woman who had complained about severe pelvic and vaginal pain for many years, but who had not been successfully diagnosed nor even determined to be terminally ill.[63]

Kevorkian's third trial took place in 1996, some five years after the deaths of Miller and Wantz. After deliberating for thirteen hours over three days, the jury acquitted him of murder in the two deaths, leading the director of Michigan's ACLU chapter to declare, "Dr. Kevorkian is simply not convictable."[64] Kevorkian also struck a triumphant tone, declaring in messianic fashion, "I've never been so convinced of being right in my life. . . . The only thing that would stop me at this is being burned at the stake. I don't like burning to death."[65] News analysts generally concluded that Kevorkian could not be convicted,[66] although some argued that regulation was desirable to prevent his questionable "back alley" practices.[67] The *New York Times* reported that the third acquittal led some prosecutors to decide that it might now be pointless to charge Kevorkian with assisted suicide.[68]

Despite this reaction, the case was not a simple matter of jury nullification of a law with which it disagreed; rather, the jury focused on the fairness of indicting Kevorkian based on a new interpretation of the common law that came long after he had relied on express statutory law to assist the two women to commit suicide. According to one juror, the jury concluded that Kevorkian had faithfully sought to determine the bounds of the law before acting, and that he never had the intent to violate the law.[69] The jury's concerns were vindicated generally when a federal district court later held that the decision by the Michigan Supreme Court to permit prosecutions for the common law crime of assisted suicide was unconstitutionally vague and violated the constitutional ban on ex post facto punishments when applied to actions that predated fair notice of this ban.[70] The district court found that the Michigan Supreme Court had "reinterpreted" the common law to such a degree in an effort to provide fair punishment in light of contemporary standards that no "reasonable person could have reasonably understood that assisting in a suicide was a crime in Michigan before the assisted suicide statute was passed."[71] In this prosecution, the issue in debate had shifted to the different issue of requiring fair notice of the reach of criminal law, which is an issue of no less importance than the political question of the legitimacy of assisted suicide.

The saga ended soon thereafter, however, when Kevorkian videotaped himself injecting Thomas Youck with a lethal dose of potassium chloride and then later appeared on the television show *Sixty Minutes* to describe his actions and to show the video.[72] Youck was nearly incapacitated at the time of his death due to Lou Gehrig's disease, and therefore he presented one of the strongest cases yet for an assisted suicide. However, Kevorkian crossed the line between assisting with a suicide and actively causing a person's death, leading to his conviction of second-degree murder and a sentence of ten to twenty-five years in prison.[73] The jury deliberated for thirteen hours, but reportedly the only question was whether to convict Kevorkian of first- or second-degree murder.[74] One of the issues on appeal was the trial judge's refusal to permit testimony by Youck's family members about his suffering and desire for Kevorkian to kill him, but the court held that consent and euthanasia are not cognizable defenses to murder charges.[75] Even if this evidence had been deemed relevant, it might not have helped Kevorkian obtain an acquittal because the speed with which Kevorkian acted and the cursory attention to Youck prior to his death caused Youck's caregiver to question publicly whether there was genuine consent at the end.[76]

Thus, in this fourth prosecution the facts and relevant law were again dramatically different, with the debate about assisted suicide not even playing a role. But it is also clear that the prosecution occurred against a background understanding that Kevorkian was pushing his earlier practices to the limit in order to test his invulnerability to prosecution, and that he was seeking conviction and martyrdom. He defended himself at the criminal trial, leading his former attorney to conclude that Kevorkian was simply bent on self-destruction and to comment ironically, "Well, I don't assist in the suicide of my clients."[77] If Kevorkian wanted martyrdom, he attained it in the end by disassociating himself from the public debate over assisted suicide that he seemed to embody. After reviewing Kevorkian's actions and statements prior to this string of cases, Robert Wade Kenny notes the wide divergence between Kevorkian's goals and rhetorical intent and the rhetorical situation that he assumed in the public debate about assisted suicide.[78] The interplay of wider public policy issues, Kevorkian's agenda, the specific facts of the case, and the legal posture of the case all converged in the criminal prosecutions. The result is justice in action, defined not as reaching the correct result about an abstract legal question, but in hermeneutically and rhetorically working through these tangled issues in specific contexts.

The Kevorkian trials exemplify the important role that the jury trial plays in contemporary American society. In *A Theory of the Trial,* Robert Burns argues that a trial structures competing linguistic practices and performances to enable the trier to make practical judgments about what is to be done in response to complex and competing accounts of facts and norms. Under this account, theorizing is simply "thinking what we do" by re-presenting the narrative construction of truth that occurs during a trial, rather than passing judgment from outside. This leads Burns to characterize judgment as the "strife" of competing claims to truth.[79]

The Kevorkian trials demonstrate that the jury responds to the competing narratives first by determining the important issues at stake and then by resolving them in a practical manner that reaffirms the integrity of both general principles and specific factual circumstances. This accords with Burns's conclusion:

> I have argued that a great advantage of the contemporary trial is its internal complexity, comprising empirical, moral, political, and strictly "legal" language and values. It is sufficiently flexible to allow, indeed to require, that the jury determine what the most important aspect of the case is.
>
> ----------
>
> The trial's constitutive rules and practices allow for delicate choices about the inevitable metalevel questions woven into the trial's different linguistic practices. If these incommensurable spheres exhaust our social perspectives, if there is no Platonic perspective from which one might determine which sphere is ultimately dominant, from which (partial) perspective ought the jury to decide which perspective is the right one? The answer seems to me clear. The jury decides the metalevel questions from the perspective of commonsense morality, rigorously applied, criticized, and sometimes challenged by the devices of the trial. The existence of such a forum is a challenge to any form of social ordering that cannot justify its distinctive principles in the language of ordinary morality.[80]

The Kevorkian juries worked through the tangled threads of legal, social, and moral issues and deliberated to results that identified the just result. The justice in action of the Kevorkian trials is perhaps best captured in the statements made by a juror who participated in one of the acquittals, during an interview on a television news show regarding Kevorkian's upcoming murder trial for Youck's death. The juror began an exchange by agreeing that the jurors did not vote to acquit Kevorkian simply as a reflection of their personal views about assisted suicide.

> Ms. Beedle [juror]: . . . I was all for Dr. Kevorkian, but I went in there doing what I was supposed to do, went by the law, and there was no law so . . .
>
> [Matt] Lauer [interviewer]: How was the testimony of the loved one, in terms of your decision? How much impact did that have on you?
>
> Ms. Beedle: Well, it crushed me. It tore at you. It was terrible, but you—you had to put that aside and follow the rules, follow the laws, what we were supposed to be doing and we all—I feel we all did that.
>
> Lauer: Ms Beedle, based on what you've heard, and I know most of it comes from those of us in the media, at this moment, knowing the law that stands in the books in Michigan now, would you vote to acquit or convict?
>
> Ms. Beedle: I would have to go through the trial, to tell you the truth.
>
> Lauer: No gut feeling?
>
> Ms. Beedle: I would have to go through it. You would have to. You would have to get all the facts . . . [81]

This exchange succinctly captures the aspirations of a just legal system defined as one that maximizes the ability of decision makers to gain rhetorical knowledge of the situation. Ms. Beedle overtly claims to follow the law—the rules—and to bracket the raw emotional appeals in the case. And yet she recognizes that she can't prejudge the Youck case because she would have to "go through" the hermeneutical-rhetorical event of the trial to "get all the facts" so as to be in a position to find the just result. There is a difference between raw emotionalism and assessing a case in terms of not only the logos, but also the pathos and ethos in evidence. Kevorkian's trials were never solely about the legitimacy of assisted suicide as a general matter, Jack Kevorkian individually, nor a static conception of what the law states. Rather, they presented a subtle and ever-shifting negotiation of these and other concerns.

Georgia Warnke contends that justice is a well-structured conversation embodying respect and tolerance rather than a stable state of affairs to be achieved. Her hermeneutical conception of justice informs the practical example provided by the Kevorkian trials. "The idea behind the notion of hermeneutic conversation is the idea that an interpretive pluralism can be educational for all the parties involved. If we are to be educated by interpretations other than our own, however, we must both encourage the articulation of those alternative interpretations and help to make them as compelling as they can be. And how can we do this except by assuring the fairness of the conversation and working to give all possible voices equal access?"[82] Whereas Warnke credits Habermas with developing a sophisticated critical philosophy that can help to identify structural deformities in social understandings, my hermeneutical-rhetorical account follows this same critical impulse back to the conversation itself. It is only within the conversation that the fairness of the conversation is problematized and then worked out. The purpose of a trial, Burns persuasively demonstrates, is to structure narratives in order to achieve a justice that is strife.

Critics might argue that justice so construed empties the concept of any normative power and collapses into a contextualist relativism, but this reading should hold no sway. The pragmatic deliberation about the requirements of justice in a given case is no more relativistic than the kind of reflection and discussion in which an individual engages when confronted by a moral dilemma about how to act in a given situation. The absence of a definitive answer to moral dilemmas does not mean that this reflection and deliberation are irrational and emotive, and no person in the midst of such a situation regards her reasoning in this way. The condition of undecidability does not mean that decisions are made without any reasonable basis. The "dialogical unendingness" in which rhetorical knowledge is encountered does not signify a "complete relativism" any more than a person's life is an arbitrary collection of life experiences.[83] In both cases we not only are already committed in certain ways, we also strive—in a manner that can be reasonable rather than just random—for a coherence and closure that we know will never be achieved absolutely. Just as a particular conversation has a history and develops a topic, so too an individual's life and social practices such as law develop criteria of reasonableness and the rhetorical means to continue the ongoing project. One is never able to isolate ethical questions in a pure form, just as the jurors in the Kevorkian trials were never simply passing on the legitimacy of proscribing assisted suicide. A just legal practice, like a life well lived, does not circle around a determinate ground of truth but instead spirals forward from a shared tradition of contested commonplaces in the form of reasonable judgments about how to proceed.

It would be a mistake to think that pressing questions of justice emerge only in the context of dramatic facts that raise the hot-button issues of the day. Even run-of-the-mill commercial cases can present triers of fact with a controversy over the justice of the social and legal relations at issue in the case. Consider the situation in which a bank is routinely foreclosing on a residence after default under a promissory note, when suddenly it is confronted by a defense raised by an elderly homeowner. The homeowner alleges that a scam artist renting a room in her home tricked her into co-signing the note that he executed in connection with a personal loan from the bank, and that she also was tricked into mortgaging her property to provide the collateral for the loan. The homeowner's lawyer now stands in court seeking an order permitting discovery of the bank's lending practices. The lawyer argues that the note should be unenforceable because at the time of the loan the bank knew that the borrower had no realistic ability to repay the loan, but that it approved the loan anyway because the non-borrowing cosigner's home equity completely covered the bank's exposure.

In these circumstances the judge certainly will not countenance a claim that the bank has an absolute duty to protect the homeowner from the thief, but it is far from clear how the judge should rule when the homeowner argues that the bank has an obligation not to make loans that certainly will result in foreclosure of the primary residence of a non-borrower without subjecting the transaction to some form of heightened scrutiny. The routine foreclosure action—generally handled with form pleadings and stock maneuvers—now requires the court to clarify duties and to assess the justice of the legal relations in order to "apply" the straightforward foreclosure statutes. The fragility of the web of legal doctrine is suddenly manifest, and openings for critical appraisals of the unhelpful myths of commercial law are widened.[84]

Justice does not depend on a technology that successfully implements the right answer to such legal disputes; it is the condition which permits the legal actors and authorities to come to know what justice demands in the situation through a process of argumentation. Lawyers are adept at making analogies, drawing distinctions, and otherwise inventively presenting their clients' claims against the backdrop of numerous confused legal notions. This critical practice can be helpfully supplemented by more far-ranging critical inquiries that challenge certain background assumptions by drawing from other, suppressed features of practice. The critical dimensions of legal practice foster rhetorical knowledge, which can be facilitated by the critical interventions of legal theorists.

Critical Legal Theory as Cultural Critique

The unavoidable critical element of legal practice is never maximally realized, which is to say that it is obvious that conditions of justice do not always prevail in society despite the pervasiveness of the legal system. In the postmetaphysical age, it is difficult to endorse the traditional conception of theory as a rational inquiry that first systematizes and then directs practice. However, it is plausible to pursue more-circumscribed theoretical efforts to facilitate the critical elements of legal practice. Although a theory of interpretation cannot deliver knowledge about a legal text in the sense that it clarifies the correct application of the text to future problems, a productive theory might alter the theoretical self-understanding of some participants in legal practice sufficiently to free them from disabling views and to increase their openness to practices that generate rhetorical knowledge and critical insight. For example, neither an originalist theory of meaning nor a hermeneutical philosophy of understanding can provide unimpeachable knowledge about the meaning of the Constitution, but a hermeneutical critique of the bogus philosophical assumptions underlying originalism might lead to a more genuine interpretive practice by removing conceptual roadblocks that inhibit robust rhetorical exchanges.[85] Although currently it is fashionable to talk about the end of theory, the concept of rhetorical knowledge invites serious reflection on the rhetorical and hermeneutical dimensions of legal practice. The first step of this theoretical project is to develop a new understanding of the potential for a theory about a particular human practice and the relationship of such a theory to the practice under consideration.

The Rhetoric of Inquiry: Critique as Practice

Theory has fallen on hard times in the postmodern era. The "hermeneutic turn" toward characterizing knowledge as situated and interpretive has contributed to growing doubts among scholars that their work as critics can effectively bring external insight to bear on the social practices that they study. The "rhetorical turn" toward characterizing knowledge as a social engagement magnifies this doubt about the efficacy of theory to chart appropriate developments in social practices by emphasizing the contingent means of persuading another to adopt one's own provisional interpretation. If lawyers and judges have no recourse to fixed and universal criteria of judgment and must engage in an ongoing rhetorical practice suspended over an illusory syllogistic safety net, it becomes difficult for the legal theorist to assert that she has developed a theoretical key for unlocking the logic of this practice. An observer seeking to evaluate or criticize a rhetorical event is no less enmeshed in an interpretive-rhetorical horizon than those whom she is studying. Consequently, "the rhetorical critic's task is at least as difficult as that of the most successful rhetor."[86] The new movement toward narrative in contemporary legal scholarship is challenging and unsettling because not only are narratives the object of inquiry, they also constitute the methodology and result of the inquiry.[87]

Theory is not precluded by the recognition that the practices under study produce only rhetorical knowledge, once we move beyond construing "theory" in its traditional, narrow sense as the construction of a system of laws that has strong predictive value. Legal theory claims no expertise derived from being insulated from the contingencies of practice. It is a comportment within legal practice, even if from the relatively removed perspective of traditional academic articles in law reviews urging doctrinal reorientations. Even as a comportment within wider social and intellectual practices, as in the case of this book and other works in legal theory that have relatively weak and indirect connections to the everyday practice of law, theory is not a special power that rises above practice.

Legal theory is best understood as a rhetorical practice seeking rhetorical knowledge, no less than the legal practice to which it is directed.

If the concept of rhetorical knowledge is viewed "only" as a rhetorical claim put forth in an argumentative dialogue about the best means of representing legal practice, it might first appear that the concept strips itself of any authoritative claim. This initial reaction, though, simply repeats the mistake of regarding legal practice either as a rational-deductive exercise or as an irrational (although perhaps ideological) exercise of power under the guise of reason. Just as the better interpretation of a statute can emerge from legal argumentation, the better representation and critique of legal practices can emerge from argumentation in a theoretical dialogue. The recent cross-disciplinary investigation of the "rhetoric of inquiry" represents a sustained effort to describe the rhetorical tools available "not just for deconstructions of objectivist pretensions, but also for much-needed, much sought-after reconstructions of inquiry in the wake of those debunkings."[88] By emphasizing "the role played by rhetorical invention in the conduct of inquiry," the movement builds on rhetorical insights to foster the exercise of good judgment by scholars as they participate in their own historically defined practices, rejecting antitheory relativism as having missed the point of the rhetorical turn.[89]

Rhetorical practices are not self-deconstructing, since they involve inventional efforts to secure reasoned adherence by refashioning the prior agreements embedded in a shared tradition. The rhetoric of inquiry movement reconstructs these practices in order to explain how they develop and to foster better practices. Herbert Simons describes the positive theoretical object of the movement as follows: the "new rhetoric of inquiry should be able to prepare the way for wiser, more judicious judgments by scholars and others engaged in the conduct of inquiry. However open-ended such rhetoric may be, it need not be unreasonable or unempirical. However capable it may be of conceiving plausible arguments for opposing claims, it need not leave us in a state of indecision. If it cannot lay claim to fixed and immutable standards of judgment, or to formal devices by which to compel assent, it can nevertheless provide ways of engaging one's hearers, of clarifying ideas and also of rendering them plausible or probable."[90] There is a role for legal theory, but it is a thoroughly rhetorical role.

The proper role of theory is obscured by theorists who are willing to take the linguistic turn as a description of social practices, but who exempt their own theoretical reconstructions from the limitations of everyday speech. For example, the analytic branch of linguistic philosophy acknowledges the primacy of language but eschews the radical implications of philosophical hermeneutics and the new rhetoric by defending a theoretical program of rigorous critique built on the new foundation stone of language. This relapse involves an assumption that language fundamentally is structured by lawlike relationships subject to theoretically guided reconstruction, missing the insight that language is a dynamic, pragmatic, and lived-through medium all the way down to everyday practices and all the way back up again to sophisticated academic theorizing about these practices. Taking the concept of rhetorical knowledge seriously means rejecting the claim that language is a new fixed point of departure for theoretical reconstruction and confronting honestly the challenging implications of regarding reason as a thoroughly pragmatic activity in all its manifestations in practice and theory.[91]

Joseph Margolis challenges scholars to address the radical themes of the new rhetoric by abandoning Aristotle's last-ditch effort to oppose the sophistic claim that rhetorical practices have no recourse to an invariant reality that grounds bivalent thinking. The analytic tradition of linguistic philosophy is a modern analogue to Aristotle's claim that dialectical arguments are distinct from lower forms of persuasion. The move to secure a role for an invariant logic of argumentation constituting the structure of language is precisely the target of the new rhetoric, which regards persuasion as the motivation of action within a particular historical context.

> [T]he entire apparatus of valid argument forms . . . applied in real-world circumstances, must be inextricably intertwined with the conditions of persuasion intrinsic to a particular society's linguistic practices—in virtue of which (alone) intended reference is consensually supported, accepted, agreed upon in the absence of theoretically compelling proofs.
>
> ----------
>
> All discourse and thought becomes encumbered, at a single stroke, by the "extra"-linguistic, historically contingent, socially

> constructed, context-ridden, inherently informal habits and practices of a community of humans. But that is the essential nerve of the "new" rhetoric.
>
> ----------
>
> Now, then, very simply put: if reference and predication cannot but be inseparable from the . . . resources of actual societies surviving, at least in large part, as a result of the contingently fortunate effects of their linguistic practices, then given the defeat of the Aristotelian conception of the relationship between the forms of argument and the force of rhetoric, the "new" rhetoric cannot be convincingly resisted.[92]

Margolis thus links the new rhetoric with the long-suppressed challenge of the sophists, and he breaks the news none too gently to the defenders of philosophical truth: after the linguistic turn, there is no place to stand with confidence in order to elaborate a theory except within the pragmatic and social accomplishments of a living language.

The rhetoric of inquiry leads some theorists to adopt the provocative posture of devaluing the role of theory altogether, providing the opposite reaction to those who strive to maintain the special status of theory. Stanley Fish has attacked the status of theory relentlessly, arguing that the timeless debate between the strong claims to truth by philosophy and the attention to historical practices by rhetoric does not shape practices so much as reflect their ongoing operations.[93] Change occurs not through the projects implemented by a subject possessed of critical self-consciousness, but as a byproduct of the unpredictable and evolving practices about which theorists make their claim. Fish argues that it is impossible to achieve the sufficiently critical self-consciousness necessary to direct the practices in which we are enmeshed, concluding that

> change cannot be engineered because persuasion is a contingent rather than a formal matter. . . . One can, of course, set out to persuade someone else, but both the career and the success of that effort will be unpredictable; you can never be sure what will work, or if anything will . . .
>
> If change cannot be engineered, neither can it be stopped.

> The failure of critical self-consciousness is a failure without consequences since everything it would achieve—change, the undoing of the status quo, the redistribution of power and authority, the emergence of new forms of action—is already achieved by the ordinary and everyday efforts by which, in innumerable situations, large and small, each of us attempts to alter the beliefs of another.[94]

Fish's approach has parallels in contemporary law-as-literature/law-as-narrative accounts, which present legal practice as a mode of storytelling that is not susceptible to theoretical elaboration. For example, Lewis LaRue traces the rhetorical features of judicial narration in several well-known cases in support of his argument that constitutional law must be regarded as fiction in some important sense. LaRue's thesis is "that judicial opinions are filled with 'stories' that purport to be 'factual' but that instead are 'fictional,' and furthermore, that these 'fictions' could not be eliminated without crippling the legal enterprise."[95] When confronting the question that naturally follows from his thesis—"well then, how do we judge which fictional accounts are good stories?"—LaRue responds with an extended description of the masterful storytelling prowess displayed in Norman Maclean's final book.

> I hope that my exposition [of Maclean's book] has not made tedious that which is elegant, for I am convinced that reading Maclean can teach one more about storytelling than all of the theorizing past or future. Lawyers and judges who tell stories, which is to say, lawyers and judges, can learn much by contemplating [the techniques employed by Maclean].
>
> ----------
>
> To one who might be disappointed [that I end only with a recounting of Maclean's book], I ask, "Why are you disappointed? Do you want a theory that distinguishes good stories from bad?"
>
> ----------
>
> [The] topic of language as a whole is too rich and too open-ended to permit good theories. By analogy, I judge that the topic of storytelling in law is likewise not the sort of practice about which there can be a theory.[96]

Fish and LaRue find theory unavailing against the rich rhetorical practices of law, and they regard the invocation of theory as misguided not because theory is pernicious but because it is simply irrelevant. To complete the domination of theory by practice, Fish acknowledges that the rhetorical deployment of a theory of meaning—originalist theory, for example—can be influential only if it is acknowledged as a move within the rhetorical practices under study, and never as a supra-practical guide.[97]

The antitheory theories of Fish and LaRue are undermined by their own rhetorical performances, however, since neither is content to leave legal practice to its own devices nor to regard practicing law as the only means of affecting legal practice. Both Fish and LaRue use a disarming rhetorical device—humility about the persuasive qualities of one's own project—to seek the adherence of their audience to their reconstructions of legal practice. The consequence of their rejection of theory is an ironic portrait of rhetorically engaged legal actors who somehow remain unaffected by the rhetorical injunctions of theory. They err by not taking seriously the idea that legal theory is a rhetorical practice and by not acknowledging that their own rhetorical efforts are theories about legal practice. The fact that LaRue wrote his book demonstrates that he regards it as more than just one story among many; he plainly regards it as a more convincing story than the received wisdom provides, a story with the potential to have consequences in the world. Although Fish correctly identifies the inevitable critical component of rhetorical practices, his effort to leave critique mysteriously and incorrigibly situated in these practices falls flat. By regarding the rhetorical claims of theoretical discourse either as one of the rhetorical resources of legal practice or as a wholly distinct academic practice, Fish misses the means by which a rhetorical claim can be about a practice without being either wholly within the practice or anchored in an extra-practice ideality. Both Fish and LaRue engage legal practice theoretically by describing the rhetorical nature of legal practice, even as they disavow theory's overblown claim to direct, justify, or rationalize practice from without. Lacking in their accounts is a description of how a practice-grounded, postmodern theoretical critique operates as an emanation from the critical experience of everyday practices. The concept of rhetorical knowledge demands a positive account of postmodern theory as an emancipatory rhetorical practice.

Offering an interesting image to emphasize the rhetorical nature of philosophical reflection, Gadamer delivers a pithy critique of the analytic tradition's effort to secure in language one last stronghold for classical theory while also rejecting the literary abandonment of philosophy. During an interview about his teaching, Gadamer noted that his classes do not appear sufficiently "philosophical" to some, but he reaffirmed the epistemic value of his multivalent approach.

> Gadamer: I must add one thing: It seems that not many philosophers are attending these lectures of mine. Those who are now drawn to analytic philosophy speak of my lectures as being vague.
>
> Question: Yes, we know you have heard that before.
>
> Gadamer: Naturally, that is also the reproach that I see in critical reviews of my written work—that I am so vague in my expression. Yet the people who write that do not realize how flattered I feel. It is not so terribly easy to speak in such a way that many ideas are awakened in a person without his being hammered on the head.
>
> Question: Do you mean that to express one's self clearly and distinctly is not necessarily the right way?
>
> Gadamer: It may be a cultivated thing to eat with a knife and fork, but that is not the right approach in philosophy.[98]

The rhetoric of philosophical inquiry, like the rhetoric of legal practice, strives mightily to suppress its rhetoricity without success. The concept of rhetorical knowledge leads inevitably to the concept of the rhetoric of inquiry, thereby debunking the theorist's self-conceptions in the same way that it has debunked the lawyer's self-conceptions. This invites the literary-rhetorical-exegetical approach exemplified in Gadamer's hermeneutical philosophy, which properly can be characterized as a postmodern theory of how understanding occurs.[99]

Critical Legal Theory as an Emancipatory Rhetorical Practice

The legal critic who chooses to write in academic journals performs a task different from the practicing lawyer who writes legal arguments to be filed in court. Even if the traditional scholarly practice of reporting on doctrinal developments can be characterized as the preparation of a "generic" brief for use by practicing lawyers who encounter the point in question, the role of the legal critic who challenges existing doctrine or otherwise engages in more theoretical endeavors remains unclear. Theoretical reflection on practices seems to be a fundamental part of the human experience, but understanding the epistemic potential of theoretical critique is made more difficult by the postmodern disavowal of strong theory. In this environment of uncertainty, the notion of the "rhetoric of inquiry" provides a starting point for clarifying the role of theory by emphasizing that legal theorists seek rhetorical knowledge about the practice of law. Theory is a productive dimension of legal studies, not because it provides a rationalistic escape from legal practice but because it operates critically across the fragmented discourse of legal practice to foster rhetorical knowledge.

Thomas Farrell and Calvin Schrag proved reliable in developing the concept of rhetorical knowledge, and they offer additional valuable insight into the relationship between critical theory and rhetorical knowledge. Farrell acknowledges the paradox arising from the recognition that rhetorical engagement is the only means for reflecting on the sustaining power of public institutions to foster civic (that is, rhetorical) life but also that any such rhetorical engagement always already will be shaped by the institutions that it seeks to assess. "The question is, may rhetoric be liberating? May it, in other words, put us in touch with a range of issues and experience outside our normalized, received opinion, our doxa? And, paradoxically, can it do this through received opinion and the traditional resources of rhetoric?"[100] Farrell elaborates a rhetorical criticism by reading Habermas's strongest theoretical claims back into Habermas's earlier critique of the transformation of the modern public sphere in which validity claims are put to the test in discourse.[101] Rhetorical criticism—the assessment of particular rhetorical events—is enriched by a wider theoretical critique of how public institutions are complicit in both creating and limiting the public space for rhetorical engagement, which in turn is informed only by the actual rhetorical practices of a given society. Farrell sets out "to show that there is no contradiction between viewing rhetoric as a normalized, institutional practice and admitting within it the possibility of new orders of realization."[102] Critical insight arises from ongoing practices, leading Farrell to conclude that reason "involves facing up to what we have done, picking up the pieces, and moving on."[103] These insights guide his persuasive critique of Habermas's universal pragmatics by drawing out the latent ambivalence in Habermas's more recent work. "We find Habermas conceding, whether by accident or design, that a domain of ideality may emerge from practice, in addition to being imposed on it. . . . Rhetoric is the primary—indeed, the only—humane manner for an argumentative culture to sustain public institutions that reflect on themselves, that learn, so to speak, from their own history. The more difficult question, of course, is how rhetoric may do this in any normatively reliable way, given the severe difficulties and distortions in many of these institutions."[104] Farrell readily concedes that an acontextual theory cannot be pulled off the shelf and pressed into service as a standard against which to test social institutions, but he reaffirms the possibilities opened by a critically motivated rhetorical reconception of practices. Offering Betty Friedan's *The Feminine Mystique* as one example of a successful rhetorical claim that linked theory and practice by means of an incisive criticism, he concludes "that the moment of truth in the best rhetoric comes when a larger vision is wedded clearly to both the critical judgment and the ordinary convictions of others, all at the same time."[105] Theory is not just practice dressed up with jargon; it is inter-practice argumentation about the field in which the practice plays itself out.

In similar fashion, Schrag argues that philosophical theorizing can disengage us from the immediacy of our rhetorical involvements sufficiently to foster insight, even though it cannot "put us in touch with the bottom of being or the ground of all meaning."[106] Under this more modest conception, reflection involves "not a move to another standpoint but ways of moving about in our everyday engagements" in a rational effort to reconfigure them.[107] Schrag explains that critical efforts emerge from the interplay of our collective practices in which we interpret, act, and express. No practice stands alone, and the multiplicity of practices provides a shifting repertoire of resources for reassessing a particular practice such as law as if from the outside. "Transversal communication possesses the resources for transhistorical assessment, evaluation, and critique without the problematic appeals to atemporal essences or transcendental conditions. . . . Socio-historical critique may indeed remain context-dependent, but this does not preclude an assessment, refiguration, or indeed overturn of different localized contexts as one discerns the play between and among them. Every context-dependency is situated within a wider context interdependency."[108] The theorist is not freed from rhetorical practices when she criticizes legal practice, but she is freed from the specific contours of legal practice by virtue of the rhetorical resources made available by the confluence of multiple human practices and discourses.[109] Farrell and Schrag both emphasize that theory is a rhetorical engagement across a variety of practices rather than an idealization that exists outside of practice.

Hans Kögler develops a similar account of political theory on the basis of Gadamer's hermeneutics, although surprisingly he does not draw from rhetorical theory. He agrees with Gadamer that all understanding, including theoretical reconstructions, is rooted in pre-understanding, but he conceives pre-understanding as the basis from which dialogic encounters proceed rather than a preexisting linguistic unity that anticipates consensus and assimilation.[110] The political theorist cannot escape her pre-understanding and achieve a god's-eye view of the symbolic structures of communication; nevertheless, critical distance emerges in the "break with the immediate self-understanding" that occurs "through the hermeneutic experience of other epochs and foreign cultures" in dialogue.[111] "An important alternative to the Gadamerian account here is the hermeneutically and dialogically possible recognition of a plurality of views, forms of life, and cultural projections of meaning. . . . Although this hermeneutic process may not ultimately lead to a single and newly shared view of what is true, the possibilities represented in alterity are nevertheless capable of challenging the structure of our customary assumptions and praxis."[112] Kögler emphasizes that in "critical interpretation, the reconstruction of the other and of her symbolic background serves as a critical foil from which to become, as it were, one's own other," through a process of "radical self-distanciation," and "that the critical-hermeneutic task [of the theorist] is to map the conceptual and methodological space in which such an interpretive practice of critical self-reflection can be most completely and productively achieved."[113] He thus proposes a "systematic use of the methodological fact of hermeneutic unfamiliarity."[114] While Kögler's fascination with methodological inquiry into social power structures betrays a Habermas-inspired optimism, his project is best conceived as providing the warrant for a theoretical critique and reconstruction of the institutionally and symbolically structured arena within which social actors seek rhetorical knowledge. Theorists do not provide answers from "outside" rhetorical engagement but instead analyze the possibilities for rhetorical engagement by cultivating a critical perspective on the social practices that shape these engagements.

These theorists converge in expressing a new understanding of the relationship between critical legal theory and cultural critique. The cultural context in which legal problems arise and are resolved inevitably is implicated in any critical enterprise, in two complementary respects. First, the changing cultural context inspires critical insight by providing distance from the commonplaces that define everyday practice. When access to higher education expanded dramatically at the same time that the diversity of the population was increasing, the "natural" approach to college admissions began to appear questionable under existing legal doctrine. Similarly, the rapid increase in the number of committed gay and lesbian partnerships that were visible to others in the community, coupled with an increasing level of activism seeking equal civil rights, shifted the perspective from which morals legislation was viewed. Second, an analysis of legal doctrine unavoidably puts cultural understandings into question by virtue of the nature of doctrinal challenges. In the affirmative action context, the notion that students should compete on fair and equal terms for admission to college generates an inquiry into the lived reality of fairness and equality in contemporary America, including the important role of the SAT in breaking down the "anti-merit old boy's network" even if now (unwittingly, perhaps) it has erected cultural criteria of its own. Similarly, the fragile substantive due process doctrine in constitutional jurisprudence mandates an initial inquiry into whether a "suspect class" has been disadvantaged by the law in question, leading to the Court's awkward discussion in *Lawrence* of the cultural significance of gay and lesbian partnerships in contemporary society.

The entwinement of cultural and legal critique does not mean that all cultural criticism operates as legal critique, or vice versa. Just as there is much to be gained by following the positivist insistence that we distinguish law and morality, it is important not to subsume legal criticism to cultural criticism. But just as law and morality have deep connections at the level of lived experience and theoretical inquiry, legal critique and cultural criticism are similarly connected. The concept of rhetorical knowledge highlights these connections while maintaining the distinctions by emphasizing that critical insight in practice is closely related to critical theorizing, but that the practices involved (legal versus cultural, for instance) may involve different audiences and distinct commonplaces.

This conception of critical theory as a practical rhetorical engagement can be sharpened by translating Nietzsche's cultural critique to the legal setting. Nietzsche's vital contribution to the theory of rhetorical knowledge is to move the analysis beyond identifying the critical dimension of practice and to focus on the work of critical legal theorists. Nietzsche never provided a critical theory of law,[115] but his philosophy provides substantial guidance when deployed as part of a description of rhetorical knowledge. Nietzsche's artist/social-critic provides a model for the activity of the lawgiver/legal-critic, who similarly must affirm life with a gay science that works genealogically rather than logically. Recent commentaries relate Nietzsche's cultural criticism to law in a creative manner that clarifies the role of critique in fostering the critical inventiveness that is an engine of rhetorical knowledge.

Roger Berkowitz draws lessons for Nietzsche's unstated legal philosophy from Nietzsche's commentary on the Code of Manu, after duly acknowledging that the historical documents used by Nietzsche have been thoroughly discredited.[116] Berkowitz argues that Nietzsche diagnosed the subordination of active lawgiving to a scientific-bureaucratic assessment of law as a tool to achieve collateral social ends. Nietzsche responded by seeking a return to a "creative and life-affirming positive law" that can no longer plausibly be grounded in abiding natural foundations nor in mere technical considerations, but rather is the accomplishment of the lawgiver who brings to voice the nature of dynamic social relations.[117] Law is necessarily a creative myth, but it is a myth that derives its legitimacy from its life-affirming characteristics, which is to say it derives its legitimacy by recognizing the natural divisions of society and refusing to participate in the politics of Ressentiment. "In short, what Nietzsche values in the Manu Code is the creative and artistic sanction of a natural and life-affirming inequality."[118] Berkowitz moves beyond Nietzsche's racist application of these themes and emphasizes the broader, philosophical point:[119]

> What Nietzsche stresses is not the specifics for any particular division of nature, but rather that nature—and with it life—demands distinction among men.
>
> ----------
>
> The ultimate end of the Manu Code must be the willful and artistic creation of a beautiful lie that makes the actuality of existence bearable.
>
> ----------
>
> The creative explosion of the art of legislation is the foundation for the positive establishment of any system of *Recht*. Positive law is, insofar as it is understood as a free and spontaneous work of art, paradoxically resistant to the efforts of the various legal sciences to subordinate law to social or political ends.[120]

Berkowitz's generous reading of Nietzsche accords with the naturalistic perspectivism that guided my reading of Nietzsche. Legitimate law is the product of a lawgiver who recognizes and advances the noble elements in a society through a positive legal mythology. The mythology expressed by the forces of Ressentiment is a "lie," no less than the lawgiver's creation, but Ressentiment is an unproductive lie that interferes with the vitality of will to power. Thus, the legal critic's project is to expose the role of the great lawgiver and to persuade one's contemporaries to abandon the unproductive myths that result from modernity's paradox that law is "an artifice that must deny its artificiality."[121]

Richard Weisberg also describes an incipient Nietzschean critical legal theory that celebrates the role of law and legal thinking. Weisberg works from *On the Genealogy of Morals*—which appears to be at once a pervasive attack on legal argumentation and an endorsement of law—to describe Nietzsche's subtle appreciation of the positive role of law.[122] Weisberg credits Nietzsche with upholding the integrity of legal documents crafted by lawgivers who are able to perceive and then facilitate the urge toward justice in a given society, and he foregrounds Nietzsche's attacks on those who would twist legal documents against their greatness. In this way, Weisberg focuses on Nietzsche's critical assessment of the hermeneutic reception of legal documents that have been rhetorically crafted by the artist-lawgiver described by Berkowitz.

Weisberg regards Nietzsche as a philosophical ally in his attacks against the deformations of Christian hermeneutics. Weisberg links early efforts by the disciples to manipulate the Torah to proclaim the coming Messiah to the recent legal hermeneutics of Vichy, France, which permitted Catholic lawyers to incorporate Naziism within the shell of the great French Civil Code. These bookends of Christian hermeneutics represent circumstances in which expediency subjects the code of a great lawgiver to an impatient reading for venal, and reactive, ends.[123] Christian hermeneutics not only overpowers the Jewish tradition of carefully reading and conserving the great Code, but it also equates the Jewish tradition with an excessive legalism that amounts to sacrilege.[124]

Weisberg is quick to assure us that Nietzsche does not counsel a blind literalism in legal traditions, for that would certainly undermine vitality. For example, the flexible hermeneutics of *Brown v. Board of Education* can be justified from a Nietzschean perspective by recalling that Nietzsche respects legal texts only "when both the original text and the interpretation that follows it are non-resentful and constitute for that reason worthy (and occasionally sacred) texts. If Brown is re-instantiating (against Plessy, specifically) the true interpretive intent of the Framers as to equality, then it is interpreting superbly according to the Nietzschean hermeneutic."[125] Similarly, Weisberg distinguishes the hermeneutic flexibility of the great Talmudic scholars (which he deems appropriately Nietzschean) from the complete disregard of all interpretive conventions by early Christian church fathers and Vichy lawyers, both of whom ignored the profundity of the Code and embodied Ressentiment.[126]

A Nietzschean critical legal theory carries forward his contribution to the model of rhetorical knowledge. Nietzsche embodies vigorous critical thinking, which is grounded by both the rhetorical and hermeneutical elements of rhetorical knowledge. Critical genealogies of law offer an alternative account of how the lawgiver can best capture the situation; they are a call to acknowledge the situation actively and positively rather than reactively. But the Nietzschean critic must also attend to the hermeneutical reception of the law by those who administer it and are subject to it. Law is a living force within society, and so the artistic creation of law must always be met by an artistic interpretation of the law. Just as Nietzsche's cultural criticism of religion proceeds from the dynamic ground of the model of rhetorical knowledge, legal critique is a development of the rhetorical knowledge at work in legal practice.

Weisberg's intriguing argument against overly flexible Christian hermeneutics but in favor of inventive Jewish hermeneutics is sensible when connected to the theory of rhetorical knowledge. Drawing the line between a subject-centered, monological imposition of meaning on a legal text and an inventive and dialogical understanding of a legal text is not accomplished methodologically. Instead, critical interventions by Nietzsche and Weisberg are rhetorically secured and validated. The theory of rhetorical knowledge shows why there is no safety net for the critic who argues that the legalisms of Vichy, France, were illegitimate and the innovations of *Brown v. Board of Education* were legitimate. This recognition does not diminish the power of critical arguments; it recognizes the source of their power.

Finally, Richard Sherwin has argued that Nietzsche's resolute affirmation of life and his refusal to engage in metaphysical flights of fancy bear important similarities to work by some of the most sophisticated legal thinkers of the Legal Realist era, including Benjamin Cardozo and Karl Llewellyn. But Sherwin emphasizes that these legal thinkers—a legendary common law judge and the author of the Sales article of the Uniform Commercial Code—show how law exceeds Nietzsche's suggestive ontological critique of metaphysics. In his opinions, Cardozo artfully "takes us into the midst of life. Lived experience rhetorically evoked, psychologically described, and ethically justified, bears the weight of judgment."[127] In the practical demands of legal judgment an ethical community is forged that tempers the lonely aspirations of the Nietzschean theorist. Law responds to the claims of persons and thereby "marks a shift from the purely aesthetic affirmation of Nietzsche's beatitude (love of what is in its totality) to the ethical aesthetic of law's beatitude (acknowledging the irreducible imperative of the naked countenance of the other before us). Therein lies the aspiration of law's beatitude, an aspiration that warrants law's legitimacy."[128] Sherwin thus brings the Nietzschean critic full circle back to the rhetorically sensitive and hermeneutically attuned experience of practicing law.

By bringing Nietzschean critique to bear on law, we can better appreciate that legal theory is an inquiry seeking rhetorical knowledge about the (rhetorical) practice of law. Theoretical inquiry proceeds in a number of different ways, but it can be broken down loosely into three different types of projects: doctrinal theory, critical theory, and philosophical theory. Doctrinal theory reconfigures some portion of existing legal doctrine in order to provide guidance to decision makers and to render practice more coherent and predictable. This effort involves more than mindlessly cataloguing and pigeonholing case precedents into established frameworks; it involves claims about the practice which seek to convince others of the utility of accepting the new characterization. Consequently, it has both descriptive and normative features. Doctrinal theory is distinguished from legal practice because it embraces a set of rhetorical tools beyond those defined by the pragmatics and institutional setting of practice, but it is closely related to the language of everyday practice.

An example of doctrinal theory is Lon Fuller's justly famous articulation of the underlying interests addressed by courts awarding damages for breach of contract. Fuller was not playing the role of a lawyer arguing that his client should receive a certain level of damages based on precedent; instead, he wrote as an academic to demonstrate that the self-understanding displayed in case precedents obscured the interests that actually were being taken into account when courts fashioned the measure of damages in particular cases. Fuller's theory about contract damages is not presented as a scientific finding about a certain factual database; rather, he makes a claim about existing practice that seeks to be a persuasive guide for clarifying and improving future practice. The intended audience of doctrinal theory is lawyers and judges: to provide the former with the understanding to make more persuasive claims in practice; to provide the latter with a better vocabulary for stating the law. Doctrinal theory is not just spinning a conceptual web of normative laws that purportedly govern the practice of law. Although such exercises can be intellectually challenging, they are far too abstracted from the rhetorical grip on practices that gives good doctrinal theory its power. Doctrinal theory inventively surveys existing representations of legal practice and the activity of lawyering in order to fashion a better representation.[129]

The second manifestation of theory is critical theory, which encompasses the theorist's effort to move beyond the doctrinal level of legal discourse in order to address the social, economic, and institutional patterns that shape legal discourse through linguistic and nonlinguistic means. Critical theory differs from doctrinal theory because it does not seek to clarify or develop doctrine but rather works to situate doctrine within broader practices that must be clarified and then challenged from a variety of perspectives. Critical theory generally is historically oriented and interdisciplinary in scope, because it reconstructs and contextualizes the seemingly self-contained dialogue of legal doctrine in a wider historical tapestry that generates themes and topics beyond those that find expression within legal dogmatics. One example of critical theory is Jay Feinman's reconstruction of the origins of the "at will" default rule regarding the duration of employment contracts.[130] Feinman links historical inquiry into the emergence and proliferation of the doctrine in nineteenth-century America to an understanding of economic, social, and political developments that shaped, directly or indirectly, this feature of legal practice.[131] In response, Deborah Ballam challenges Feinman's "orthodox" critical reading that the "at will" rule suddenly was adopted by courts amid the economic conditions of the nineteenth century, and she argues that the "at will" rule consistently was followed due to economic conditions that differentiated America from England as far back as the early colonial period.[132] Ballam's argument represents a competing critical theory, engaged in a rhetorical confrontation with Feinman's work in an attempt to secure the adherence of her (academic) audience. Critical theory thus represents a suspension of the "ordinary science" of legal practice to revive questions that never have been dealt with adequately or that have been placed beyond question after temporarily being resolved.

Critical intervention does not issue from a stable normative realm outside legal practice but rather emerges from the cross-practice inventions that result from interdisciplinary inquiry. A critical theory might be closely linked with a doctrinal theory, in which case its interdisciplinarity is suppressed in favor of fostering legal reform,[133] or a critical theory might be more closely tied to broader philosophical themes, in which case points of legal doctrine primarily will be discussed as examples of a wider thesis.[134] The intended audience for a critical theory largely determines its positioning on this continuum. At one end of the spectrum, the audience is composed of a small subset of practicing lawyers and judges for whom the critical argument might serve as a persuasive motivation to reargue basic features of the doctrinal landscape; at the other end, the audience is comprised of a small subset of academics who seek to problematize legal practice more generally. Critical theory affects legal practice when a rough consensus forms among prominent critics and translates to a new orientation or attitude among lawyers and judges. For example, it is now a commonplace in employment law cases effecting a change in doctrine for courts to historicize classical case law doctrine as representing a bygone social and economic structure, in part due to the efforts by Feinman and others to demystify the origins and purposes of the "at will" rule.[135]

Finally, philosophical theory represents claims about the nature of legal practice in the widest sense of explaining the practice of law as a whole. Traditionally, this involves a conceptual analysis that clarifies what we designate by the term "law" and develops the general features of a legal system. The premier example of a traditional philosophical theory in this century is H. L. A. Hart's exposition of the concept of law. More-recent works rooted firmly in the hermeneutic turn and the rise of postmodern thinking eschew conceptual analysis in favor of a phenomenological account of the epistemic dimension of law, with the goal being to capture the experience of legal actors by describing the experience of legal reasoning and assertions of legal authority rather than to clarify conceptual terminology.[136] Philosophical theory is only tangentially connected to day-to-day legal practice, and may make reference to legal doctrine only to supply a clarifying example in the course of a theoretical reconstruction. Philosophical theory often is more closely related to critical theory, since a philosophical orientation might yield critical insight into features of legal practice, but it also can connect with doctrinal theory and legal practice. Arthur Corbin's wonderful article challenging traditional applications of the parol evidence rule is a case in point. Corbin propounds the "context" theory of meaning in the course of arguing against traditional applications of the parol evidence rule, criticizing courts for feeling constrained by the "semantic stone wall" of plain textual meaning instead of recognizing that the meaning of words depends on "verbal context and surrounding circumstances and purposes in view of the linguistic education and experience of their users and their hearers or readers (not excluding judges)."[137] But this deceptively doctrinal point is backed by a bold theoretical statement: "This is true whether the words are in a statute, a contract, a novel by Henry James, or a poem by Robert Browning. A word has no meaning apart from these factors; much less does it have an objective meaning, one true meaning."[138] Corbin's assertions, premised on his experience as a lawyer rather than on academic linguistic philosophy, are briefly stated before he offers an assessment and critique of the traditional application of the parol evidence rule by courts. Thus, Corbin's article is a work of philosophical theory regarding the nature of legal (and nonlegal) language that remains closely tied to ongoing doctrinal arguments in legal practice and whose intended audience is practicing lawyers and judges as much as legal academics.

Similarly, the storytelling/narrative movement that swept through the academy at the end of the twentieth century undoubtedly has effected a shift in the orientation and vocabulary of professors and casebook writers, and it may well slowly filter into general consciousness and partially shape some doctrinal elaboration. An interesting, even if highly aberrational, example can be found in a sentencing memorandum written by senior district judge Jack Weinstein. Weinstein begins by declaring that his memorandum "is largely devoted to explaining how a sentencing judge—and a trier of fact generally—reaches a decision. The case presents an opportunity to observe, explain, and discuss forensic decision-making."[139] Weinstein acknowledges that "storytelling" techniques figure into the trier's method of reaching a conclusion on the basis of proffered items of evidence, and he assesses the record, in part, as a story.[140] Judge Weinstein was prompted to draft an extensive and exhaustive explanation of his decision-making process when the sentence originally imposed by him was vacated on appeal for lack of an evidentiary basis. The court of appeals had held that Judge Weinstein improperly determined that a drug smuggler's sentence could be based on the quantity of drugs discovered when the smuggler was arrested, multiplied by the number of smuggling trips taken before he was captured. After Judge Weinstein reimposed the same sentence and filed his lengthy justification, the court of appeals again vacated the sentence, but not before conceding (tongue in cheek?) that "his comprehensive opinion is a valuable addition to the legal literature on the subject of evidence in particular and judicial decisionmaking in general."[141] The jurisprudential implications of this exchange are raised to the level of surface discourse and are none too small. It is unavoidable that one would respond to this invocation of the narrative movement by asking how a higher court reviews the trial judge's "story" about the defendant's "story," and also how a trial judge can be honest about the nature of his decision-making process while still remaining within the framework of legal practice as it is traditionally understood.

It is helpful to explore the rhetorical dimension of each of these theoretical practices and to reaffirm the usefulness of each mode of theorizing. In no case does the theorist escape from rhetorical practice to the high ground of theoretical laws, but the theorist is also not just practicing law or engaging in a wholly distinct academic practice. Legal theory is a rhetorical practice that opens legal practice to other practices and discourses, and so the linkage of legal theory and legal practice remains indissoluble even though the two never collapse into a unitary practice. It would be a mistake to construct a hierarchy of relationships—for instance, practice is "real," doctrinal theory less so, all the way "up" to "abstract" philosophical theory—because these modalities of theory are interwoven in a continuous fabric of argumentative deliberation that has intrinsic connections with legal practice. It would be foolish to leave legal practice to its own devices to foster justice, because the rhetorical challenges and clarifications that foster critical invention in practice are given vitality through a vigorous theoretical discourse that feeds on the rhetorical dynamism of practice.

It should be clear that legal theory conceived as an expression of rhetorical knowledge is differentiated from the model of scientific theory. Although legal theorizing often invokes logical and empirical support within the course of argumentation, legal theory never will achieve the status of a scientific theory with strong claims to representational and predictive values. Thus, the law and economics movement during the past several decades can best be understood as a theoretical effort to deliver rhetorical knowledge rather than as an attempt to ground legal theory in scientific theory. Law and economics is a conjunction of all three types of legal theory, since it includes descriptive accounts of a purported internal logic of doctrinal development, critical accounts of legal discourse from more broad-based social understandings of political economy, and (increasingly) philosophical accounts of the nature of human interaction and communication. The empirical, economic, and sociological claims prominent in this theorizing represent an inter-practice rhetorical engagement rather than the subjugation of legal practice by economic "science." Thus, one would not confuse judicial opinions written by Judge Richard Posner with his law and economics scholarship, nor would one confuse his books with economic scholarship. Posner is a legal theorist and judge who utilizes doctrinal theory and critical theory that relies on economic claims deployed within broader argumentation. The scare quotes around "science" signal the obvious: much of economics is rhetorically secured rather than logical-empirical.[142] This helps to explain why economics has found such a strong connection with legal theory and even legal practice. Economics, thus construed, lends important insights to legal theory.[143] Rhetorical claims in favor of efficiency and rational allocation undoubtedly have had a strong influence on legal practice, but this influence is secured rhetorically no less than the influence of conceptions such as democracy and liberty, even though the economic concepts being employed lay claim to scientific-empirical status. Legal theory is not reducible to the more specialized mode of reasoning employed in academic economic theory, but economic theory plainly plays a role in the types of legal theory described above.

By refusing to be co-opted by the grandiose claims of scientific rationality, legal theorists are not consigned to unreasoning speculations divorced from empirical claims and objective knowledge. The rhetorical nature of legal theory does not mean that it is a subjective undertaking, any more than the rhetorical nature of legal practice means that legal reasoning or adjudication are subjective activities. Theorists can lay claim to providing a better description or critique of legal practice even as they acknowledge the rhetorical dimension of their activity. Of course, if one accepts the philosophical theory outlined in this paper, a theorist will be more persuasive to the extent that she explicitly embraces the rhetorical character of her theory. The urge to overreach the rhetorical possibilities of theory is strong, and often it is manifested by a theorist's grandiose effort to merge philosophical, critical, and doctrinal theory into a single compelling argument.[144] Although such grand efforts can themselves be important rhetorical interventions and are not unproductive per se, a legal theorist, no less than a conversation partner, needs above all to retain a sense of limit and humility.

Steven Mailloux has elaborated a self-reflexive definition of rhetorical theory that upholds the possibility of having an emancipatory effect without presuming an eschatological dialectic or an indubitable ground of critique. Mailloux wants to have his antifoundationalism and his theory, too, by incorporating the "philosophical insights of neopragmatism without falling into a relativist despair or political quietism."[145] As one critic summarizes, "exploring realms of practice, including theory itself, remains not only possible but imperative" in the absence of foundational guarantees, and Mailloux argues successfully that "there is a role for theory redefined: that, in fact, the theorizing *is* the process of historicizing interpretive practices."[146] As Mailloux explains, under "rhetorical hermeneutics the traditional distinction between doing theory and doing history breaks down. . . . Rhetorical histories thus replace foundationalist theory."[147] Noting the intersection of Gadamer's philosophical hermeneutics and Perelman's new rhetoric in the concept of traditionary force,[148] Mailloux argues that theory involves a historical project in several senses. Theory is the recovery of the "historical sets of topics, arguments, tropes, ideologies, and so forth which determine how texts are established as meaningful through rhetorical exchanges" by describing "the historical circumstances of various rhetorical exchanges," but simultaneously it must also locate "itself within, not above, its own history" by reconstructing its "agonistic relationship to other theories."[149] Applied to the legal context, a critical theory would be thoroughly rhetorical only if it situated itself within the realm of critical theories as a means of orienting itself to a persuasive historical reconstruction of a setting within which legal rhetorics play out. Kathryn Abrams's argument for a "reasonable woman" standard in sexual harassment law provides one example of a thoroughly rhetorical critical theory, especially in light of her subsequent reconsideration of some of her theoretical claims and their implementation by some courts.[150]

And so, to Professor LaRue's rebuke—"Do you want a theory that distinguishes good stories from bad?"—one might respond, "yes and no." The hermeneutical and rhetorical dimension of human understanding precludes a master theory that can regulate rhetorical exchanges according to criteria that remain above question. But it is equally a mistake to underestimate the significance that theorizing holds for the practice of law. Theory and practice are distinguishable but not distinct. Rhetorical knowledge is sought in ongoing practical and theoretical engagements that always place demands on the lawyer, judge, or theorist by posing questions.[151] One can hardly imagine the law without natural law, legal positivism, legal realism, critical theory (including feminism and critical race theory), law and economics, or pragmatism. To deride these theoretical projects as just stories is to undervalue the power of rhetorical knowledge. To deride these theoretical projects as stories entirely distinct from the practice of law is to undervalue the rhetorical openness of the practice of law.

A Research Agenda to Facilitate Rhetorical Knowledge

Mailloux's description of a rhetorical theory is clarified by recasting it in terms of the three types of legal theory identified above. A multifaceted but integrated legal theory in the sense proposed by Mailloux would entail several different projects. It is rare for a single theorist to provide a historical reconstruction and persuasive argument that encompasses all three types of theory simultaneously, and so this schema is offered as an orientation from which scholars might pursue more narrowly tailored inquiries. Philosophical legal theory takes account of the rhetorical, hermeneutical, deconstructive, and linguistic features of the communicative exchanges comprising legal practice, thereby developing an account of the capabilities that enable legal practice to move forward. Critical legal theory dislodges doctrine from its ethereal conceptual realm and resituates it in the institutional and cultural settings that serve as the forum for the communicative possibilities identified in philosophical theory, thereby exposing how rhetorical capabilities are facilitated and hindered in practice and tracing the effects of institutional influences on the actions of legal actors. Doctrinal legal theory moves within doctrinal ambiguities and contradictions to create opportunities for new deployments of commonplaces in response to changing needs and conceptions. There is no earth-shaking revelation in this account, but if these projects coalesce as part of a wider rhetorical project of theorizing about law, they will maximize their persuasive power and provide impetus for change.

Gadamer and Perelman both make "openness to reconsideration" a hallmark of their philosophies, and this maxim serves as the only normative guide that philosophical theory can provide to practitioners and to theorists. Hermeneutical openness is a confused notion that does not lead to logically deduced prescriptions, especially when the ideal of openness is informed by an understanding of rhetorical activity. However, hermeneutical openness can serve as a theoretical commonplace that can be incredibly productive for the foreseeable future. Theorists can translate the philosophical norm of hermeneutical openness (which is subject to further elaboration by means of philosophical theory) into a research agenda for continued critical theory and doctrinal theory. This agenda does not require a completely new form of scholarship; instead, it provides a new context and guiding force to disparate scholarly endeavors already under way, promising to deliver the elusive and much-sought-after synthesis of theoretical discourse.

Ed Rubin's proposal for a new paradigm of legal scholarship serves as a good starting point for exploring the potential that the concept of rhetorical knowledge holds for defining a new research agenda. Rubin argues that a commitment to the "microanalysis of institutions" might provide sufficient "common ground" to overcome the current "conceptual disarray of legal scholarship," much in the same manner that the Legal Process synthesis was able to overcome the unsettling effects of Legal Realism.[152] Rubin demonstrates that both law and economics scholarship and contemporary critical theory (especially "outsider" scholarship) have preserved some of the core tenets of Legal Process, even as they speak past each other. "They both are concerned with practical problems of governance, they both focus on the relative effectiveness of institutions in solving these problems, and they both display a particular concern with the judiciary and with the mechanism of legal rights."[153] Admitting that the political motives of the adherents of both perspectives widely diverge, Rubin nevertheless believes that a synthesis on the level of methodology may be possible because the underlying disciplines that inform these schools of legal theory—economics and critical sociology—have begun to converge on institutional analysis as a method of inquiry. However, Rubin paints a rather fanciful picture of the substantive features of such a new synthesis, suggesting that the debate over the competing norms of efficiency and social justice would be a productive focal point for the assessment of public institutions, since the new synthesis would mandate a broad and inclusive representation of all views in the debate.[154] The problem with Rubin's account is that it lacks any justification for, or description of, a broadly inclusive debate that would address specific instances of the question "how much justice should be purchased at the cost of how much efficiency?"[155] nor does he explain why his framing of the question exhibits a thoroughly economic approach to the clash of values by seeking an efficient trade-off between achieving social justice and maximizing economic efficiency.

The concept of rhetorical knowledge supplies a necessary emendation of Rubin's proposed new synthesis. Philosophical elucidation of the rhetorical knowledge at work in legal practice and legal theory provides the backing for the claim that open argumentation over conflicting values is the appropriate "methodology" for scholarly inquiry. Moreover, this philosophical orientation ensures that no theorist labors under the mistaken impression that there is a fixed optimum balance of these incommensurable values, thereby reinforcing the thesis that a vibrant rhetorical practice is the end rather than simply the methodology of inquiry. In some respects the concept of rhetorical knowledge only renders the assumptions of Rubin's argument explicit, but important clarifications also follow from this explicit grounding.

Gadamer has long been challenged by his critics to attend more to the institutional and cultural setting of interpretive activities, and Georgia Warnke has led the way by pursuing this inquiry without relapsing into Habermasian grand theory. The new rhetoric often has found its disciplinary home in departments of communication studies, with the result that scholars such as Thomas Farrell have pursued the new rhetoric with a focus on the institutional settings of public rhetorical engagements. In this intellectual environment it should be plain that the concept of rhetorical knowledge invites precisely the focus on the "microanalysis of institutions" that Rubin sees as a unifying theme of contemporary scholarship, but it does so in a manner that provides more concentrated guidance.

Legal institutions can and should be tested against the criterion of facilitating rhetorical knowledge. The resulting inquiry would consist of an interplay between participants in the legal system arguing that their claims are receiving insufficient attention and legal theorists arguing about the capacity for legal institutions to address competing claims successfully. Rubin suggests that the debate over mandated access to banking services in poor communities serves as an example of an issue that is better addressed under the rubric of a microanalysis of institutions, and he argues that practical analyses of how various proposals would play out in the real world will clarify the inherent trade-off between social justice and economic efficiency.[156] But this manner of synthesis begins by accepting relatively stagnant perspectives that must be integrated in a pluralistic solution to the problem of community banking—precisely the type of substantive compromise that increasingly seems implausible, notwithstanding the shared focus on the microanalysis of institutions. By developing the concept of rhetorical knowledge as the starting point of theoretical inquiry, legal theorists can eschew the urge to synthesize their work in favor of orienting it toward a continual self-reflexive mode of challenges and argumentation.

Working from the concept of rhetorical knowledge, critical legal theorists should track the rhetorical constructions embodied in law and economics scholarship and critical race theory as potentially fruitful inventions that can always be challenged and interrogated, both internally and by other discourses. The purpose of legal theory is not to reach consensus by fashioning a compromise between views but rather to foster interdisciplinary dialogue that unsettles the (sometimes) unproductive commonplaces that have evolved in each school of thought. A doctrinal theorist should elaborate these themes by exploring the complex rhetorical devices at work in legislative debates, regulatory rule making, and judicial lawmaking, thereby uncovering the doctrinal tensions that invite inventive responses in light of changing circumstances. A unified research agenda should not be purchased at the cost of a settled scale of values; it should be manifested in the effort to uncover previously suppressed assumptions in the process of revisiting the hierarchy of values implicit in legal practice at any given time.[157]

A microanalysis of legal institutions informed by the concept of rhetorical knowledge would not pursue a dubious cost-benefit analysis of incommensurable values but rather would seek to render rhetorical practices relatively more transparent and therefore subject to more vigorous reassessment. Consider a simple problem within contemporary contract law doctrine: the ubiquitous use of standard form contracts that are rarely read, and even more rarely understood, by the parties purportedly bound by them. An array of doctrinal topics (including the "duty to read," the parol evidence rule, and the defense of unilateral mistake) connects with more general principles (including the modified-objective theory of interpretation, the need for certain and predictable relational obligations, and the concern for overreaching by more sophisticated parties) in a variety of contexts (the sale of insurance policies, routine transactions with car repair shops, and the sale of supplies by one business to another) to raise this problem as an issue requiring resolution. A theoretical reconstruction that is too specific would lose sight of the degree to which the rhetoric of contract law writ large figures into the specific contextual rules of dealing with form contracts, but a grand theory of the underlying principles of contract law misses the variety of responses taken by legislatures, regulators, and courts in these different contexts. This project necessarily brings a wide range of rhetorical claims within its scope, from linguistic analyses of how clear the meaning of an insurance policy is for a speaker having average native competence in the English language to a philosophical inquiry into the nature of interpretation. The principal question would be how social and legal institutions facilitate the generation of rhetorical knowledge about competing claims regarding whether persons should be deemed contractually bound under certain circumstances. The factors to be balanced, and not just the balancing itself, are thrown open to question by this reorientation.

It is not difficult to reconceive much of contemporary legal theory in terms of this broad description of an agenda for research informed by the theory of rhetorical knowledge. Perhaps the most pressing need in legal theory is to develop a sophisticated account of the dynamic conceptual structure of legal argumentation practiced by lawyers and judges and a corresponding account of the conceptual structure of argumentation practiced by legal theorists. Perelman's effort to catalogue the principal argumentation forms is being continually refined and extended by rhetorical scholars.[158] These investigations may provide extremely useful guidance that will gird a new description of legal theory that comports with the postmodern account of rhetorical knowledge that I have constructed based on Gadamer's philosophical hermeneutics, Perelman's new rhetoric, and Nietzsche's naturalist perspectivism.

Conclusion

Joining Gadamer, Perelman, and Nietzsche in Dialogue

> How do I know what I think till I see what I say, somebody asks, kidding the Philistines. But I can't think the question so stupid. How do I know what I think unless I have seen what I say?
>
> *Wallace Stegner*
> *All the Little Live Things*

I conclude that we must join Gadamer, Perelman, and Nietzsche in dialogue. This seemingly straightforward conclusion should be understood in several different ways. In one sense, we can clarify the nature of rhetorical knowledge by joining together the philosophical investigations of these three thinkers. Combining the insights of philosophical hermeneutics, the new rhetoric, and Nietzschean critique generates a more persuasive account of rhetorical knowledge by emphasizing synergistic features of each approach. The critical dimension of hermeneutical understanding is underscored by Gadamer's focus on the inventiveness of conversational discourse, and the critical bite of rhetorical inquiry emerges from Perelman's careful refusal to permit his inquiry to collapse into crude methodologism. These critical openings are clarified by challenging them with the radical critique embodied by Nietzsche. Nietzsche exemplifies the critical theorist working rhetorically rather than demonstratively, but his critical exuberance also leaves many fundamental questions confused or unanswered. When we join the complementary projects undertaken by Gadamer and Perelman, and then subject them to interrogation by Nietzsche, a more complete and persuasive picture of rhetorical knowledge emerges.

My conclusion also can be understood in a different and more challenging manner, although this alternative meaning becomes apparent only in light of the argument in this book. Rhetorical knowledge is gained when I join with Gadamer, Perelman, and Nietzsche to investigate how we participate in legal practice and how we persuade others of our resulting understandings. By attending to the various arguments, general themes, and evocative styles in numerous texts authored by Gadamer, Perelman, Nietzsche, and those who draw inspiration from them, I have attempted in this book to embody hermeneutical understanding. In this sense, one joins these thinkers not as one would join lengths of pipe to create a new fixture, but as one would join an ongoing conversation with the aim of learning from one's conversation partners.

This latter sense of "joining" is deeper still, especially when one's interlocutors speak only through texts that must be hermeneutically appropriated. Developing arguments from textual sources always involves an inventive reordering and emendation by the reader that is responsive to the rhetorical power of the texts. By joining together the arguments of various thinkers, one necessarily joins them in a conversational give-and-take that is best described as a rhetorical engagement, rather than as a passive absorption of the wisdom of the text. This is not an esoteric or invariably profound experience; this is what a good lawyer does every time she writes a brief. Hermeneutical appropriation and rhetorical elaboration define legal reasoning; consequently, legal reasoning is a practical engagement that gives rise to critical insight that only later seeks to interrogate this practice as if from outside the practice. This book is my lawyer's brief: if successful, it will enact the hermeneutical and rhetorical themes that I discuss by modeling the hermeneutical openness and the rhetorical inventiveness that girds my model of rhetorical knowledge. I cannot hope to overpower my readers with a demonstration of the correct answers to the dilemmas of contemporary legal theory, but I can aspire to provoke them to follow a path of thinking that has yielded knowledge for me, or perhaps at a minimum to inspire them to forge a more productive path in response to my failure.

Rhetorical knowledge is a productive starting point for thinking about legal practice and legal theory. Proceeding from this orientation, theorists will be better equipped to explore the rich potential for achieving knowledge in the practice and critical appraisal of law. I have described the concept of rhetorical knowledge in some detail, but there are no simple solutions, nor can I invoke any special claim to authority beyond my ability to deliver a persuasive account. It seems fitting, then, to conclude by recalling Gadamer's description of the role played by the philosopher, for it is his circumspect and pragmatic rhetorical insight that in the end must inform every sophisticated theoretical undertaking that seeks to be relevant to the living community about which it speaks.

> [Philosophical hermeneutics] limits the position of the philosopher in the modern world. However much he may be called to draw radical inferences from everything, the role of prophet, of Cassandra, of preacher, or of know-it-all does not suit him.
>
> What man needs is not just the persistent posing of ultimate questions, but the sense of what is feasible, what is possible, what is correct, here and now. The philosopher of all people, must, I think, be aware of the tension between what he claims to achieve and the reality in which he finds himself.
>
> ----------
>
> But I will stop here. The ongoing dialogue permits no final conclusion. It would be a poor hermeneuticist who thought he could have, or had to have, the last word.[1]

Notes

Introduction

Epigraphs. The following copyright holders granted express permission or acknowledged fair use for the excerpts used as epigraphs in this introduction: Aspen Publishers for an excerpt from page 126 of Mieczyslaw Maneli, *Perelman's New Rhetoric as Philosophy and Methodology for the Next Century* (Dordrecht, Holland: Kluwer, 1994); *Yale Journal of Law and the Humanities* and Fred Dallmayr for excerpts from pages 507, 508, 520, 524, and 514 of Fred Dallmayr, "Self and Other: Gadamer and the Hermeneutics of Difference," 5 *Yale Journal of Law and the Humanities* 507 (1993); and the Regents of the University of California for excerpts from pages 61 and 67 of Christoph Cox, *Nietzsche: Naturalism and Interpretation* (Berkeley: University of California Press, 1999).

1. In particular, conservative groups immediately began a public relations campaign designed to persuade President Bush not to nominate White House counsel Alberto Gonzales to fill an expected Supreme Court vacancy, given Gonzales's moderate support of affirmative action (Dinan and Hallow). This sentiment immediately carried over to other decisive issues such as abortion, with conservative groups again finding fault with Gonzales for lending support to the recent liberal rulings (Hurt). When Justice Sandra Day O'Connor announced her retirement in 2005, conservative groups again insisted that Gonzales, then attorney general, would be an inappropriate selection for the Court.

Chapter 1

Epigraph. The following copyright holder granted express permission or acknowledged fair use for the excerpt used as an epigraph in this chapter: Yale University Press for an excerpt from page xx of Walter Jost and Michael J. Hyde, "Prologue," in *Rhetoric and Hermeneutics in Our Time: A Reader,* ed. Walter Jost and Michael J. Hyde (New Haven: Yale University Press, 1997).

1. Gadamer, *Truth and Method* xxviii–xxix.

2. Gadamer, *Truth and Method* 231–42, 254–64.

3. Gadamer, *Truth and Method* 264. Gadamer describes his philosophical project as working through the implications for hermeneutical philosophy of Heidegger's radical undermining of scientistic ideology.

4. Gadamer writes: "Philosophical hermeneutics takes as its task the opening up of the hermeneutical dimension in its full scope, showing its fundamental significance for our entire understanding of the world and thus for all the various forms in which this understanding manifests itself: from interhuman communication to manipulation of society; from personal experience by the individual in society to the way in which he encounters society; and from the tradition as it is built of religion and law, art and philosophy, to the revolutionary consciousness that unhinges tradition through emancipatory reflection" ("On the Scope and Function of Hermeneutical Reflection 18). See also Madison 25 ("Hermeneutical theory is a veritable crossroads"). In an autobiographical essay, Gadamer acknowledges that he derives a "special sort of satisfaction" from seeing his hermeneutical philosophy extended to various fields of inquiry ("Reflections" 17).

5. The overview of Gadamer's philosophy in this section is necessarily brief and conceptual. I have engaged in more detailed explorations of the relevance of philosophical hermeneutics to legal theory in a number of articles. See Mootz, "A Future Foretold: Neo-Aristotelian Praise of Postmodern Legal Theory"; "Psychotherapeutic Practice as a Model for Postmodern Legal Theory"; "Law in Flux: Philosophical Hermeneutics, Legal Argumentation, and the Natural Law Tradition"; "Rhetorical Knowledge in Legal Practice and Theory"; "Legal Classics: After Deconstructing the Legal Canon"; "Rethinking the Rule of Law: A Demonstration That the Obvious Is Plausible"; and "The Ontological Basis of Legal Hermeneutics: A Proposed Model of Inquiry Based on the Work of Gadamer, Habermas, and Ricoeur."

6. Gadamer, *Truth and Method* 383.

7. Gadamer, *Truth and Method* 385, 387–88.

8. Gadamer argues that it is a profound mistake to read the Platonic dialogues as embodying principled arguments that compel adherence, since they obviously fail on this level.

> It is unavoidable that philosophy, which never finds its object already at hand but must itself provide it, does not move within systems of propositions whose logical formalization and critical testing for conclusiveness and univocity might somehow deepen its insights. . . . To illustrate this point with an example, if one analyzes with logical methods the arguments in a Platonic dialogue, shows inconsistencies, fills in gaps, unmasks false deductions and so

> on, one can achieve a certain gain in clarity. But does one learn to read Plato by proceeding in this way? Does one make his questions one's own? Does one succeed in learning from Plato instead of just confirming one's own superiority? . . . Simple logical rigor is not everything. (Gadamer, "Reflections" 38–39)

Georgia Warnke carefully links Gadamer's analysis of conversation to his ontological claims about the dialogic structure of understanding, and she critically analyzes the remaining ambiguities in Gadamer's account (*Gadamer* 100–103, 168–71).

9. Gadamer, *Truth and Method* 270–71. Ironically, Gadamer invokes the idea of prejudice to challenge the overriding prejudice of Enlightenment thought, namely "the prejudice against prejudice itself, which denies tradition its power" (*Truth and Method* 270).

10. Gadamer, "Text and Interpretation" 26.

11. *Truth and Method* 312–24.

12. *Truth and Method* 388. It is important not to misunderstand Gadamer's analogy by concluding that the reader and the author each constitute a horizon, and that the "fusion" is just the reader's recovery of the author's intended meaning. A reader cannot even begin to hypothesize about the historical intentions of an author until she has engaged the text and allowed it to pose a question to her, which is the experience that Gadamer attempts to capture with his term "fusion of horizons." See Garrett.

13. *Truth and Method* 312–24.

14. In an interview at the end of his career, Gadamer acknowledges the importance to him of Heidegger's recuperation of Aristotle's *Rhetoric* but explains his lack of formal attention to rhetoric in his lectures and writings as simply a matter of not being "able to do everything" (Gadamer, "Heidegger as Rhetor: Hans-Georg Gadamer Interviewed by Ansgar Kemmann" 62).

15. *Truth and Method* 312–24.

16. Schaeffer 101.

17. Schaeffer 150–51.

18. Schaeffer's critique (117–22) is on point when he suggests that by employing a more explicitly rhetorical account Gadamer could have better responded to Jürgen Habermas's challenges without appearing to abandon the potential for critical theorizing.

> For Gadamer, tradition, and the prejudices of which it is composed, is revised by a dialectical interaction with texts, especially classical texts. For Vico, on the other hand, the *sensus communis* is revised by social action under the

influence of eloquence. It is not dialectic that challenges, but imagination that reconstellates, *sensus communis.*

> The hurly-burly of oral debate not only applies the *sensus communis* to concrete problems, but also tests and reshapes the *sensus communis* itself. The *sensus communis* cannot be merely a static set of values embodied in a literary canon. . . . The *sensus communis* is constantly reinterpreted and reshaped by the decisions of the community. Vico conceives of these decisions as constituting a kind of jurisprudence, a kind of developing interpretive context with which the values contained in classical texts meet the problems of daily life. In short, rhetoric transmits the *sensus communis;* eloquence transmutes it; the community tests it. (Schaeffer 114–15)

My argument, in chapter 2, under "Philosophical Hermeneutics and Critical Insight," is that Gadamer is best read as making just these claims.

19. *Truth and Method* 19–20.

20. *Truth and Method* 23–24.

21. *Truth and Method* 21.

22. Gadamer, "Relevance of the Beautiful" 17.

23. *Truth and Method* 19. Gadamer links ancient rhetoric with the lived experience of the life world in "Hermeneutics as a Theoretical and Practical Task" 119–22, and in "The Expressive Power of Language" 350.

24. Gadamer, Interview: "Writing and the Living Voice" 71; this text is based on interviews conducted in November 1983 and July 1986. See generally Gadamer, *Dialogue and Dialectic.*

25. Gadamer, "Expressive Power" 348.

26. *Truth and Method* 485.

27. Dockhorn 160.

28. Madison 164. By and large, the importance of the rhetorical tradition to the argument in *Truth and Method* was overlooked by commentators. However, Jean Grondin also places particular emphasis on Gadamer's use of the rhetorical tradition to elucidate "a concept of truth that remains aware of its attachment to human finitude" (49). See also Verene, "Gadamer and Vico on *Sensus Communis* and the Tradition of Humane Knowledge."

29. Gadamer, "The Phenomenological Movement" 114–18.

30. Bineham, "Displacing Descartes" 309.

31. Madison 32–35. See generally Gallagher, arguing that Gadamer follows Aristotle by distinguishing phronesis from the clever application of preexisting rules by defining it as the ability to "work out the rules for the situation" within a particular

"sub-discourse" or "conversation" (304); and Dascal, urging a cross-disciplinary encounter between the quasi-empirical focus of pragmatics in linguistic studies and the ontological focus of Gadamer's philosophical hermeneutics.

32. "On the Scope and Function" 20–25. Gadamer goes so far as to emphasize that "the rhetorical and hermeneutical aspects of human linguisticality completely interpenetrate each other" (25). He explains:

> Clearly the ability to speak has the same breadth and universality as the ability to understand and interpret . . . Hermeneutics may be precisely defined as the art of bringing what is said or written to speech again. What kind of art this is, then, we can learn from rhetoric.
>
> ----------
>
> [Because] the being of the interpreter pertains intrinsically to the being of what is to be interpreted . . . the orator always has to link up with something like [a prior, sustaining agreement] if his persuading and convincing in disputed questions is to succeed. So, too, any understanding of another's meaning, or that of a text, is encompassed by a context of mutual agreement, despite all possible miscomprehensions; and so too does any understanding strive for mutual agreement in and through all dissent. ("Hermeneutics as a Theoretical and Practical Task" 119, 136)

Gadamer cites Perelman's work in this passage, acknowledging that rhetorical studies are illuminating because the hermeneutical recovery of meaning is always predicated on the interpreter finding common ground with the text, much as an orator must find common ground with her audience in order to speak effectively.

33. Gadamer, "Expressive Power" 348; Gadamer, "Hermeneutics as a Theoretical and Practical Task" 123–24.

34. A similar account is given by H. P. Rickman, who contends that an effective lecture originally delivered to a specific, known audience—such as Aristotle's *Nicomachean Ethics*—presents entirely different challenges to the task of understanding when read by later audiences removed from the rhetorical immediacy of its original presentation (100–111). Rickman also looks to Vico as an important bridge for understanding this new dimension of rhetoric: "Vico's principle that the mind can understand what the human mind can create is the link which connects hermeneutics and rhetoric" (111). It is important not to misunderstand this insight, as Rickman perhaps does, by permitting it to devolve into Schleiermacher's narrow conception that hermeneutical recovery of meaning is the inverse of rhetorical production, in other words, that hermeneutics amounts to reconstructing the rhetorical intentions of the author. See Gadamer, *Truth and Method* 188–89. Rather, Gadamer argues that

the contemporary interpreter has more in common with the rhetor than with the audience, since the interpreter must render the text meaningful by establishing a shared basis of understanding from which to proceed (Dockhorn 168–69).

35. Gadamer, "Hermeneutics as a Theoretical and Practical Task" 93. Gadamer criticizes the dismissal of rhetoric as "ornate prattle" by modern scientific consciousness and recalls the central role of rhetoric in Greek democracy and Roman republicanism ("Culture and Media" 179–80).

36. Gadamer, "On the Scope and Function" 23–24.

37. Gadamer, "Hermeneutics as a Theoretical and Practical Task" 127. See generally Gadamer, *Truth and Method* 324–41 ("The Exemplary Significance of Legal Hermeneutics").

38. "Culture and Media" 188.

39. "Culture and Media" 177, 179.

40. Gadamer writes: "It is not only our tiny Europe or its appendages that are at issue. At stake now is a global human task and the question of what the living conditions and life expectations for humanity look like in the breathtaking technological development and transformation of the natural as well as of the social world" ("Culture and Media" 174).

41. Gadamer, *Truth and Method* xxxvii–xxxviii.

42. *Truth and Method* 567–69. Gadamer offers another extended discussion of rhetoric in the same context of defending his approach against Habermas's critique. In "On the Scope and Function of Hermeneutical Reflection," he demonstrates that the scientistic claims of critical sociology fail for the same reason that scientistic approaches to rhetoric and hermeneutics fail to capture the full scope of the experiences of persuasion and understanding. It is not happenstance that Gadamer invokes rhetoric extensively in the latter essay, since he is not only rebutting Habermas's critical theory but also absorbing and responding to Klaus Dockhorn's review of *Truth and Method.* Gadamer readily accepts Dockhorn's thesis that the entire argument of *Truth and Method* is suffused with the concepts of the rhetorical tradition (Gadamer, "On the Scope and Function" 43 nn. 3, 6, and 7); see Dockhorn 161, as a helpful clarification of his thesis. In more recent commentary on his philosophy, Gadamer highlights the rhetorical themes that guided his thinking, bringing to the forefront what earlier was only suggested. See Gadamer, "Reflections" 30; and Gadamer, "Reply to Donald Phillip Verene" 154–55.

43. *Truth and Method* 569 n. 27.

44. "On the Scope and Function" 23–24.

45. See "Praise of Theory." (The speech was originally given in Bonn on 3 June 1980.)

46. "Praise of Theory" 24.

47. Gadamer, "Science and the Public Sphere" 68. (Lecture originally given in Marburg in 1977.)

48. "Praise of Theory" 31.

49. Gadamer, "Hermeneutics as Practical Philosophy" 92. See also Gadamer, "Hermeneutics as a Theoretical and Practical Task" 113.

50. Gadamer summarizes his discussion of Aristotle: "[I]f we relate Aristotle's description of the ethical phenomenon, and especially the virtue of moral knowledge to our own investigation, we find that his analysis in fact offers a kind of *model of the problems of hermeneutics.* We too determined that application is neither a subsequent nor merely an occasional part of the phenomenon of understanding, but codetermines it as a whole from the beginning" (*Truth and Method* 324). I provide a more detailed exegesis and critique of Gadamer's reading of Aristotle on the connections between practice and theory in "A Future Foretold: Neo-Aristotelian Praise of Postmodern Theory."

51. Gadamer, "The Diversity of Europe: Inheritance and Future" 221.

52. *Truth and Method* 319–20.

53. *Truth and Method* 519.

54. *Justice and Interpretation* 12.

55. *Justice and Interpretation* viii.

56. *Justice and Interpretation* 133.

57. *Justice and Interpretation* 132, 137.

58. Warnke emphasizes: "Does the rationality of hermeneutic conversation require more [than remaining open to other discourses]? I have suggested that it does, for if we allow for systematically distorted interpretations of meaning, such as those offered of American history by the Ku Klux Klan, we cannot assume that all interpretive conversations will be equally educational" (*Justice and Interpretation* 160). Warnke argues that the purpose of political theory is to critique those features of society that render the political conversations of its inhabitants unfair and to bring to voice those perspectives that have been silenced (155).

59. Perelman, *The New Rhetoric and the Humanities: Essays on Rhetoric and Its Applications* 56; Conley 296–97; Dearin 156.

60. As Perelman puts the point, "Descartes claims that disagreement is both a sign of error and a lack of rationality" (*New Rhetoric and the Humanities* 112). Edgar Bodenheimer traces the intellectual legacy of Cartesian philosophy and Perelman's rejoinder (392–403).

61. Perelman, *New Rhetoric and the Humanities* 112.

62. *New Rhetoric and the Humanities* 125.

63. Perelman and Olbrechts-Tyteca, *The New Rhetoric: A Treatise on Argumentation* 1.

64. Perelman confirms that in "the debate between Plato and Aristotle, I have no

hesitation in placing myself on the side of Aristotle" (*Justice, Law, and Argument: Essays on Moral and Legal Reasoning* 88–89). Ever the iconoclast, I. F. Stone argued that Socrates was executed by Athens for the simple reason that he was an enemy of democracy and an open society, as particularly revealed in his denigration of rhetorical engagement as compared to Aristotle's more temperate and commonsensical approach (90–97). Stone notes that Socrates could easily have won acquittal by appealing to principles of free speech, but that "he would have found it repugnant to plead a principle in which he did not believe; free speech for him was the privilege of the enlightened few, not of the benighted many. He would not have wanted the democracy he rejected to win a moral victory by setting him free" (230). Even if the divergence between Socrates/Plato and Aristotle in their conceptions of a democratic, rhetorical public life was not this stark, Stone makes a persuasive case that an important divergence existed.

65. Perelman emphasizes that his "new rhetoric" is premised on the understanding that argumentation "is manifest in discussion as well as in debate, and it matters not whether the aim be the search for truth or the triumph of a cause, and the audience may have any degree of competence" (*New Rhetoric and the Humanities* 12). This marks a departure from Aristotle to the extent that Perelman rejects a clear distinction between dialectical reasoning and rhetorical persuasion. See Jacob 1641; Joy 276–77; and Grosse vii. This feature of Perelman's philosophy is debated in Crusius, criticizing Perelman for rejecting the distinction (23) and Bator, defending Perelman's battle against the "historical attempt to create a clear, albeit artificial distinction between dialectic and rhetoric" (43).

66. Perelman and Olbrechts-Tyteca 62. This position has been summarized in a variety of ways. See, e.g., Dearin 175 ("From Perelman's point of view, it is possible to justify both one's criteria and their application. Justification involves, simply, the securing of the adherence of the appropriate audience. The means by which this is achieved are the techniques of argument identified and exemplified in the new rhetoric."); and Pavcnik 482 ("It is between these two poles—absolute constraint and absolute freedom—that the field of argumentation lies.").

Perelman's lead has been followed by a number of scholars, as evidenced in recent definitions of rhetoric as reasoned argumentation. Douglas Walton writes:

> The analysis of argumentation schemes is very much affected by the recognition of practical reasoning as a distinctive type of reasoning, as distinguished from what might be called theoretical or discursive reasoning.
>
> ----------
>
> Practical reasoning is a goal-directed sequence of linked practical inferences that seeks out a prudent line of conduct for an agent in a set of particular circumstances known by the agent.

> In this pragmatic framework, two participants are reasoning together in a goal-directed, interactive, conventionalized framework called a dialogue. An argument is considered good (correct, reasonable) to the extent that it contributes to the goal of the dialogue. An argument is evaluated as bad (incorrect, fallacious) to the extent that it blocks the goals of the dialogue. (11, 1)

Cf. Eemeren, et al., who write, "Argumentation is a verbal and social activity of reason aimed at increasing (or decreasing) the acceptability of a controversial standpoint for the listener or reader, by putting forward a constellation of propositions intended to justify (or refute) the standpoint before a rational judge" (5).

67. Perelman and Olbrechts-Tyteca 62; Perelman, *New Rhetoric and the Humanities* 118–22; and Perelman, *Justice, Law, and Argument* 92.

68. Gaonkar 58.

69. Gaonkar 63 n. 13.

70. Perelman, *New Rhetoric and the Humanities* 117–18.

71. Perelman, *Justice, Law, and Argument* 59.

72. *New Rhetoric and the Humanities* 120, 121, 123.

73. *Justice, Law, and Argument* vii, 96–105; *New Rhetoric and the Humanities* 133–41.

74. *New Rhetoric and the Humanities* 31.

75. Perelman, *New Rhetoric and the Humanities* 82–89. Perelman's friend and collaborator, Mieczyslw Maneli, reports that Perelman was beginning to develop the ontological features of his approach just prior to his death (4). This biographical information confirms what is evident on the face of Perelman's writings: he was concerned with the lived experience of reasonable social interaction rather than with the more limited project of outlining a methodology for advancing that interaction through rhetorical analysis.

76. Perelman and Olbrechts-Tyteca 26; Perelman, *New Rhetoric and the Humanities* 43–45. Against the tendency to caricature the "Cartesian tradition" of rationality, it is necessary to recall that Jürgen Habermas argues strenuously against postmodern theory as the outcome of the rhetorical assault upon reason, and he offers a postmetaphysical defense of philosophy and rationality. See Habermas, *The Philosophical Discourse of Modernity.* The sophisticated challenges by critical theorists such as Habermas are taken up in chapter 2 of this book.

77. Perelman and Olbrechts-Tyteca 512; Perelman, *Justice, Law, and Argument* 108; and Maneli 28.

78. *Justice, Law, and Argument* 129; Maneli 85–95. As summarized by Donald Hermann, "While legal reasoning cannot be assimilated to formal logic nor utilize scientific demonstration, neither can it be dismissed as mere subjectivism and exercise of unrestrained power. The argumentation which is the ultimate method of legal rea-

soning necessarily employs reasons which are ultimately tested by their effect in persuading" (509).

79. According to Perelman and Olbrechts-Tyteca, "[o]nly the existence of an argumentation that is neither compelling nor arbitrary can give meaning to human freedom, a state in which a reasonable choice can be exercised" (514). Pavcnik argues that Dworkin's "right-answer thesis" cannot be sustained except as an aspirational recognition that legal decision making is "a responsible intellectual activity" and that legal decisions "are always responsible human acts, ones that create law in the fullest sense of the word" (502–4).

80. Perelman and Olbrechts-Tyteca 6–7. Perelman expressly disclaims an intent to follow an Aristotelian conception of rhetoric, seemingly adopting the prevailing view that "Aristotelian rhetoric—in spite of heroic twentieth-century efforts by a host of scholars to defend it as whole, good, noble, and necessary—is a degraded, low-class thing" (Neel 70). Perelman explains that his new rhetoric abandons the Aristotelian focus on a specific audience and moves beyond the development of techniques for persuading the ignoramuses in the public square (*New Rhetoric and the Humanities* 57–58).

Perelman's reading of Aristotle is widely accepted, but some scholars have argued that Aristotle's position is more subtle, and that he recognized to some degree the epistemic significance of civic discourse. Richard Burke argues that Aristotle's "*Rhetoric* along with his *Politics,* should be read as a justification of this assumption against both Plato's elitism and the cynicism of most prior teachers of rhetoric, who apparently taught it (as some advertising manuals do today) as an art of manipulating the emotions of the audience" (19). Burke's interpretation finds support in the following passage from Aristotle's *Rhetoric:*

> [O]ne should be able to argue persuasively on either side of a question, just as in the use of syllogisms, not that we may actually do both (for one should not persuade what is debased) but in order that it may not escape our notice what the real state of the case is and that we ourselves may be able to refute if another person uses speech unjustly. None of the other arts reasons in opposite directions; dialectic and rhetoric alone do this, for both are equally concerned with opposites. Of course the underlying facts are not equally good in each case; but true and better ones are by nature always more productive of good syllogisms and, in a word, more persuasive.
>
> ----------
>
> In addition [it is clear] that it is a function of one and the same art to see the persuasive and [to see] the apparently persuasive. (Aristotle, *On Rhetoric* 34–35 [1354b–1355a])

Aristotle's translator, George Kennedy, acknowledges the apparent incongruity of these passages with Aristotle's later emphasis on style and arousing the emotions (G. A. Kennedy 28). Eugene Garver persuasively demonstrates that the conflict arises only because contemporary readers are inattentive to Aristotle's claim that rhetoric is an ethical activity subordinate to politics and thus inevitably requires a judicious use of civic emotions in determining the proper course of action (*Aristotle's Rhetoric: An Art of Character* 104–38). As Garver explains:

> The emotions are the form in which we perceive practical particulars. In any but the easiest cases, it is not simple to determine whether the emotional coloring of an issue is enabling or corrupting. It is characteristic of the realm of praxis that there be no theoretical standpoint, outside the practical situation itself, for making such decisions.
>
> ----------
>
> [T]he need for rhetoric comes not from the weakness of audiences but from the complexity and indeterminacy of the world. The emotions can be constitutive of particular judgments because they are constitutive of the enterprise of judging and deliberating. (*Aristotle's Rhetoric* 106, 109)

Given the subject matter of deliberative rhetoric, not all appeals to emotions are illegitimate, but there are illegitimate uses of emotion. As two commentators aptly summarize, "rhetoric is, in terms of a minimal but classic definition, the art or science of persuasion. . . . Rhetoric, however, has always been more than merely the art of persuasion. . . . [I]t also represents certain philosophical assumptions about the nature of humanity" (Roberts and Good 2).

81. As Perelman explains, "wanting to convince someone always implies a certain modesty on the part of the initiator of the argument. . . . He acknowledges that he must use persuasion, think of arguments capable of acting on his interlocutor, show some concern for him, and be interested in his state of mind" (Perelman and Olbrechts-Tyteca 16). "Recourse to argumentation assumes the establishment of a community of minds, which, while it lasts, excludes the use of violence" (55).

82. Perelman and Olbrechts-Tyteca 17.

83. *New Rhetoric and the Humanities* 13–14.

84. *New Rhetoric and the Humanities* 48–50.

85. Perelman and Olbrechts-Tyteca 19.

86. See Berman xi ("Professor Perelman's 'universal audience' . . . is 'common sense' in the seventeenth-century English meaning of that phrase."); Crosswhite 166 (arguing that the universal audience "represents a '*sensus communis*' rather than being an abstraction that stands above the agreements reached by actually existing

groups"); Barker 484–85 (contrasting Perelman's use of audience with the abstract conceptual analysis dominant in philosophy generally and exemplified in Rawls's theory of justice).

87. Crosswhite emphasizes that the rhetor's comportment toward an "undefined universal audience" enables the rhetorical construction of a "universal audience" in the course of argumentation (170).

88. Perelman, "The New Rhetoric and the Rhetoricians: Remembrances and Comments" 191. William Kluback interprets Perelman's statement as a reference not to the power of the rhetor's subjective will but to the rhetor's participation in a tradition which pulls all participants toward idealizations while simultaneously preserving "the freedom and truth of the plurality of audiences in their limitations" (317, 326).

89. Alexy 160–63.

90. Crosswhite 172.

91. Conley 301–3.

92. Habermas, "Postscript to *Between Facts and Norms*" 144 n. 11.

93. Guy Haarscher compares the work of Perelman and Habermas in "Perelman and Habermas."

94. Perelman and Olbrechts-Tyteca 65–95.

95. Perelman, *Justice, Law, and Argument* 100, 61, 132.

96. Perelman describes commonplaces as storehouses for arguments that most generally pertain to the quality or quantity of the matter under discussion (Perelman and Olbrechts-Tyteca 83–95). The bulk of his treatise describes the various techniques of argumentation, such as using examples and analogies (185–508). Douglas Walton attempts to provide a tighter, systematic account of the proper use of argument forms than Perelman provides, although Walton shares Perelman's point of departure (Walton 46–110).

97. Perelman and Olbrechts-Tyteca 75, 85.

98. Perelman, *Justice, Law, and Argument* 169–70.

99. Perelman, *New Rhetoric and the Humanities* 131; Perelman, *Justice, Law, and Argument* 27–28 (construing the principle of inertia in legal practice as a central aspect of justice). Richard Burke emphasizes this same point by defending the rhetorical device of "appeal to authority" as a perfectly reasonable argument capable of persuading an audience (18). However, the informal logic at work in argumentation means that neither the application of this argument to particular disputes nor its probability of succeeding in persuading a particular audience can be charted in advance. "Instead of saying that an appeal to authority or majority opinion is fallacious unless certain other conditions are present, the textbooks should say that these are

plausible arguments, and therefore should persuade a rational person, unless a stronger argument to the contrary is available with a reasonable expenditure of time and effort" (Burke 24). For a general discussion of the argument from authority, see Perelman and Olbrechts-Tyteca 305–10. As Perelman notes, most attacks on arguing from authority in fact amount to attacks on the authority in question rather than on the nature of the argumentative strategy (307).

100. McBride 516–17; Bodenheimer 414–17.

101. Thus, although Perelman argues that "all audiences, of all kinds, have to take loci into account" (Perelman and Olbrechts-Tyteca 85), his claim that the inventive and responsive nature of rhetorical engagement opens the possibility for critique leads to the conclusion that "the opportunity for reconsideration, innovation, rejection, and amendment appears as a moment in the basic structure of every legal problem" (Jacob 1643). Perelman makes this same point in a different context, arguing that the commonplaces utilized by professional historians—the conception of historical periods and analytical perspective brought to bear on the data—can never be "entirely put aside [since the] only way to do without them is to replace them with others," but also emphasizing that the contingent quality of such periodization makes "dialogue among historians both possible and indispensable" (*New Rhetoric and the Humanities* 155–57).

102. Perelman, *New Rhetoric and the Humanities* 33. I have expanded this conception of natural law and drawn connections with contemporary legal theory in Mootz, "Law in Flux."

103. Perelman, *Justice, Law, and Argument* 125–29.

104. *Justice, Law, and Argument* 81.

105. *Justice, Law, and Argument* 98, 123, 125–26.

106. Hermann 469.

107. Perelman, *Justice, Law, and Argument* 38–39, 94, 127. As John Valauri emphasizes, Perelman does not oppose rules and equity as two distinct approaches; rather, he views them as two necessary features of a unified legal practice that may be deemed just (577–78).

108. Perelman, *Justice, Law, and Argument* 145.

109. Perelman repeats this theme throughout his collection of essays, but in particular see *Justice, Law, and Argument* 114–19, 146, 174.

110. Perelman contends that the philosopher makes arguments of a different type to the extent that she addresses the universal audience rather than addressing the participants in a lawsuit within a particular legal system, but nevertheless the philosopher is employing rhetorical rationality no less than a lawyer or judge (*Justice, Law, and Argument* 72). There are also important institutional differences. Perelman

notes that the demand for stability within the legal system requires that res judicata play an important role, whereas in philosophy there can be no principle of res judicata (53, 75).

111. Joy 273. See also Bruce Krajewski's *Traveling with Hermes: Hermeneutics and Rhetoric* and Walter Jost and Michael J. Hyde's *Rhetoric and Hermeneutics in Our Time: A Reader.*

112. For example, Kathy Eden chronicles the "profound interaction between rhetoric and hermeneutics" in the tradition stretching from ancient Greece to medieval humanism (102).

113. Examples include Ramsey Eric Ramsey, who argues that Heidegger's philosophy—and particularly his consideration of Aristotle's Rhetoric—provides an antidote to the methodologism of modern communication studies (266–76); and Michael R. Heim, who adopts Heidegger's recovery of Aristotle's analysis of deliberative-practical rhetoric (181–95).

114. Two leading commentators have argued that Heidegger's synthesis of rhetoric and hermeneutics provides the intellectual backdrop for the contemporary advances in both disciplines.

> [T]o observe and disclose the relationship between hermeneutics and rhetoric, one must describe it ontologically [in the manner initiated by Heidegger].
>
> ----------
>
> Rhetoric's ontological relationship with hermeneutics occurs when understanding becomes meaningful, when interpretation shows it "as something." . . . If the hermeneutical situation is the "reservoir" of meaning, then rhetoric is the selecting tool for making-known this meaning. . . . Without the hermeneutical situation there would be a meaningless void; without rhetoric the latent meaning housed in the hermeneutical situation could never be actualized.
>
> ----------
>
> [Consequently,] [a]ll knowledge, when it is acquired, is contextual, a product of the hermeneutical situation, and therefore founded in rhetoric—the making-known of primordial interpretive understanding. (Hyde and Smith 354–56)

115. Jeffery Bineham asserts that "Gadamer's appropriation of [key Aristotelian] concepts locates hermeneutics within a rhetorical tradition" ("Displacing Descartes" 309); Enrico Berti traces the "rehabilitation of practical philosophy" exemplified in the work of Gadamer and Perelman to the resurgence of interest in the Aristotelian tradition (30–31). Robert Scott argues that Gadamer's and Perelman's shared em-

phasis on the idea that understanding and knowledge always involve contextual application—an idea they both derive from Aristotle—provides the essential linkage of rhetoric and hermeneutics in contemporary thought (266).

116. Bineham, "Displacing Descartes" 300–305; Bineham, "The Hermeneutic Medium" 1–16.

117. Scott 259.

118. George Dillon describes the many challenges that have been raised against the notion that scientific discourse is "pure" or less structured rhetorically than other academic discourse (52–62).

119. Kuhn 98–110, 118–30, 163–68.

120. Burke 22. Donald McCloskey draws on a colloquial expression to make this same argument in the context of economics, arguing that the alliance of economics with the delimited world of scientific knowledge has been for the worse. "The modernist attempt to get along with fewer than all of the resources of human reasoning puts one in mind of the Midwestern expression, 'few bricks short of a load.' It means cracked, irrational. The modernist program of narrowing down our arguments in the name of rationality was a few bricks short of a load. To admit now that metaphor and story figure also in human reasoning is to become more, not less, rational, because of putting more of what persuades serious people under scrutiny. Modernism was rigorous about part of reasoning and angrily irrational about the rest" (137, 146).

121. *Nicomachean Ethics* 5 [1094b].

122. An example of such a statute can be found at *Conn. Gen. Stat.* § 46b-172(b) (Supp. 1998) (providing that the filing of a written acknowledgment of paternity and a written waiver of the right to a hearing, to counsel, and to the results of a blood test shall result in a final judgment that is res judicata after three years). In *Bleidner v. Searles,* 19 Conn. App. 76, 83–84 (1989), the court interpreted this statute to mean that there is no absolute right to contest the acknowledgment within the three-year period when the putative father was represented by counsel at all times and therefore is presumed to have filed the acknowledgment voluntarily and with an understanding of the legal ramifications of doing so.

123. See, e.g., *Cal. Fam. Code* §§ 7540, 7541 (West 1994) (upheld as constitutional in *Michael H. v. Gerald D.,* 491 U.S. 110 (1989)).

124. I make this argument in a symposium essay on the contributions that modern linguistics might make to legal practice. See Mootz, "Desperately Seeking Science" 1012–18.

125. *Truth and Method* 283.

126. Michael Gagarin explains: "One obstacle to appreciating the work of the Sophists is, of course, that much of our evidence comes directly or indirectly from

this hostile source, Plato. In the fourth century, Plato won the struggle against Isocrates and perhaps others to control the content of the emerging discipline, philosophy. By this victory, Plato succeeded in controlling our view of the Sophists not just as bad philosophers, but as not really philosophers at all" (4).

127. Aristotle, *On Rhetoric* 39 [1356a].

128. Aristotle, *On Rhetoric* 39 n. 46 (translator's commentary).

129. Schiappa 185.

130. J. Poulakos 189.

131. Conley 5–46.

132. Eemeren et al. 29–30.

133. J. Poulakos 14–15.

134. Schiappa 147. Schiappa contends that a "different picture of their teachings emerges" once "it is accepted that the Sophists' theorizing concerned *logos* rather than *rhêtorikê* per se." He argues that the "Sophists were representatives of an intellectualist movement that favored abstract thinking over . . . the poetic mind. The Sophists were continuing and expanding a 'movement' started by the presocratic philosophers, teaching and speaking in a culture still dominated by preliterate practices and modes of thinking" (56).

135. Schiappa 13, 169–70.

136. Schiappa 199, 162–68.

137. Schiappa 185.

138. Schiappa 113, 103–16.

139. J. Poulakos 188.

140. Gagarin 24–25.

141. Gene Garver argues that this is sufficient to save rhetoric from the Sophists, and marks the achievement of Aristotle's *Rhetoric* (*Aristotle's Rhetoric* 206–31). As Garver explains, "By limiting the art of rhetoric to argument, Aristotle has made the practice of rhetoric rational. But by confining the excellence of rhetoric to the means of persuasion, and saying nothing about the ends to which rhetoric is put, he has avoided moralizing the difference between good and bad rhetoric. He thus need not deny the competitive and controversial side of rhetoric that comes from the diverse ends that rhetoric serves" ("Philosophy, Rhetoric, and Civic Education in Aristotle and Isocrates" 208).

142. T. Poulakos 57. David Depew comments on Aristotle's segregation of these elements in Isocrates' conception of rhetoric: In "criticizing Isocrates, Aristotle pays him a backhanded compliment. He cooptively incorporates within his own philosophy of human affairs the meanings that Isocrates (but not Plato) assigned to key terms, notably *phronēsis.* At the same time, he constricts the conditions of applicability of these terms in a distinctly non-Isocratean way, subordinating practical reason

(*praxis*) to theoretical *theōria* reason, and in turn subordinating technical reason (*technē*) to practical" *(Depew 158).*

143. Haskins 8, 87.

144. Haskins 57–79.

145. Haskins 67.

146. King 311.

147. Garver, *Aristotle's Rhetoric* 237.

148. *Aristotle's Rhetoric* 232–48.

149. *Aristotle's Rhetoric* 178, 180, 184.

150. Bineham, "Hermeneutic Medium" 13–14.

151. Cascardi 225.

152. Dillon 38 (quoting Ingram 156). See Perelman and Olbrechts-Tyteca 117.

153. Farrell 62, 257.

154. Schrag, *Communicative Praxis and the Space of Subjectivity* 170.

155. *Communicative Praxis* 179.

156. *Communicative Praxis* 193.

157. Schrag, *The Resources of Rationality: A Response to the Postmodern Challenge* 175–76.

158. Cohen 94, 107.

159. Gagarin 31.

160. Schrag, *Resources of Rationality* 121–22, 140 (quoting and discussing Gadamer, "On the Scope and Function" 25).

161. Scott 261.

162. Gadamer, *Truth and Method* 365, 375.

163. Gadamer, "To What Extent Does Language Preform Thought?" 542–44. This is what Gadamer means when he insists that the lesson of the Platonic dialogues is that "dialectic is the art of having a conversation with oneself and fervently seeking an understanding of oneself. It is the art of thinking" ("Reflections" 33).

164. Billig, "Psychology, Rhetoric and Cognition" 121.

165. Billig, "Psychology, Rhetoric and Cognition" 124, 133.

166. Schrag, *Communicative Praxis* 172.

167. Abortion also has played a peculiar role in American politics and social life for the past quarter century, but although there is an abundance of political gamesmanship, there seems to be far less double-talk, resulting in the particularly vitriolic quality of the debate. Elsewhere I have discussed the abortion controversy with respect to philosophical hermeneutics. See Mootz, "Rethinking the Rule of Law" 183–93.

168. Perelman and Olbrechts-Tyteca 75.

169. Warren Sandmann 638 (quoting McGee 1–16).

170. Sandmann 657.

171. I discuss the problem of affirmative action from the perspective of natural law theory in Mootz, "Law in Flux" 363–67.

172. Thomas Conley relates several accounts of rhetorical exchanges in ancient Greece to underscore the ambivalence over rhetoric that existed then and persists today, arguing that these episodes reveal that rhetorical power reverberates with the "tensions between privilege and correctness, right and might, power and persuasion, and persuasion and ignorance" (3).

173. Willem Witteveen made this point in the discussion period after I presented a paper on this topic at the Joint International Meeting of the Law and Society Association and the Research Committee on Sociology of Law, convened in Glasgow, Scotland, on 10–13 July 1996. Willem helpfully reminded me of the nature of the contemporary wariness of rhetoric. Paralleling this mindset on the academic Left is the equally anti-rhetorical, elitist traditionalism on the Right, which fears the disintegration of received wisdom if it is subjected to democratic assessment.

174. Conley 21.

175. J. Poulakos 113–49.

176. J. Poulakos 131–32.

177. Weinreb, "Natural Law and Rights" 298.

178. Weinreb, "The Moral Point of View" 208–9.

179. Weinreb, "The Case for Natural Law Reexamined—1993" 10.

180. Weinreb, *Natural Law and Justice.*

181. Gadamer, *Truth and Method* 361.

182. Weinreb, *Oedipus at Fenway Park: What Rights Are and Why There Are Any* 191.

183. Weinreb, *Oedipus at Fenway Park* 190.

184. *Oedipus at Fenway Park* 193.

185. *Oedipus at Fenway Park* 193.

186. *Regents of Univ. of Cal. v. Bakke,* 438 U.S. 265 (1978).

187. Compare *Hopwood v. Texas,* 78 F.3d 932 (5th Cir. 1996) (holding that educational diversity is not a compelling state interest justifying the race-conscious admissions), with *Smith v. University of Washington, Law School,* 233 F.3d 1188 (9th Cir. 2000) (holding that educational diversity is a compelling state interest that justifies race-conscious admissions).

188. *Bakke,* 438 U.S. at 311–12.

189. *Bakke,* 438 U.S. at 314.

190. *Bakke,* 438 U.S. at 315.

191. *Grutter v. Bollinger,* 123 S. Ct. 2325 (2003).

192. *Gratz v. Bollinger,* 123 S. Ct. 2411 (2003).

193. *Grutter,* 123 S. Ct. at 2336.

194. *Grutter,* 123 S. Ct. at 2337 (quoting and analyzing *Bakke,* 438 U.S. at 306–315 (Powell, J.)).

195. *Grutter,* 123 S. Ct. at 2340.

196. Consolidated Brief of Lt. Gen. Julius W. Becton Jr., et al., as Amici Curiae in Support of Respondents, at *5 and *16 (filed 21 February 2003; available on Westlaw database at 2003 WL 1787554) ["Consolidated Military Brief"].

197. Consolidated Military Brief, at *11.

198. *Grutter,* 123 S. Ct. at 2340–41.

199. *Grutter,* 123 S. Ct. at 2338.

200. *Grutter,* 123 S. Ct. at 2365, 2366 (Rehnquist, C.J., dissenting).

201. *Gratz,* 123 S. Ct. at 2411, 2433 (Ginsburg, J., dissenting). Justice Ginsburg thereby responds to Justice Thomas's critique of the Court's willingness to defer to the educational judgment of the University of Michigan after refusing to defer to the educational judgment of the Virginia Military Institute in maintaining a military school open only to men. See *U.S. v. Virginia,* 518 U.S. 515 (1996). Justice Thomas had suggested that context matters, but that it is the context of contemporary, hypocritical notions of political correctness that matters: "Apparently where the status quo being defended is that of the elite establishment—here the Law School—rather than a less fashionable Southern military institution, the Court will defer without serious inquiry and without regard to the applicable legal standards" (*Grutter,* 123 S. Ct. at 2359 (Thomas, J., dissenting)). Logically, Justice Thomas's critique carries great force. There appears to be no justification for requiring a school to change what it deems to be an essential part of its character and educational mission to prohibit gender-based admissions that are judged under an intermediate level of scrutiny, while the Court is unwilling to require an institution to jettison its elitist admissions policies instead of using race-conscious admissions standards that are subject to the strict scrutiny standard of review. The point, of course, is that the persuasive context is determined by whether the policies are designed to include formerly excluded persons (underrepresented minorities at the University of Michigan, for instance) or are in fact the very policies of exclusion that create inequalities (admitting only men to an institution of higher education).

202. *Grutter,* 123 S. Ct. at 2350, 2361–62 (Thomas, J., dissenting).

203. *Grutter,* 123 S. Ct. at 2347.

204. *Grutter,* 123 S. Ct. at 2343.

205. *Grutter,* 123 S. Ct. at 2365, 2367 (Rehnquist, C.J., dissenting).

206. *Grutter,* 123 S. Ct. at 2370–71 (Kennedy, J., dissenting).

207. *Grutter,* 123 S. Ct. at 2368–69 (Rehnquist, C.J., dissenting).

208. *Grutter,* 123 S. Ct. at 2344.

209. *Grutter,* 123 S. Ct. at 2367 (Rehnquist, C.J., dissenting) (emphasis in original).

210. Justice Thomas makes reference to this history, but he does so in the context of his color-blind argument that it is impermissible for the University of Michigan to decide that it has "too many" white law students (*Grutter,* 123 S. Ct. at 2360 (Thomas, J., dissenting)). This point carries much greater persuasive weight if the law school practices appear to operate in a manner that amounts to finding that the entering class might have "too many" Hispanics.

211. *Bakke,* 438 U.S. at 296–97.

212. *Grutter,* 123 S. Ct. at 2366 (Rehnquist, C.J., dissenting).

213. *Grutter,* 123 S. Ct. at 2362 (Thomas, J., dissenting).

214. *Grutter,* 123 S. Ct. at 2362 n. 11 (Thomas, J., dissenting).

215. *Grutter,* 123 S. Ct. at 2363 (Thomas, J., dissenting).

216. *Gratz,* 123 S. Ct. at 2431–33 (O'Connor, J., concurring).

217. *Gratz,* 123 S. Ct. at 2433 (Thomas, J., concurring).

218. *Gratz,* 123 S. Ct. at 2442 (Souter, J., dissenting).

219. *Gratz,* 123 S. Ct. at 2446 (Ginsburg, J., dissenting).

220. *Gratz,* 123 S. Ct. at 2430 n. 22. Justice Ginsburg responds by restating her primary point: "In my view, the Constitution, properly interpreted, permits government officials to respond openly to the continuing importance of race," and that among "constitutionally permissible options, those that candidly disclose their consideration of race seem to me preferable to those that conceal it" (*Gratz,* 123 S. Ct. at 2446 n. 11 (Ginsburg, J., dissenting)).

Chapter 2

Epigraph. The following copyright holder granted express permission or acknowledged fair use for the excerpt used as an epigraph in this chapter: State University of New York Press for an excerpt from page 26 of Hans-Georg Gadamer, "Text and Interpretation," trans. Dennis J. Schmidt and Richard Palmer, in *Dialogue and Deconstruction: The Gadamer-Derrida Encounter,* ed. Diane P. Michelfelder and Richard E. Palmer (Albany: State University of New York Press, 1989).

1. Mindful of the inevitable oversimplifications attendant on "charting" similarities between two philosophers, I believe that it is appropriate and helpful to note the relationship between the key concepts employed by Gadamer and Perelman. Gadamer, focusing on conversation as a model, employs the concept of "truth" in a manner similar to Perelman's use of "universal audience" in his model of persuasion. Gadamer's use of "common sense" or "prejudice" relates to Perelman's use of "commonplace" or "loci." Gadamer's distinction between "authority" and "authoritarian" relates to Perelman's distinction between "persuasion" and "violence." Gadamer's central theme that understanding always involves application relates to Perelman's central theme that practical philosophy is always embedded in politics.

2. Madison 26–35.
3. Madison 26, 35.
4. Madison 35.
5. Fairfield 286.
6. Altieri 91.
7. Altieri 23.
8. Farrell 232–49.
9. Farrell 248–49.
10. Farrell 232, 236.
11. Farrell 140.
12. Farrell 135.
13. Farrell 213.

14. The following argument that Gadamer's philosophy explicitly and necessarily includes a strong critical gesture has been a consistent theme in my prior work. See Mootz, "The Ontological Basis of Legal Hermeneutics" 602–5; Mootz, "Rethinking the Rule of Law" 159–64; Mootz, "Psychotherapeutic Practice" 299–395; and Mootz, "The Quest to Reprogram Cultural Software: A Hermeneutical Response to Jack Balkin's Theory of Ideology and Critique" 945–89.

15. Gadamer, *Truth and Method* 277–307.

16. In "Aesthetics and Hermeneutics," Gadamer describes the experience of the work of art as the "shattering and demolition of the familiar" (104). Gadamer defines classic literary texts by their power of overcoming the subjectivism of the reader. "The interpreter, who gives his reasons, disappears—and the text speaks" ("Text and Interpretation" 51). Gadamer's thesis helps explain the controversies surrounding the teaching of books like *The Adventures of Huckleberry Finn* in public schools. Although the banalities associated with the battle lines drawn around "political correctness" predominate the discussion, one might ask why the issue is deemed to be so important. It seems plain that critics regard the book as dangerous precisely because its real-life (ambiguous) portrayal of race in language and settings now removed from contemporary discourse would prove threatening to students. On one hand, the book might be presented to students too young and unsophisticated to meet the critical challenge posed by the text; on the other hand, the book might be too challenging for any reader within the context of contemporary American social and political reality. In either case, the critical force of a classic text is reaffirmed and feared as a decentering tool perhaps too powerful to be contained, which is precisely Gadamer's point as to why such encounters are necessary and beneficial.

17. Gadamer, *Truth and Method* 383–89.

18. Gadamer admits as much. In the closing to the preface of the second edition of *Truth and Method,* Gadamer concedes the one-sided nature of his hermeneutical

universalism, but he defends his approach as a necessary "corrective" to the "will of man" that aspires to "eschatological consciousness" of all that is contained within tradition (*Truth and Method* xxxviii–xxxix).

19. Cascardi 226.

20. In Mootz, "Legal Classics: After Deconstructing the Legal Canon" 1016–23, I describe Gadamer's conception of a classical text as one that refuses to submit to reverent, repetitive readings and instead invites a dialogic encounter in the form of a series of questions and answers posed and proposed by both reader and text.

21. "Text and Interpretation" 33–35.

22. Gadamer, "On the Scope and Function" 29.

23. Farrell 202–8.

24. Farrell 210–11.

25. Goodrich, "The Role of Linguistics in Legal Analysis" 531. In *Legal Discourse: Studies in Linguistics, Rhetoric, and Legal Analysis,* Goodrich describes his project as placing "the communicative or rhetorical functions of law within their institutional and socio-linguistic contexts" (205).

26. Goodrich, "Historical Aspects of Legal Interpretation" 334; Goodrich, *Legal Discourse* 210. Goodrich places Gadamer's hermeneutics within the glossator-philological tradition of biblical hermeneutics rather than recognizing it as part of the rhetorical tradition that emphasizes the inventiveness of language ("Historical Aspects" 348–49). This is a surprising angle of attack in light of Goodrich's emphasis that critical inquiry reveals the hermeneutical openness of texts rather than "seeing through them" from a privileged perspective (*Legal Discourse* 208–9).

27. *Legal Discourse* 111.

28. *Legal Discourse* 113.

29. *Legal Discourse* 120–23.

30. *Legal Discourse* 125. Goodrich is careful to emphasize that he is not arguing in favor of a crude Marxist analysis of law (158–67).

31. *Legal Discourse* 158–67.

32. *Legal Discourse* 113.

33. *Legal Discourse* 175–82. Goodrich's psychoanalytic account of legal language seeks to "move from the analysis of textual figures to that of the emotions, conflicts or repressed histories that underpin them" (Goodrich, "Jani Anglorum: Signs, Symptoms, Slips and Interpretation in Law" 113). Subsequently, Goodrich links rhetoric and psychoanalytic theory as strategies for exploring the intradiscourse of legal practice:

> [A] theme of the present study is to pursue the deflections or screenings instituted by the mask, façade, or image of law. . . . The specific strategy of

this study is that of thinking historically of psychoanalytic jurisprudence. Using the earliest theoretical discipline associated with law, namely rhetoric, the study progresses to a genealogy of the image in law . . .

[Another] theme, although I am uncertain of its success, is that of the return of the repressed within the discourse of law. . . . The recollection of institutional repression offers a positive politics, a wealth of resources, of fragments and contaminations of the science of doctrine, the purity of reason or the ideality of law. It offers the possibility of a criticism or critical legal studies that rereads and rewrites doctrinal scholarship and, by implication, the future of professional practice through the epistemological other of legal knowledge.

Rhetoric, which studies the tropes and figures of language simultaneously and necessarily, studies also the unconscious of the institution as the long-term significance of its figures and as the symptoms of the culture, work, and affect of law. (*Oedipus Lex: Psychoanalysis, History, Law* 10–13, 183)

More recently, Goodrich attempts to make good on the goal of recollecting "institutional repression" in the effort to develop a "positive politics" (Goodrich, *Law in the Courts of Love: Literature and Other Minor Jurisprudences*). For example, Goodrich recovers the intimate linkage of legal judgment and divine authority in centuries past in order to bring to consciousness the severe repression that accompanied the formalization of secularized legal procedures.

[T]he history of spiritual law and of its incorporation within the secular jurisdiction gives evidence of an aspect of legal genre which is forgotten at the exorbitant cost of instituting a discourse which no longer recollects either its purpose or its transformative power as a law that writes itself upon the soul. While, in a relatively banal sense, the language of legal justification and of precedent is self-evidently replete with narratives of the good community and of the myriad proprieties of behavior, such features of ethical governance and justice, such rhetorics of penitence and improvement, are deemed jurisprudentially to be incidental or simply rhetorical. (*Law in the Courts of Love* 126)

34. *Legal Discourse* 183–204. Goodrich explains that the "purpose of this interdisciplinary study would not be that of juxtaposing legal knowledge with that of other, essentially separate, knowledges (pluridisciplinary), nor would it be that of absorbing other disciplines or sciences into legal expertise (transdisciplinary) for the purposes of providing a further technical dimension of legitimation to legal discourse. The

interdisciplinary study of law is aimed rather at breaking down the closure of legal discourse and at critically articulating the internal relationships it constructs with other discourses" (*Legal Discourse* 212).

35. *Legal Discourse* 127–28, 171–74. Goodrich argues that a properly understood rhetorical tradition poses radical questions about how ideology is maintained through institutional practices by asking "what politics does this discourse enshrine and what are the political effects of this text—not simply what does it say, but what does it do, by what means and to whom?" ("Historical Aspects" 354).

36. "Historical Aspects" 353.

37. Michael Billig notes that "the rhetorical perspective suggests that common sense or ideology is not, as is supposed in some sociological accounts, a unitary block, rather like a giant schema, which is imposed on the stimulus world and which acts to prevent thought. Instead, common sense will be dilemmatic, in that it contains contrary themes and common places, and these will ensure that members of the community have the resources to think and argue about their social worlds" ("Psychology, Rhetoric and Cognition" 127).

38. Perelman equates the dogmatic view of natural law with the overblown claims of rationality generally (*Justice, Law, and Argument* 32). This invites the intriguing question: can there be a "natural law" of the reasonable? I believe that Perelman answers this question in the affirmative. For my efforts to draw connections between hermeneutical philosophy and (nontraditional, nontheistic) natural law philosophy, see Mootz, "Law in Flux" 311–82.

39. Perelman, *Justice, Law, and Argument;* Mootz, "Rethinking the Rule of Law" 131–32 (discussing Gadamer's philosophy). Steven Mailloux makes a strong argument in the context of literary theory against equating the absence of foundational norms guiding critique with political quietism, echoing Gadamer and Perelman. "No universal, objective idea of Justice and no ahistorical foundationalist theory of how such Justice should be implemented is necessary for specific interpretations, arguments, and resistances to take place. All such practices are historically grounded in specific rhetorical and political situations that provide the contemporary (and only) available arguments and justifications for defending, reforming, or revolutionizing the status quo" (*Rhetorical Power* 169).

40. "The emancipatory power of reflection claimed by the psychoanalyst is a special rather than general function of reflection and must be given its boundaries through the societal context and consciousness, within which the analyst and also his patient are on even terms with everybody else" (Gadamer, "On the Scope and Function" 41–42), and so psychoanalysis constitutes only a "limit situation for hermeneutics," rather than a scientific model able to assert precedence over the hermeneutical

situation (Gadamer, "Hermeneutics as Practical Philosophy" 108). See also Gadamer, "What Is Practice?: The Conditions of Social Reason" 78–79; and Kögler 228–29.

41. Mootz, "Psychotherapeutic Practice."

42. Perelman, *Justice, Law, and Argument* 114–19.

43. *Justice, Law, and Argument* 53, 78–81, 117.

44. The reading of Nietzsche that follows is an abbreviation of the more detailed argument in my monograph "Nietzschean Critique and Philosophical Hermeneutics."

45. In "The Antichrist," Nietzsche indicts religion because it obscures reality (Nietzsche, "The Antichrist" §15), and his famous announcement of the "death of God" reinserts man in the natural world as a creature having no special ontological status (Cox 74–75).

46. Nietzsche, *Beyond Good and Evil* §§13, 36, 259.

47. Certainly the most prominent example is Maudemarie Clark's *Nietzsche on Truth and Philosophy.*

48. Cox 16–27.

49. Nietzsche, *Beyond Good and Evil* §21; Nietzsche, *The Gay Science* §§108–12, 344, 373.

50. *Gay Science* §57.

51. Cox 27; Vattimo, *Nietzsche: An Introduction* 43–58.

52. Cox 214.

53. Cox 163.

54. Hales and Welshon 58.

55. Hales and Welshon 63–65.

56. Cox 138–39.

57. Nietzsche, *On the Genealogy of Morals: A Polemic* III, 12.

58. Mootz, "Nietzschean Critique" 986–91.

59. Hales and Welshon 34.

60. Hales and Welshon 35.

61. Vattimo, *Nietzsche* 124.

62. *Gay Science* 374.

63. Nietzsche, *Beyond Good and Evil* 2.

64. Hales and Welshon summarize: "If there is no absolute knowledge in most of the sense that can reasonably be assigned to that phrase, the appropriate response is 'so what?' There is still knowledge—robust, honest, decent, genuine, *perspectival* knowledge. And, says Nietzsche, this is all we really need" (124).

65. Nietzsche, *Ecce Homo: How One Becomes What One Is* 59.

66. Thomas 15.

67. Nietzsche's texts on rhetoric and language, and particularly his early lecture on ancient rhetoric, are collected in *Friedrich Nietzsche on Rhetoric and Language*.

68. Nietzsche, *Gay Science* §107.

69. Thomas 114. Thomas is quoting Nietzsche's self-description of his genealogical method in *Ecce Homo* (84).

70. Nietzsche, *Gay Science* §290.

71. Cox 53.

72. Cox 55–56. Cox is quoting from Nietzsche, *Gay Science* §2.

73. I have developed this comparison of ontological perspectivism and fusion of horizons in more detail in Mootz, "Nietzschean Critique" 1002–8.

74. Nietzsche, *Gay Science* §321.

75. *Gay Science* §§276, 304.

76. I have noted the surprising lack of scholarship comparing and contrasting Nietzsche and Gadamer (Mootz, "Nietzschean Critique" 999–1002). I recently discovered an excellent article that contends that "Nietzsche and Gadamer are much more embroiled in each other's positions than either might expect" (Davey 45). Davey concludes:

> Nietzschean hermeneutics lacks a consciousness of its substantive historical dimension which philosophical hermeneutics offers a means of exposing. The latter can remind its counterpart that within history there can be no creativity *ex nihilo* and that in being fueled by the historical tradition it wishes to escape from, its "toward which" pole inevitably acknowledges its dependence on and the force of tradition. On the other hand, the hermeneutics of *pathos* points its counterpart towards both the necessity of creatively renewing traditions and of understanding that without the creative projection of meaning there would be no meaning to be open to. (57)

Davey specifically rejects a crude deconstructionist reading of Nietzsche that converts that instability of meaning into a basis for mere playing, engendering precisely the nihilism that Nietzsche feared. "It turns the hermeneutic thinker into a confused Hamlet swamped in a plethora of interpretive possibilities, unable to act decisively and creatively upon the tradition that ontologically speaking bears him up" (56).

77. Vattimo expressly grants "Nietzsche a significant role in that philosophical strand which begins with Schleiermacher, develops through Dilthey and German Historicism, and continues through to Heidegger and post-Heideggerian hermeneutics (i.e., to Gadamer, Ricoeur and Pareyson, to name only the most important figures)," and he predicts "that the study of Nietzsche's philosophy will lead to a more

precise definition of the strangely unified character of 'hermeneutics' as a philosophical strand in nineteenth- and twentieth-century culture" (*Nietzsche* 5–6).

78. Vattimo, *The End of Modernity: Nihilism and Hermeneutics in Postmodern Culture* 164; Vattimo, *After Christianity* 119.

79. Vattimo, *The Transparent Society* 9, 40–42.

80. Vattimo, *Transparent Society* 113, 114.

81. Snyder l.

82. Vattimo, "Philosophy, Metaphysics, Democracy" 5.

83. "Philosophy, Metaphysics, Democracy" 7.

84. Vattimo, *After Christianity* 17. In other words, the "fact is that the decline of the great metanarratives . . . has put an end, too, to the strong reasons for philosophical atheism" (*After Christianity* 86).

85. Vattimo, *Beyond Interpretation: The Meaning of Hermeneutics for Philosophy* 54.

86. Vattimo, "The Trace of the Trace" 79.

87. *Gay Science* §§78, 358, 377.

88. *Beyond Good and Evil* §280.

89. Nietzsche, "Twilight of the Idols" §39.

90. *Bowers v. Hardwick,* 478 U.S. 186 (1986).

91. *Romer v. Evans,* 517 U.S. 620 (1996).

92. *Boy Scouts of America v. Dale,* 530 U.S. 640 (2000).

93. *Lawrence v. Texas,* 123 S. Ct. 2472 (2003).

94. In *Rhetoric, Language, and Reason,* Michel Meyer advocates an approach to philosophy that he characterizes as "problematology," which is devoted to investigating the central role played by questions in reasoning and to overcoming the traditional privileging of answers as the focus of philosophy.

95. *Bowers,* 478 U.S. at 190.

96. *Bowers,* 478 U.S. at 190.

97. *Bowers,* 478 U.S. at 191–93. Chief Justice Burger's infamous concurring opinion emphatically underscores the narrow holding that "there is no such thing as a fundamental right to commit homosexual sodomy" (*Bowers,* 478 U.S. at 196 (Burger, C.J., concurring)) but makes it more clear that he sees no role for the Court to "cast aside millennia of moral teaching" (*Bowers,* 478 U.S. at 197).

98. *Bowers,* 478 U.S. at 200, 206, 214 (Blackmun, J., dissenting).

99. The separate dissenting opinion authored by Justice Stevens focuses on the selective enforcement of the statute against gays and directly takes up the question of the constitutionality of targeting disfavored groups through application of broadly worded statutes. "A policy of selective application must be supported by a neutral and legitimate interest—something more substantial than a habitual dislike for,

or ignorance about, the disfavored group" (*Bowers,* 478 U.S. at 219 (Stevens, J., dissenting)).

100. *Romer,* 517 U.S. at 631–32 (contrasting the "strict scrutiny" review by the Colorado Supreme Court with the "rational basis" review employed by the Court).

101. Justice Kennedy reasoned:

> First, the [constitutional] amendment [enacted by referendum] has the peculiar property of imposing a broad and undifferentiated disability on a single named group, an exceptional and, as we shall explain, invalid form of legislation. Second, its sheer breadth is so discontinuous with the reasons offered for it that the amendment seems inexplicable by anything but animus toward the class it affects; it lacks a rational relationship to legitimate state interests.
>
> ----------
>
> A law declaring that in general it shall be more difficult for one group of citizens than for all others to seek aid from the government is itself a denial of equal protection of the laws in the most literal sense.
>
> ----------
>
> We must conclude that Amendment 2 classifies homosexuals not to further a proper legislative end but to make them unequal to everyone else. This Colorado cannot do. A State cannot so deem a class of persons a stranger to its laws. (*Romer,* 517 U.S. at 632, 633, 659)

102. *Romer,* 517 U.S. at 644 (Scalia, J., dissenting) (emphasis in original).

103. *Dale,* 530 U.S. at 648–49.

104. *Dale,* 530 U.S. at 652–53.

105. *Dale,* 530 U.S. at 683–84 (Stevens, J., dissenting).

106. *Dale,* 530 U.S. at 684 (Stevens, J., dissenting).

107. *Dale,* 530 U.S. at 696–700 (Stevens, J., dissenting). Stevens notes that the Boy Scouts might have a different case if Dale's advocacy for gay rights was connected to his leadership role with the Scouts, or if the Boy Scouts was committed to expel any person—regardless of that person's sexual orientation—who openly advocated for gay rights. Instead, he concludes, the "only apparent explanation for the majority's holding . . . is that homosexuals are simply so different from the rest of society that their presence alone—unlike any other individual's—should be singled out for special First Amendment treatment," a perspective that he later labels an "atavistic opinion" (*Dale,* 530 U.S. at 696, 701 (Stevens, J., dissenting)).

108. *Dale,* 530 U.S. at 701 (Souter, J., dissenting).

109. Gadamer, *Truth and Method* 365.

110. Justice Scalia declares that the "case most relevant to the issue before us

today is not even mentioned in the Court's opinion," and then declares the *Bowers* holding to be "unassailable, except by those who think that the Constitution changes to suit current fashions" (*Romer,* 517 U.S. at 640–41 (Scalia, J., dissenting)).

111. Justice Stevens hints at this dimension of the case after noting that the state conceded that application of the statute to married couples would be unconstitutional and that it in fact was declining to continue the prosecution of the named defendant, Michael Bowers (*Bowers,* 478 U.S. at 220 n. 13 (Stevens, J., dissenting)). ("Indeed, at this [early] stage [of the litigation], it appears that the statute indiscriminately authorizes a policy of selective prosecution that is neither limited to the class of homosexual persons nor embraces all persons in that class, but rather applies to those who may be arbitrarily selected by the prosecutor for reasons that are not revealed either in the record of this case or in the text of the statute.") Subsequent details about the facts leading to the arrest of Michael Hardwick confirm that he was targeted for arrest as a result of antigay animus that could be officially expressed by virtue of the broad and facially neutral criminal prohibition against sodomy (Coleman 89–92, providing a succinct description of the events leading to Hardwick's arrest as related by Hardwick in an interview).

112. *Romer,* 517 U.S. at 641 (Scalia, J., dissenting).

113. *Bowers,* 478 U.S. at 196.

114. *Romer,* 517 U.S. at 644 (Scalia, J., dissenting).

115. "I do not mean to be critical of these [municipal] legislative successes [by gays and lesbians]; homosexuals are as entitled to use the legal system for reinforcement of their moral sentiments as is the rest of society. But they are subject to being countered by lawful, democratic countermeasures as well" (*Romer,* 517 U.S. at 646 (Scalia, J., dissenting)).

116. *Romer,* 517 U.S. at 651–53 (Scalia, J., dissenting).

117. In *Hurley v. Irish-American Gay, Lesbian and Bisexual Group of Boston,* 515 U.S. 557 (1995), the Court held that organizers of a private St. Patrick's Day parade could not be compelled under state public accommodations law to allow the participation of GLIB.

118. Vattimo, *After Christianity* 51.

119. Another example of this kind of announcement occurs repeatedly in the Court's death penalty jurisprudence. In *Callins v. Collins,* 510 U.S. 1141 (1994) (denial of certiorari), Justice Blackmun offered a particularly dramatic critique by stating: "From this day forward, I shall no longer tinker with the machinery of death" (*Callins,* 510 U.S. at 1145 (Blackmun, J., dissenting)). Blackmun rehearses the development of the Court's intricate case law, juxtaposing his personal beliefs against the death penalty and his efforts over a twenty-year period to work through the doctrine in a reasonable manner. In the end, he concludes, the doctrinal paths are impassable and

compel the conclusion that the death penalty simply cannot be administered in a just and fair manner that also precludes arbitrariness, and therefore is in all cases unconstitutional. Justice Blackmun's doctrinal journey provides another example of the critical potential of working through a tradition, and also the Nietzschean posture of declaring that the tradition has outlived its usefulness and must be carried on in a new manner. The point is that Blackmun's critical perspective does not come from a truthful perspective outside a useless tradition of legal argumentation, but emerges from the argumentation. As with Nietzsche, though, if Justice Blackmun's critique in this case proves to be accurate, it will do so only posthumously.

Justice Scalia, concurring in the denial of certiorari, wrote in response to agree that the Court's jurisprudence is impossible, but to respond to this situation by leaving the question to legislatures and juries (*Callins,* 510 U.S. at 1141–43 (Scalia, J., concurring)). Again, he attempts to divest law of political dimensions, and to divest politics of legal dimensions, in an attempt to avoid (or at least push over to another realm) the uncertainty that flows from the hermeneutical and rhetorical character of reasoning.

120. *Lawrence,* 123 S. Ct. at 2476 (noting the defendants' conviction under Tex. Pen. Code § 21.06, which is entitled "Homosexual Conduct").

121. Petition for Writ of Certiorari at 12–13, *Lawrence v. Texas,* 123 S. Ct. 661 (2002) (No. 02–102) ["*Lawrence* Cert. Petition"].

122. *Lawrence* Cert. Petition at 4.

123. *Lawrence* Cert. Petition at 17.

124. *Lawrence* Cert. Petition at 28.

125. *Lawrence,* 123 S. Ct. at 2482.

126. *Lawrence,* 123 S. Ct. at 2475.

127. *Lawrence,* 123 S. Ct. at 2478.

128. *Lawrence,* 123 S. Ct. at 2478.

129. *Lawrence,* 123 S. Ct. at 2478–80 (concluding that sodomy laws generally targeted predatory behavior, and that the historical premises of the *Bowers* opinion "are not without doubt, and, at the very least, are overstated"); *Lawrence,* 123 S. Ct. at 2480–83 (concluding that the claims about laws targeting gays and lesbians are similarly overbroad).

130. *Lawrence,* 123 S. Ct. at 2480.

131. *Truth and Method* 327.

132. *Lawrence,* 123 S. Ct. at 2484.

133. *Lawrence,* 123 S. Ct. at 2484.

134. *Lawrence,* 123 S. Ct. at 2484 (O'Connor, J., concurring).

135. *Lawrence,* 123 S. Ct. at 2487 (O'Connor, J., concurring).

136. *Lawrence,* 123 S. Ct. at 2487 (O'Connor, J., concurring).

137. *Lawrence,* 123 S. Ct. at 2482.

138. *Lawrence,* 123 S. Ct. at 2491 (Scalia, J., dissenting).

139. Garver, *For the Sake of Argument: Practical Reasoning, Character and the Ethics of Belief.*

140. *Lawrence,* 123 S. Ct. at 2491–93 (Scalia, J., dissenting).

141. *Lawrence,* 123 S. Ct. at 2498 (Scalia, J., dissenting).

142. *Lawrence,* 123 S. Ct. at 2497 (Scalia, J., dissenting).

143. *Lawrence,* 123 S. Ct. at 2497 (Scalia, J., dissenting).

144. *Lawrence,* 123 S. Ct. at 2498 (Thomas, J., dissenting).

145. *Lawrence,* 123 S. Ct. at 2497 (Scalia, J., dissenting).

Chapter 3

Epigraph. The following copyright holders granted express permission or acknowledged fair use for the excerpts used as an epigraph in this chapter: *University of Pennsylvania Law Review* and William S. Hein & Company, Inc., for an excerpt from page 205 of Karl Llewellyn, "On Philosophy in American Law" 82 *University of Pennsylvania Law Review* 205 (1934).

1. Consider the fact that Richard Posner now styles himself a legal pragmatist. In "Practically Unreasonable: A Critique of Practical Reason," Nancy Levit criticizes Posner's invocation of pragmatism from within a subjectivist metaphysics designed to buttress his ideological program. A recent collection of essays entitled *Rhetoric, Sophistry, Pragmatism* connects ancient sophistry and rhetoric to the modern resurgence of philosophical pragmatism in more challenging and interesting ways.

2. Peter Goodrich states: "Law is a literature which denies its literary qualities. It is a play of words which asserts an absolute seriousness; it is a genre of rhetoric which represses its moments of invention or fiction" (*Law in the Courts of Love* 112); Willem J. Witteveen asserts: "Rhetoric is an important surface phenomenon of legal activity, easily visible to the untrained eye. But once one becomes knowledgeable in law, rhetoric disappears from view. . . . Specialized research is then needed to draw attention to legal rhetoric" (212); Gerald B. Wetlaufer argues: "[T]he particular rhetoric that law embraces is the rhetoric of foundations and logical deductions . . . [and] is one that relies, above all else, upon the denial that it is rhetoric that is being done" (1555).

As a consequence of this wrongheaded self-understanding, the familiar bifurcation of rhetoric and reason becomes a staple in judicial rhetoric. See, e.g., *McAllister Bros., Inc. v. United States,* 890 F.2d 582, 585 (2d Cir. 1989): "The rhetoric of the appellants' brief . . . betrays the weakness of [its] arguments." This view is articulated as a jurisprudential principle by Judge Richard Posner, who argues that rhetorical flair is to be sharply distinguished from moral correctness and scientific validity (498–530). James Aune provides a concise rejoinder to Posner's simplistic delimitation and then dismissal of rhetoric:

> Posner's impoverished view of rhetoric seems to go hand in hand with his reification of the role of the market in law and politics.
>
> ----------
>
> Posner's is a history of rhetoric from which Isocrates, Cicero, and Quintilian, among others, are absent. He constructs a history of rhetoric in which the "extremes" of Plato and Aristotle are seen as unrealistic, leaving the sophistic rhetoric of Protagoras as winner by default. (659, 662)

3. Garver, *For the Sake of Argument* (demonstrating that Aristotle's *Rhetoric* can help to explain why practical reasoning in legal analysis can be contingent, emotional, and interested, and yet still an exercise of reason); Garver, "Why Should Anybody Listen? The Rhetoric of Religious Argument in Democracy" (arguing that rhetorical principles suggest how religious arguments can sometimes be more rational in public debate than their secular counterparts, and suggesting how democratic deliberation might become more receptive to religious argument); Balkin, "A Night in the Topics: The Reason of Legal Rhetoric and the Rhetoric of Legal Reason" (contending that the recurring forms of legal argument identified by semiotic inquiry are "topics" in the classical rhetoric sense); Jacob, "Ancient Rhetoric, Modern Legal Thought, and Politics: A Review Essay on the Translation of Viehweg's 'Topics and Law' " (discussing Viehweg's insight that rhetorical studies can identify the topics used in legal argumentation but cannot build a rhetorical methodology that generates singular answers); Scallen, "Evidence Law as Pragmatic Legal Rhetoric: Reconnecting Legal Scholarship, Teaching and Ethics" (discussing how classical rhetorical philosophy informs how she teaches evidence law); Scallen, "Classical Rhetoric, Practical Reasoning, and the Law of Evidence" (rhetorical insights permit us to clarify the choices made available by positive law and to justify choices persuasively); Stamatis, "Justice without Law: A Postmodern Paradox" (reasoning by persuasion can achieve justice despite the absence of a deductive legal order); Zoeller, "Is the Life in the Law Worth Living?: Some Critical Remarks on Plato's *Gorgias*" (arguing for the dignity of legal practice despite its variance from the "standards of philosophical truth-pursuit"); Klemm, "Gorgias, Law, and Rhetoric" (championing the life of Socrates as a dialogic encounter as a model for law rather than the metaphysical message espoused by him).

4. A branch of the narrative movement in law has looked closely at the narrative story-building aspect of the lawyer-client relationship, particularly in the area of poverty law. Critics describe the constitutive function of story building but argue that poverty lawyers all too often don't hear their clients' stories because they im-

mediately translate them into preestablished legal categories. See, e.g., White, "Subordination, Rhetorical Survival Skills, and Sunday Shoes: Notes on the Hearing of Mrs. G"; Alfieri, "Reconstructive Poverty Law Practice: Learning the Lessons of Client Narrative."

In response, one commentator, Cathy Lesser Mansfield, argues that this is precisely the lawyer's job—to rework lay narratives in order to achieve the client's goals—and notes that lawyers are not journalists or biographers.

This fascinating dialogue would benefit from a new view informed by the concept of rhetorical knowledge, since lawyers (and not just poverty lawyers) can refashion their clients' stories in tired ways rather than inventively, and since clients (and not just poor clients) can remain trapped within ineffectual narratives of their experience. Rhetorical knowledge arising from a deliberative process and leading to a jointly constructed story is the goal of representation and should be fostered. White, Alfieri, and Mansfield appear to emphasize only certain features of this complex relationship. For example, Mansfield is too quick to conclude that clients obtain only victory or defeat from their lawyers rather than a slightly modified self-understanding (928), since the rhetorical knowledge that is gained (or not) in effective legal representation will have some effect on the self-understanding of both the client and the lawyer.

A similar criticism of civil rights litigation strategies and the representation of clients by committed civil rights lawyers was voiced by Derrick Bell in his attack on the integration focus that fueled the litigation culminating in *Brown v. Board of Education.* In "Serving Two Masters: Integration Ideals and Client Interests in School Desegregation," Bell questions whether civil rights lawyers advanced their own litigation interests at the expense of their clients' educational goals. Bell insists that civil rights lawyers pursued the legal goal of establishing abstract equality by court decree rather than attending more closely to their clients' practical desire to have their children educated in good schools. The dilemma of how best to attack segregated and unequal schooling underscores the rhetorical principle that there is not a single "reasonable" solution to social problems and that persuasive appeals will shift focus over time. In this regard, it is important to note that Bell never argues that *Brown* and its principles are "wrong" in some absolute sense (see "Law, Litigation, and the Search for the Promised Land" 233–35, in which Bell reviews Mark V. Tushnet's *The NAACP's Legal Strategy against Segregated Education, 1925–1950*), although he does argue that *Brown*'s rhetorical strategies have proved to be ineffectual in eliminating racism and therefore are unproductive. In his recent contribution to a book that invited leading scholars to rewrite the *Brown* decision, Bell goes so far as to write a hypothetical dissenting opinion that castigates the majority for failing to go far enough in its cultural-legal critique ("Bell, J., dissenting"). Bell's recent book, *Silent Covenants:*

Brown v. Board of Education *and the Unfulfilled Hopes for Racial Reform,* provides a critique of the integrationist ideology of *Brown* and challenges the received wisdom about the significance of the case. Bell does not despair, however, and continues to argue that different rhetorical strategies might be effective in breaking down to some degree the inescapable continuing racism in American society. See Taylor, "Racism as 'The Nation's Crucial Sin': Theology and Derrick Bell," which compares Bell's "racial realism" about the permanence of racism yet his insistence on struggling to combat this reality with Reinhold Niebuhr's theology of sin, and concludes that methodologically both embrace critique and the potential for redemption through critical engagement.

5. This is the guiding insight of the idea of "principled negotiation" developed by the Harvard Negotiation Project to facilitate more effective negotiation practices (Fisher, Ury, and Patton).

6. I have made this same point in hermeneutical terms (Mootz, "Rethinking the Rule of Law" 162 n. 345, quoting Amy Gutmann's "Can Virtue Be Taught to Lawyers").

7. "How a judge conceives of his profession and of his role within that profession will figure very prominently in the vision he has of the audience he is addressing" (Christie 347–48).

8. Greenshaw 867–72.

9. Greenshaw 896.

10. Greenshaw 866.

11. Gadamer, *Truth and Method* 326.

12. *Truth and Method* 330, 341.

13. Perelman, *Justice, Law, and Argument* 81.

14. Mailloux, "Introduction: Sophistry and Rhetorical Pragmatism" 20.

15. Frug 926.

16. Wetlaufer 1561 n. 44.

17. Wetlaufer 1590–97.

18. Wetlaufer 1593.

19. D. Kennedy 548–52.

20. D. Kennedy 551.

21. Gadamer, "To What Extent Does Language Preform Thought?" 546, 549.

22. "The hermeneutical situation is not a regrettable distortion that affects the purity of understanding, but the condition of its possibility" (Gadamer, *Truth and Method* 472).

23. Jacob 1656–57.

24. Gaonkar 60.

25. Bernard Jacob describes Viehweg's argument that rhetorical studies can only shed light on topicality as a procedure of argumentation and cannot develop a science of legal argumentation by systematizing the topics into a hierarchy of logical relationships (1656–57). As Jacob elaborates: "[I]t is the orientation of topics to problems that is important to Viehweg. And it follows from this orientation that he is not invoking passive lists of topics; nor is he focusing on the logical arrangement of the topics. Instead, he is particularly interested in the use of topics in finding the solution of problems, that is, he is interested in the role of topics in rhetorical invention. . . . It is in finding arguments, rhetorical invention or the practice of struggling with varieties of models for the treatment of a problem, that the topics find a use" (1660). In *Arguing and Thinking: A Rhetorical Approach to Social Psychology,* Michael Billig adopts a similar approach in arguing that social psychologists will never be able to "map" the use of maxims in social discourse due to the complex inventiveness at work.

26. Schrag, *Resources of Rationality* 57.

27. Perelman, *Justice, Law, and Argument* 20.

28. *Justice, Law, and Argument* 109.

29. Gadamer, *Truth and Method* 465.

30. Gadamer, "The Science of the Life-World" 189.

31. Gadamer, "Text and Interpretation" 26.

32. *People v. Kevorkian,* 527 N.W.2d 714 (Mich. 1994); *People v. Kevorkian,* 534 N.W.2d 172 (Mich. App. 1995); *Kevorkian v. Thompson,* 947 F. Supp. 1152 (E.D. Mich. 1997).

33. *Quill v. Koppell,* 80 F.3d 716 (2d Cir. 1996) (holding that there is no fundamental right to assisted suicide but that criminal statutes cannot survive the rational basis test under the Equal Protection Clause) and *Compassion in Dying v. State of Washington,* 79 F.3d 790 (9th Cir. 1996) (en banc) (holding that criminal laws against assisted suicide violate substantive due process rights).

34. *Washington v. Glucksberg,* 521 U.S. 702 (1997); *Vacco v. Quill,* 521 U.S. 793 (1997). The unavoidable rhetorical depth of these judicial considerations is revealed most clearly in Justice Souter's concurring opinion in *Glucksberg,* which openly embraces the challenging character of fundamental rights jurisprudence and eschews the pretense of legal decision making as dispassionate and orderly elaboration. For an extended discussion of Souter's opinion as an exemplar of rhetorical knowledge, see Mootz, "Law in Flux" 367–82.

35. Aristotle distinguished deliberative rhetoric—when the audience is asked to judge an action to be taken in the future by engaging in political or ethical reasoning—from judicial rhetoric—when the audience is asked to judge an action in the past (*On Rhetoric* 47–50 [1358b]). With the advent of the common law system and its

doctrine of stare decisis and the tremendous expansion of the system of judicial review in later American legal practice, this distinction is no longer very helpful in characterizing the nature of legal adjudication.

36. The factual account of the Kevorkian trials in the following pages is drawn primarily from news reports. Many news reports are collected at www.kevork.org, and the Detroit Free Press reporters who covered these cases gathered their reporting into an informative book titled *The Suicide Machine.*

37. *People v. Kevorkian,* 527 N.W.2d at 174.

38. *People v. Kevorkian,* 527 N.W.2d at 739.

39. *Compassion in Dying v. State of Washington,* 79 F.3d at 816.

40. *Quill v. Koppell,* 80 F.3d at 727–31.

41. *Cruzan v. Director, Mo. Dept. of Health,* 497 U.S. 261 (1990).

42. *Washington v. Glucksberg; Vacco v. Quill.*

43. This fact is perhaps best illustrated in Kevorkian's unsuccessful defamation suit against the American Medical Association. Kevorkian sued after the AMA characterized him as a "killer" who was engaged in "criminal activities," despite Kevorkian's third acquittal (*Kevorkian v. American Medical Ass'n,* 602 N.W.2d 233, 235 (Mich. App. 1999)). Although accusations of illegal conduct traditionally are considered defamatory per se, the court of appeals determined that the defendants were entitled to summary judgment. The court concluded that Kevorkian was "libel proof," because his "reputation in the community, if not the nation, is such that the effect of more people calling him either a murderer or a saint is de minimis," and that he benefited from negative statements in seeking to publicize his activities (*Kevorkian v. American Medical Ass'n,* 602 N.W.2d at 239). The court concluded that the statements about Kevorkian in effect were legally protected opinions about the advisability of legalizing assisted suicide.

> Plaintiff's very celebrity (or notoriety, if you will) derives exclusively from his participation in a national debate over the propriety of assisted suicide—whether it is more akin to an act of mercy or to an act of homicide. Having exercised his leadership on behalf of one side of this debate, and having contributed substantially to the awareness of the American people of this debate, it is now more than a little disingenuous for plaintiff to accuse those on the opposite side of this debate of defamation. Such alleged defamation is grounded here in nothing more than the fact that defendants are in disagreement with plaintiff's position: they would characterize plaintiff's conduct differently than plaintiff would characterize it. Where an alleged defamatory statement, occurring in the course of a public debate initiated or perpetuated by plaintiff himself, is focused precisely on a matter lying at the heart of the debate, it is

> hard to understand how tort law could be implicated. Indeed, it is hard to imagine anything that could more effectively chill legitimate public debate. (*Kevorkian v. American Medical Ass'n,* 602 N.W.2d at 240)

The court plainly identifies the man Kevorkian with the public policy issue of assisted suicide in finding that traditional libel per se does not apply to his actions.

44. Lessenberry, "Death Becomes Him."
45. "Kevorkian May Have Tried to Sidestep Law"; Lessenberry.
46. Loven, "Kevorkian Jurors Describe Prayers, Tears."
47. "Tape of Suicidal Man Brings Tears to Eyes of Kevorkian Jury."
48. Loven.
49. Loven; Donaldson.
50. Engram, "Coping/Mortal Matters."
51. Walsh, "Jury Acquits Kevorkian in Two Suicides."
52. Walsh.
53. Lessenberry.
54. Loven.
55. Walsh.
56. "Tape of Suicidal Man."
57. Loven.
58. Donaldson.
59. *People v. Kevorkian,* 517 N.W.2d 293 (Mich. App. 1994).
60. *People v. Kevorkian,* 527 N.W.2d at 739.
61. *The Suicide Machine* describes how frequently Kevorkian violated his stated rules and norms in his assisted suicides (58–66). Kevorkian alarmed even his supporters in 1996 when he helped Judith Curren to die. Curren was suffering from a painful but nonterminal muscle condition (most likely chronic fatigue syndrome, but that was not clearly established); she was obese, depressed, and bedridden; she had made allegations of spousal abuse shortly before her suicide; and her husband was reportedly facing severe financial distress. See Jacobson, "Kevorkian Methods Face New Attacks: Massachusetts Woman's Suicide Refuels Public Doubts about Discretion"; Brasier, "Kevorkian's Choice of 'Suicide' Patients Raises Moral Concerns"; Lipkin, "A Troubling Death" (commentary/letter by the president of the Chronic Fatigue Syndrome Society of Illinois).
62. *People v. Kevorkian,* 534 N.W.2d at 174.
63. *People v. Kevorkian,* 534 N.W.2d at 294.
64. Akre, "Jurors Acquit Kevorkian in 3rd Assisted-Suicide Trial."
65. Akre.
66. "Dr. Death Beats Rap Again."

67. Orentlicher, "Learning Lessons of Life and Death from Kevorkian."

68. "Kevorkian Encountering Fewer Hurdles in Suicides."

69. Akre. In a later interview, jury foreman Dean Gauthier related that "the major issue for us was the fact that Dr. Kevorkian helped [Wantz and Miller] commit their suicides in 1981 [and] unfortunately there wasn't an interpretation of the common law until 1994. So in the essence, the acts happened prior to the law's interpretation. So therefore we found him not guilty simply by—by that means" (Gauthier).

70. *Kevorkian v. Thompson.* Technically, this court's injunction did not apply to Kevorkian and his ongoing state prosecutions under the *Younger* abstention doctrine, but the court adjudicated the constitutionality of the common law charge of assisted suicide under Michigan law with respect to Janet Good. Good was the former president of the Michigan Hemlock Society seeking to legalize assisted suicide, and was dying of pancreatic cancer at the time.

71. *Kevorkian v. Thompson,* 947 F. Supp. at 1178.

72. The facts are described in greater detail in *People v. Kevorkian,* 639 N.W.2d 291, 297–300 (Mich. App. 2001).

73. *People v. Kevorkian,* 639 N.W.2d at 331 ("Simply put, consent and euthanasia are not recognized defenses to murder").

74. Crumm, "Jury Didn't Waver in Deciding Guilt."

75. *People v. Kevorkian,* 639 N.W.2d at 329–32.

76. Marker and Hamlon, "Prisoner Number 284797."

77. Swickard, "Feiger: Crusader Now Seeks Martyr's Robe."

78. Kenny, "The Rhetoric of Kevorkian's Battle."

79. Burns 181–82.

80. Burns 239, 244.

81. Beedle.

82. Warnke, *Justice and Interpretation* 157.

83. Gadamer, "Science of the Life-World" 188–89.

84. This example is drawn from my experience as a litigator before joining the academy. My argument in favor of a discovery motion seeking information from the bank about its loan practices and foreclosure rates was confronted by the judge's predictable response that such information was completely irrelevant to the foreclosure action at hand. This motion argument represents only one of many instances in my experience when the apparently solid rules of commercial law were put under stress in a manner that forced recourse to argumentation about justice, not in poetic terms about abstract ideals, but in concrete terms about the legitimacy of each party's claim. My argument didn't go over very well on this particular day, but on other days during my practice, the system would shake—sometimes for the benefit of my clients and sometimes not. Lawyers capture the reality of their collective fate

with a well-worn witticism: "I'm going to practice law until I get it right." Of course, lawyers will continue to practice law collectively for the foreseeable future because getting it "right" doesn't mean reaching a stasis; it is a quality of dynamism.

85. Mootz, "The New Legal Hermeneutics" 130–38.

86. Hyde and Smith 362.

87. Ewick and Silbey 201–4.

88. Simons, Preface vii. See also Roberts and Good, Introduction.

89. Simons, Preface viii.

90. Simons, Introduction 17.

91. This does not mean that rhetorical practices cannot be compared to locate basic shared features, and Perelman's new rhetoric is expressly generalist in its account of rhetorical practices. Paul Wangerin argues that the structure of persuasive argument largely is field invariant but cautions against narrow readings that fail to capture the multidimensional character of argumentation (204). The philosophical and empirical work to catalogue the commonplaces and lines of argumentation must always be regarded as provisional and suggestive rather than final and complete, however, due to the living character of language.

92. Margolis 138.

93. In *Doing What Comes Naturally: Change, Rhetoric, and the Practice of Theory in Literary and Legal Studies,* Fish characterizes the debate as an unending and unresolvable "tug-of-war between two views of human life and its possibilities" (501).

94. Fish, *Doing What Comes Naturally* 463–64.

95. LaRue 8.

96. LaRue 135, 148.

97. Fish, "Play of Surfaces: Theory and the Law" 297.

98. Gadamer, Interview: "The German University and German Politics: The Case of Heidegger" 7.

99. Mootz, "Is the Rule of Law Possible in a Postmodern World?" 293–98.

100. Farrell 231.

101. Farrell 197–202.

102. Farrell 83.

103. Farrell 17.

104. Farrell 213.

105. Farrell 267.

106. Schrag, *Communicative Praxis* 4.

107. Schrag, *Communicative Praxis* 53.

108. Schrag, *Resources of Rationality* 173.

109. Raymie McKerrow offers a similar account of rhetorical criticism by comparing the decentered rhetorical critic to the decentered rhetor in the public square,

arguing that both might evidence reasonable developments of the traditions they take up.

> The critic engages in critique not as a centered subject originating thought but as a contributor to the universe of discourse. As inventors of texts, the critic's role is to re-present texts from a collection of fragmentary episodes. . . . The goal in this process is not to produce a master text encompassing all known and possible conditions of its making. Rather, the goal is to pull together those fragments whose intersection in real lives has meaning for social actors—meaning that confirms them as either subjects empowered to become citizens or social actors with a potential to enact new relations of power. As such, the invented text functions to enable historicized subjects to alter the conditions of their lived experience.
>
> ----------
>
> For social actors embedded in a set of social practices that define as they constrain, a critique of freedom illuminates the possibilities of a new existence. The social actor, in this latter sense, has influence over those considerations. To care for oneself includes the remaking of social practices within which one is inscribed. (62–65)

For McKerrow, not only are critical assessments of rhetorical practices possible in the postmodern world, but they are an expression of the sense of self that remains after the deconstruction of the insular modernist ego (64–65).

110. Kögler 84.

111. Kögler 245.

112. Kögler 148–49.

113. Kögler 252, 169, 254.

114. Kögler 229.

115. Anton Schütz asserts, "There is no such thing as a philosophical theory of law in Nietzsche's work" (497); Jonathan Yovel states, "Indeed, Nietzsche devoted very limited work to law. . . . It is the worthy individual that matters, not society, and law is inherently social" (641).

116. Berkowitz 1133–34. Anton Schütz emphasizes the danger attendant on referring to a work that is suffused with Nietzsche's Aryan elitism, arguing that it "would be a categorical error doubled by a lack of due consideration" to treat Nietzsche's discussion as a "theory of law" (497).

117. Berkowitz 1135–37.

118. Berkowitz 1140.

119. In a similar manner, Adam Geary charts contemporary uses of Nietzsche's

philosophy in African thinking despite the racist context of Nietzsche's thought, concluding: "Nietzsche is not absolved of racism, but becomes readable as a thinker who opens a style of thinking, that can ultimately be related to the most radical ways of settling accounts with the racist structures of the western tradition" (923).

120. Berkowitz 1141, 1144, 1147.

121. Berkowitz 1134. In a related manner, Kyron Huigens argues that Nietzsche's attacks on asceticism can be extended to legal criticism in order to address the crisis of law being cast adrift from natural law foundations without finding a safe harbor in positivist science (563–66). Huigens insists that Nietzsche embraces an affirmation of life that is too often obscured by postmodern obsessions over the indeterminacy of language that results from perspectivism, and he relates this (a connection not understood by Nietzsche) to Aristotle's dynamic virtue ethics and the fostering of individual excellence (564). This reading instantiates law in the social process of facilitating individual flourishing, and opens the way for applications to legal systems that extend beyond the truncated and prejudiced world Nietzsche inhabited. Indeed, the dynamism of Nietzsche's thought provides both an intellectual attack on and an example of moving beyond the timelessness and essentialism that has clouded legal understanding.

122. Weisberg 3–4.

123. Weisberg 7–8.

124. Anton Schütz presents a persuasive argument that Nietzsche all too often is bound up with the Christian hermeneutics decried by Weisberg, and that his attacks on the Jews are equivalent to attacks on legalism. In the end, Schütz concludes, "Nietzsche accuses Christianity of being insufficiently Christian, insufficiently anti-legal (insufficiently anti-Jewish), of having abandoned its own foundational evangelic task of eradicating all 'vindictive,' that is to say, legal elements" (524–25). This does not necessarily undermine Weisberg's reading, as Nietzsche appears to alternate between finding a vitalistic interpretive in ancient (including Jewish) traditions and also finding one in the inspiration for the Christian tradition. It is the practices of all these traditions that Nietzsche finds unsatisfactory.

125. Weisberg 14.

126. Weisberg 14–15.

127. Sherwin 701.

128. Sherwin 702.

129. A masterful text in this tradition is Karl Llewellyn's "On Our Case-Law of Contract: Offer and Acceptance."

130. Feinman, "The Development of the Employment at Will Rule."

131. Feinman 129–35.

132. Ballam, "Exploding the Original Myth Regarding Employment-at-Will: The

True Origins of the Doctrine"; Ballam, "The Traditional View on the Origins of the Employment-at-Will Doctrine: Myth or Reality?"

133. A good example of this approach is Kathryn Abrams's "Gender Discrimination and the Transformation of Workplace Norms." Abrams explicitly locates her work within contemporary feminist theory (1185–97), but her focus is on the specific context of the workplace and even more specifically on the problems that arise when courts define sexual harassment without taking into account how a "reasonable woman" would understand and react to certain behavior (1197–220). Abrams's critical theory is then more readily accommodated to the development of legal doctrine by courts, even if the courts do not absorb the full depth of her feminist critique. See, e.g., *Ellison v. Brady,* 924 F.2d 872, 879 (9th Cir. 1991) (citing Abrams and adopting the "reasonable woman" standard for sexual harassment litigation).

134. One of the classics in this tradition is Roberto M. Unger's "The Critical Legal Studies Movement." Although his article is more than one hundred pages long, Unger does not discuss a single judicial opinion, statute, or regulation. Instead, his discussion concerns broad principles and concepts. For example, he utilizes contract doctrine to exemplify his broader critical project of debunking objectivism and formalism, attempting to capture all of contract doctrine within a wider, "single, cohesive set of ideas" (617).

135. In one of the leading cases establishing the cause of action for wrongful discharge, the court began with the premise that the "law governing the relations between employer and employee has evolved over the years to reflect changing legal, social and economic conditions" (*Monge v. Beebe Rubber Co.,* 316 A.2d 549, 551 (N.H. 1974)). *Monge* was decided before Feinman's article was published, but it cited other leading academic criticisms of the "at will" rule and it in turn was cited by Feinman as an example of the contemporary stresses on the rule that suggested the need for an understanding of its origins (Feinman 118 n. 2). Several courts have explicitly adopted Feinman's sociohistorical characterization of the "at will" rule and its development. See, e.g., *Magnan v. Anaconda Indus., Inc.,* 479 A.2d 781, 783–84 (Conn. 1984); *Shearin v. E. F. Hutton Group, Inc.,* 652 A.2d 578, 585 (Del. Ch. 1994); *Darlington v. General Elec.,* 504 A.2d 306, 309 (Pa. Super. Ct. 1986).

136. This book offers a philosophical theory along these lines. Ronald Dworkin generally is described as adopting an interpretivist posture in his attempt to steer a course between the conceptual analysis dominant in both positivist and natural law theories and the vacuity of an "antitheory" pragmatist approach (see Dworkin's *Law's Empire*). Dworkin's work proves frustrating because he glides over the difficult philosophical issues raised by his discussion, but his rhetorical approach has made his writing accessible not just to practicing lawyers but also to the citizenry at large. Consequently, Dworkin's body of work would be an interesting focus for a

hermeneutical-rhetorical consideration of the role of audience and the relationship of theory and practice.

137. Corbin 187.

138. Corbin 187.

139. *U.S. v. Shonubi,* 895 F. Supp. 460, 464 (E.D.N.Y. 1995).

140. *U.S. v. Shonubi,* 895 F. Supp. at 487–490.

141. *U.S. v. Shonubi,* 103 F.3d 1085, 1092 (2d Cir. 1997).

142. Deirdre N. McCloskey, *If You're So Smart: The Narrative of Economic Expertise;* Donald N. McCloskey, "The Rhetoric of Economic Expertise."

143. "Some economists claim that they have put together the whole puzzle. They are wrong, of course. But a condemnation of extremist rhetoric does not demand the condemnation of economic discourse itself any more than listening to Jimmy Swaggert should lead us to condemn religion or listening to the Butthole Surfers should lead us to condemn music" (Heald 305).

144. Peter Goodrich's sophisticated interdisciplinary theory falls victim to this problem. Although his erudite scholarship is extremely thought provoking on many fronts, in the end it appears too much for him to integrate his postmodern philosophical orientation, critical deconstructions of existing doctrine, and doctrinal analysis into a narrative that purports to unravel ideological formations by seeing through history. Goodrich's historical readings would be more persuasive if couched in the more circumspect and inviting approach taken by Steven Mailloux and described in the text following this note reference.

145. Jarratt 208.

146. Jarratt 207.

147. Mailloux, *Rhetorical Power* 130.

148. Mailloux, *Rhetorical Power* 17 n. 24.

149. Mailloux, *Rhetorical Power* 167, 148, 166.

150. Abrams, "Gender Discrimination"; Abrams, "Social Construction, Roving Biologism, and Reasonable Women."

151. Gadamer places particular emphasis on the idea that hermeneutical understanding always involves the response to a question and the posing of a question seeking a response (*Truth and Method* 362–79). This is generalized to a philosophical claim of central importance in his work: "It is clear that the structure of the question is implicit in all experience" (362).

152. Rubin 1393–94.

153. Rubin 1411.

154. Rubin 1429–30.

155. Rubin 1432.

156. Rubin 1430–33.

157. In a recent article, two authors attempt to bring law and economics scholarship and critical race theory scholarship to bear on the modern American workplace for the purpose of working through how issues of diversity are handled and investigating the potential efficacy of legal intervention. See Carbado and Gulati's "The Law and Economics of Critical Race Theory."

158. Recent additions to the literature include Eemeren, et al., *Fundamentals of Argumentation Theory: A Handbook of Historical Backgrounds and Contemporary Developments;* Douglas N. Walton, *Argumentative Schemes for Presumptive Reasoning.* In the legal context, see Brewer, "Exemplary Reasoning: Semantics, Pragmatics and the Rational Force of Legal Argument by Analogy."

Conclusion

Epigraph. The following copyright holder granted express permission or acknowledged fair use for the excerpt used as an epigraph in this chapter: Brandt & Hochman Literary Agents, Inc., on behalf of Wallace Stegner for an excerpt from page 11 of Wallace Stegner, *All the Little Live Things* (1967).

1. Gadamer, *Truth and Method* xxxviii, 579.

Works Cited

Books, Articles, Interviews

Abrams, Kathryn. "Gender Discrimination and the Transformation of Workplace Norms." *Vanderbilt L. Rev.* 42.4 (1989): 1183–1248.

———. "Social Construction, Roving Biologism, and Reasonable Women." *DePaul L. Rev.* 41.4 (1992): 1021–40.

Akre, Brian S. "Jurors Acquit Kevorkian in 3rd Assisted-Suicide Trial." *Austin American-Statesman* 15 May 1996: A15.

Alexy, Robert. *A Theory of Legal Argumentation: The Theory of Rational Discourse as Theory of Legal Justification.* Trans. Ruth Adler and Neil MacCormick. Oxford: Clarendon Press, 1989.

Alfieri, Anthony. "Reconstructive Poverty Law Practice: Learning the Lessons of Client Narrative." *Yale L. J.* 100.7 (1991): 2107–47.

Altieri, Charles. "Toward a Hermeneutics Responsive to Rhetorical Theory." *Rhetoric and Hermeneutics in Our Time: A Reader.* Ed. Walter Jost and Michael J. Hyde. New Haven: Yale Univ. Press, 1997.

Aristotle. *Nicomachean Ethics.* Ed. and trans. Roger Crisp. Cambridge: Cambridge Univ. Press, 2000.

———. *On Rhetoric.* Trans. George A. Kennedy. Oxford: Oxford Univ. Press, 1991.

Aune, James Arnt. "On the Rhetorical Criticism of Judge Posner." *Hastings Constitutional L. Quarterly* 23.3 (1996): 658–69.

Balkin, J. M. "A Night in the Topics: The Reason of Legal Rhetoric and the Rhetoric of Legal Reason." *Law's Stories: Narrative and Rhetoric in the Law.* Ed. Peter Brooks and Paul Gewirtz. New Haven: Yale Univ. Press, 1996. 211–24.

Ballam, Deborah A. "Exploding the Original Myth Regarding Employment-at-Will: The True Origins of the Doctrine." *Berkeley J. of Employment and Labor Law* 17.1 (1996): 91–130.

———. "The Traditional View on the Origins of the Employment-at-Will Doctrine: Myth or Reality?" *American Business L. J.* 33.1 (1995): 1–50.

Barker, Evelyn M. "A Neo-Aristotelian Approach to Dialectical Reasoning." *Revue Internationale de Philosophie* 34 (1980): 482–89.

Bator, Paul G. "The 'Good Reasons Movement': A 'Confounding' of Dialectic and Rhetoric?" *Philosophy and Rhetoric* 21.1 (1988): 38–47.

Beedle, Cameron. Interview by Matt Lauer, *The Today Show,* NBC, 9 Dec. 1998. Transcript, 1998 WL 23219707 (Westlaw database).

Bell, Derrick. "Bell, J., dissenting." *What Brown v. Board of Education Should Have Said: The Nation's Top Legal Experts Rewrite America's Landmark Civil Rights Decision.* Ed. Jack M. Balkin. New York: New York Univ. Press, 2001. 185–200.

———. "Law, Litigation, and the Search for the Promised Land." *Georgetown L.J.* 76.1 (1987): 229–350.

———. "Serving Two Masters: Integration Ideals and Client Interests in School Desegregation." *Yale L.J.* 85.4 (1976): 470–516.

———. *Silent Covenants: Brown v. Board of Education and the Unfulfilled Hopes for Racial Reform.* Oxford: Oxford Univ. Press, 2004.

Berkowitz, Roger. "Friedrich Nietzsche, the Code of Manu, and the Art of Legislation." *Cardozo L. Rev.* 24.3 (Mar. 2003): 1131–49.

Berman, Harold J. Introduction. *Justice, Law, and Argument: Essays on Moral and Legal Reasoning.* By Chaim Perelman. Dordrecht, Holland: D. Reidel Publishing Company, 1980. ix–xii.

Berti, Enrico. "Aristotle's Renaissance as an Example of the Essential Tension between Tradition and Innovation." *Philosophical Inquiry* 16.3–4 (1994): 26–37.

Billig, Michael. *Arguing and Thinking: A Rhetorical Approach to Social Psychology.* Cambridge: Cambridge Univ. Press, 1987.

———. "Psychology, Rhetoric and Cognition." In Roberts and Good, *The Recovery of Rhetoric: Persuasive Discourse and Disciplinarity in the Human Sciences.* 119–36.

Bineham, Jeffery L. "Displacing Descartes: Philosophical Hermeneutics and Rhetorical Studies." *Philosophy and Rhetoric* 27.4 (1994): 300–12.

———. "The Hermeneutic Medium." *Philosophy and Rhetoric* 28.1 (1995): 1–16.

Bodenheimer, Edgar. "Perelman's Contribution to Legal Methodology." *Northern Kentucky L. Rev.* 12.3 (1985): 392–417.

Brasier, Lori L. "Kevorkian's Choice of 'Suicide' Patients Raises Moral Concerns." *Toronto Star* 2 Sept. 1996: F4.

Brewer, Scott. "Exemplary Reasoning: Semantics, Pragmatics and the Rational Force of Legal Argument by Analogy." *Harvard L. Rev.* 109.5 (1996): 923–1028.

Burke, Richard J. "A Rhetorical Conception of Rationality." *Informal Logic* 6 (1984): 17–25.

Burns, Robert P. *A Theory of the Trial.* Princeton: Princeton Univ. Press, 1999.

Carbado, Devon W., and G. Mitu Gulati. "The Law and Economics of Critical Race Theory." *Yale L.J.* 112 (2004):1757–1828.

Cascardi, Anthony J. "The Place of Language in Philosophy; or, the Uses of Rhetoric." *Philosophy and Rhetoric* 16.4 (1983): 217–27.

Christie, George C. "The Universal Audience and Predictive Theories of Law." *Law and Philosophy* 5.3 (1986): 343–50.

Clark, Maudemarie. *Nietzsche on Truth and Philosophy.* Cambridge: Cambridge Univ. Press, 1990.

Cohen, Tom. "The 'Genealogies' of Pragmatism." In Mailloux, *Rhetoric, Sophistry, Pragmatism.* 94–108.

Coleman, Thomas J., Jr. "Disordered Liberty: Judicial Restrictions on the Rights to Privacy and Equality." *Thomas Marshall L. Rev.* 12 (Fall 1986): 81–108.

Conley, Thomas M. *Rhetoric in the European Tradition.* Chicago: Univ. of Chicago Press, 1990.

Corbin, Arthur L. "The Interpretation of Words and the Parol Evidence Rule." *Cornell L. Quarterly* 50.2 (1965): 161–90.

Cox, Christoph. *Nietzsche: Naturalism and Interpretation.* Berkeley: Univ. of California Press, 1999.

Crosswhite, James. "Universality in Rhetoric: Perelman's Universal Audience." *Philosophy and Rhetoric* 22.3 (1989): 157–73.

Crumm, Charles. "Jury Didn't Waver in Deciding Guilt." *Oakland Press* 27 Mar. 1999: A5.

Crusius, Timothy W. "A Case for Kenneth Burke's Dialectic and Rhetoric." *Philosophy and Rhetoric* 19.1 (1986): 23–37.

Dallmayr, Fred. "Self and Other: Gadamer and the Hermeneutics of Difference." *Yale J. of Law and the Humanities* 5.2 (1993): 507–29.

Dascal, Marcelo. "Hermeneutic Interpretation and Pragmatic Interpretation." *Philosophy and Rhetoric* 22.4 (1989): 239–59.

Davey, Nicholas. "Hermeneutic Passions: Gadamer versus Nietzsche on the Subjectivity of Interpretation." *International Journal of Philosophical Studies* 2.1 (1994): 45–60.

Dearin, Ray D. "Justice and Justification in the New Rhetoric." *Practical Reasoning in Human Affairs: Studies in Honor of Chaim Perelman.* Ed. James L. Golden and Joseph J. Pilotta. Dordrecht, Holland: D. Reidel Publishing Company, 1986. 155–85.

Depew, David. "The Inscription of Isocrates into Aristotle's Practical Philosophy." In Poulakos and Depew, *Isocrates and Civic Education.* 157–85.

Dillon, George L. *Contending Rhetorics: Writing in Academic Disciplines.* Bloomington: Indiana Univ. Press, 1991.

Dinan, Stephen, and Ralph Z. Hallow. "Conservatives Slam Split Race Rulings; Urge Bush to Pick Supreme Court Nominee with Care." *Washington Times* 25 June 2003: A1.

Dockhorn, Klaus. "Hans-Georg Gadamer's *Truth and Method.*" Trans. Marvin Brown. *Philosophy and Rhetoric* 13.3 (1980): 160–80.

Donaldson, Gail. Interview by Phil d'Aneri, *All Things Considered,* National Public Radio, 2 May 1994. Transcript, 1994 WL 8679950 (Westlaw database).

"Dr. Death Beats Rap Again." *National L. J.* 27 May 1996: A8.

Dworkin, Ronald M. *Law's Empire.* Cambridge, Mass.: Belknap Press, 1986.

Dzwonkowski, Ron, ed. *The Suicide Machine.* Detroit, Detroit Free Press, 1997.

Eden, Kathy. *Hermeneutics and the Rhetorical Tradition: Chapters in the Ancient Legacy and Its Humanist Reception.* New Haven: Yale Univ. Press, 1997.

Eemeren, F. H. van, et al. *Fundamentals of Argumentation Theory: A Handbook of Historical Backgrounds and Contemporary Developments.* Mahwah: L. Erlbaum, 1996.

Engram, Sara. "Coping/Mortal Matters." *Baltimore Evening Sun* 3 Aug. 1992: B8.

Ewick, Patricia, and Susan S. Silbey. "Subversive Stories and Hegemonic Tales: Toward a Sociology of Narrative." *Law and Society Review* 29.2 (1995): 197–226.

Fairfield, Paul. "Truth without Methodologism: Gadamer and James." *American Catholic Philosophic Quarterly* 67.3 (1993): 285–98.

Farrell, Thomas B. *Norms of Rhetorical Culture.* New Haven: Yale Univ. Press, 1993.

Feinman, Jay M. "The Development of the Employment at Will Rule." *American J. of Legal History* 20 (1976): 118–35.

Fish, Stanley Eugene. *Doing What Comes Naturally: Change, Rhetoric, and the Practice of Theory in Literary and Legal Studies.* Durham: Duke Univ. Press, 1989.

———. "Play of Surfaces: Theory and the Law." *Legal Hermeneutics: History, Theory, and Practice.* Ed. Gregory Leyh. Berkeley: Univ. of California Press, 1992. 297–316.

Fisher, Roger, William Ury, and Bruce Patton. *Getting to Yes: Negotiating Agreement without Giving In.* 2d ed. New York: Penguin Books, 1991.

Frug, Jerry. "Argument as Character." *Stanford L. Rev.* 40.4 (1988): 869–927.

Fuller, Lon L., and William R. Perdue Jr. "The Reliance Interest in Contract Damages." *Yale L. J.* 46 (1936): 52, 373 (parts 1 and 2).

Gadamer, Hans-Georg. "Aesthetics and Hermeneutics." *Philosophical Apprenticeships.* Trans. Robert R. Sullivan. Berkeley: Univ. of California Press, 1976. 95–104.

———. *The Beginning of Knowledge.* Trans. Rod Coltman. New York: Continuum, 2001.

———. *The Beginning of Philosophy.* Trans. Rod Coltman. New York: Continuum, 1998.

———. "Culture and Media." *Cultural-Political Interventions in the Unfinished Project of Enlightenment.* Ed. Axel Honneth et al. Trans. Barbara Fultner. Cambridge, Mass.: MIT Press, 1992. 171–88.

———. *Dialogue and Dialectic: Eight Hermeneutical Studies on Plato.* Trans. P. Christopher Smith. New Haven: Yale Univ. Press, 1980.

———. "The Diversity of Europe: Inheritance and Future." In Gadamer, *Hans-Georg Gadamer on Education, Poetry, and History: Applied Hermeneutics.* 221–36.

———. *The Enigma of Health: The Art of Healing in a Scientific Age.* Trans. Jason Gaiger and Nicholas Walker. Stanford: Stanford Univ. Press, 1996.

———. "The Expressive Power of Language." *Publications of the Modern Language Association of America* 107 (1992): 348–52.

———. *Gadamer in Conversation: Reflections and Commentary.* Trans. Carsten Dutt and Richard E. Palmer. Ed. Richard E. Palmer. New Haven: Yale Univ. Press, 2001.

———. *Hans-Georg Gadamer on Education, Poetry, and History: Applied Hermeneutics.* Ed. Dieter Misgeld and Graeme Nicholson. Trans. Lawrence Schmidt and Monica Reuss. Albany: State Univ. of New York Press, 1992.

———. "Heidegger as Rhetor: Hans-Georg Gadamer Interviewed by Ansgar Kemmann." Trans. Lawrence Kennedy Schmidt. Interviews conducted 1999–2001. *Heidegger and Rhetoric.* Ed. Daniel M. Gross and Ansgar Kemmann. Albany: State Univ. of New York Press, 2005. 47–64.

———. "Hermeneutics as Practical Philosophy." *Reason in the Age of Science.* By Gadamer. Trans. Frederick G. Lawrence. Cambridge, Mass.: MIT Press, 1981. 88–112.

———. "Hermeneutics as a Theoretical and Practical Task." *Reason in the Age of Science.* By Gadamer. Trans. Frederick G. Lawrence. Cambridge, Mass.: MIT Press, 1981. 113–38.

———. *Hermeneutics, Religion, and Ethics.* Trans. Joel Weinsheimer. New Haven: Yale Univ. Press, 1999.

———. *The Idea of the Good in Platonic-Aristotelian Philosophy.* Trans. P. Christopher Smith. New Haven: Yale Univ. Press, 1986.

———. Interview: "The German University and German Politics: The Case of Heidegger." In Gadamer, *Hans-Georg Gadamer on Education, Poetry, and History: Applied Hermeneutics.* 3–14.

———. Interview: "Writing and the Living Voice." In Gadamer, *Hans-Georg Gadamer on Education, Poetry, and History: Applied Hermeneutics.* 63–71.

———. "On the Scope and Function of Hermeneutical Reflection." Trans. G. B. Hess and R. E. Palmer. *Philosophical Hermeneutics.* Trans. and ed. David E. Linge. Berkeley: Univ. of California Press, 1976. 18–43.

———. "The Phenomenological Movement." Trans. G. B. Hess and R. E. Palmer. *Philosophical Hermeneutics.* Trans. and ed. David E. Linge. Berkeley: Univ. of California Press, 1976. 130–81.

———. "Praise of Theory." *Praise of Theory: Speeches and Essays.* Trans. Chris Dawson. New Haven: Yale Univ. Press, 1998. 16–36.

———. "Reflections on My Philosophical Journey." Trans. Richard E. Palmer. *The Philosophy of Hans-Georg Gadamer.* Ed. Lewis Edwin Hahn. Chicago: Open Court, 1997. 3–63.

———. "The Relevance of the Beautiful: Art as Play, Symbol, and Festival." *The Relevance of the Beautiful and Other Essays.* Trans. Nicholas Walker. Ed. Robert Bernasconi. Cambridge: Cambridge Univ. Press, 1986.

———. "Reply to Donald Phillip Verene." Trans. Matthias Lütkehermölle and Dennis J. Schmidt. *The Philosophy of Hans-Georg Gadamer.* Ed. Lewis Edwin Hahn. Chicago: Open Court, 1997. 154–55.

———. "Science and the Public Sphere." *Praise of Theory: Speeches and Essays.* Trans. Chris Dawson. New Haven: Yale Univ. Press, 1998. 62–70.

———. "The Science of the Life-World." *Philosophical Apprenticeships.* Trans. Robert R. Sullivan. Berkeley: Univ. of California Press, 1976. 182–97.

———. "Text and Interpretation." Trans. Dennis J. Schmidt and Richard Palmer. *Dialogue and Deconstruction: The Gadamer-Derrida Encounter.* Ed. Diane P. Michelfelder and Richard E. Palmer. Albany: State Univ. of New York Press, 1989. 21–51.

———. "To What Extent Does Language Preform Thought?" *Truth and Method* (Supplement II). Trans. Joel Weinsheimer and Donald G. Marshall. 2d rev. ed. New York: Crossroad, 1989. 542–49.

———. *Truth and Method.* Trans. Joel Weinsheimer and Donald G. Marshall. 2d rev. ed. New York: Crossroad, 1989.

———. "What Is Practice?: The Conditions of Social Reason." *Reason in the Age of Science.* By Gadamer. Trans. Frederick G. Lawrence. Cambridge, Mass.: MIT Press, 1981. 69–87.

Gagarin, Michael. *Antiphon the Athenian: Oratory, Law, and Justice in the Age of the Sophists.* Austin: Univ. of Texas Press, 2002.

Gallagher, Shaun. "The Place of Phronesis in Postmodern Hermeneutics." *Philosophy Today* (Fall 1993): 298–305.

Gaonkar, Dilip Parameshwar. "The Revival of Rhetoric, the New Rhetoric, and the Rhetorical Turn: Some Distinctions." *Informal Logic* 15.1 (1993): 53–64.

Garrett, Jan Edward. "Hans-Georg Gadamer on 'Fusion of Horizons.'" *Man and World* 11 (1978): 392–400.

Garver, Eugene. *Aristotle's Rhetoric: An Art of Character.* Chicago: Univ. of Chicago Press, 1994.

———. *For the Sake of Argument: Practical Reasoning, Character and the Ethics of Belief.* Chicago: Univ. of Chicago Press, 2004.

———. "Philosophy, Rhetoric, and Civic Education in Aristotle and Isocrates." In Poulakos and Depew, *Isocrates and Civic Education.* 186–213.

———. "Why Should Anybody Listen? The Rhetoric of Religious Argument in Democracy." *Wake Forest L. Rev.* 36 (Summer 2001): 353–99.

Gauthier, Dean. Interview by Matt Lauer, *The Today Show,* NBC, 9 Dec. 1998. Transcript, 1998 WL 23219707 (Westlaw database).

Geary, Adam. "African Nietzsche: Poetry, Philosophy and African Legal Thinking." *Cardozo L. Rev.* 24.3 (Mar. 2003): 903–23.

Goodrich, Peter. "Historical Aspects of Legal Interpretation." *Indiana L. J.* 61.3 (1986): 331–54.

———. "Jani Anglorum: Signs, Symptoms, Slips and Interpretation in Law." *Politics, Postmodernity and Critical Legal Studies: The Legality of the Contingent.* Ed. Costas Douzinas, Peter Goodrich, and Yifat Hachamovitch. London: Routledge, 1994. 105–44.

———. *Law in the Courts of Love: Literature and Other Minor Jurisprudences.* London: Routledge, 1996.

———. *Legal Discourse: Studies in Linguistics, Rhetoric, and Legal Analysis.* New York: St. Martin's Press, 1987.

———. *Oedipus Lex: Psychoanalysis, History, Law.* Berkeley: Univ. of California Press, 1995.

———. "The Role of Linguistics in Legal Analysis." *Modern L. Rev.* 47.5 (1984): 523–34.

Greenshaw, Leigh Hunt. "'To Say What the Law Is': Learning the Practice of Legal Rhetoric." *Valparaiso Univ. L. Rev.* 29 (1995): 861–96.

Grondin, Jean. "Hermeneutics and Relativism." Trans. Mildred Mortimer. *Festivals of Interpretation: Essays on Hans-Georg Gadamer's Work.* Ed. Kathleen Wright. Albany: State Univ. of New York Press, 1990. 42–62.

Grosse, W. Jack. "Chaim Perelman and the New Rhetoric." *Northern Kentucky L. Rev.* 12.3 (1985): vii–xv.

Gutmann, Amy. "Can Virtue Be Taught to Lawyers." *Stanford L. Rev.* 45.6 (1993): 1759–71.

Haarscher, Guy. "Perelman and Habermas." *Law and Philosophy* 5.3 (1986): 331–42.

Habermas, Jürgen. *The Philosophical Discourse of Modernity: Twelve Lectures.* Trans. Frederick G. Lawrence. Cambridge, Mass.: MIT Press, 1987.

———. "Postscript to *Between Facts and Norms.*" Trans. William Rehg. *Habermas, Modernity, and Law.* Ed. Mathieu Deflem. London: Sage Publications, 1996. 135–50.

Hales, Steven D., and Rex Welshon. *Nietzsche's Perspectivism.* Urbana: Univ. of Illinois Press, 2000.

Hart, H. L. A. *The Concept of Law.* 2d ed. Oxford: Oxford Univ. Press, 1994.

Haskins, Ekaterina V. *Logos and Power in Isocrates and Aristotle.* Columbia, S. C.: Univ. of South Carolina Press, 2004.

Heald, Paul J. "Economics as One of the Humanities." *Southern California Interdisciplinary L. J.* 4.2 (1995): 293–322.

Heim, Michael R. "Philosophy as Ultimate Rhetoric." *Southern J. of Philosophy* 19.2 (1981): 181–95.

Hermann, Donald H. J. "Legal Reasoning as Argumentation." *Northern Kentucky L. Rev.* 12.3 (1985): 467–510.

Huigens, Kyron. "Nietzsche and Aretaic Legal Theory." *Cardozo L. Rev.* 24.2 (Jan. 2003): 563–86.

Hurt, Charles. "Abortion Foes Poised for Court Vacancy; Seek to Avoid 'Another David Souter.'" *Washington Times* 26 June 2003: A7.

Hyde, Michael J., and Craig R. Smith. "Hermeneutics and Rhetoric: A Seen but Unobserved Relationship." *Quarterly J. of Speech* 65.4 (1979): 347–63.

Ingram, David. "The Possibility of a Communication Ethic Reconsidered: Habermas, Gadamer, and Bourdieu on Discourse." *Man and World* 15.2 (1982): 149–61.

Jacob, Bernard E. "Ancient Rhetoric, Modern Legal Thought, and Politics: A Review Essay on the Translation of Viehweg's 'Topics and Law.'" *Northwestern Univ. L. Rev.* 89.4 (1995): 1622–77.

Jacobson, Sherry. "Kevorkian Methods Face New Attacks: Massachusetts Woman's Suicide Refuels Public Doubts about Discretion." *Dallas Morning News* 25 Aug. 1996: A1.

Jarratt, Susan C. "In Excess: Radical Extensions of Neopragmatism." In Mailloux, *Rhetoric, Sophistry, Pragmatism.* 206–27.

Jost, Walter, and Michael J. Hyde, eds. *Rhetoric and Hermeneutics in Our Time: A Reader.* New Haven: Yale Univ. Press, 1997.

Joy, Morny. "Rhetoric and Hermeneutics." *Philosophy Today* 32 (1988): 273–85.

Kennedy, Duncan. "Freedom and Constraint in Adjudication: A Critical Phenomenology." *J. of Legal Education* 36.4 (1986): 518–62.

Kennedy, George A. Introduction. *On Rhetoric.* By Aristotle. Oxford: Oxford Univ. Press, 1991. 3–22.

Kenny, Robert Wade. "The Rhetoric of Kevorkian's Battle." *Quarterly J. of Speech* 86.4 (Nov. 2000): 386.

"Kevorkian Encountering Fewer Hurdles in Suicides." *New York Times* 17 Oct. 1997: A26.

"Kevorkian May Have Tried to Sidestep Law." *Seattle Times* 17 May 1993: A5.

King, Andrew. "The Rhetorical Critic and the Invisible Polis." *Rhetorical Hermeneutics: Invention and Interpretation in the Age of Science.* Ed. Alan G. Gross and William M. Keith. Albany: State Univ. of New York Press, 1997. 299–314.

Klein, Wayne. *Nietzsche and the Promise of Philosophy.* Albany: State Univ. of New York Press, 1997.

Klemm, David E. "Gorgias, Law, and Rhetoric." *Iowa L. Rev.* 74.4 (1989): 819–26.

Kluback, William. "The Implications of Rhetorical Philosophy." *Law and Philosophy* 5.3 (1986): 315–29.

Kögler, Hans Herbert. *The Power of Dialogue: Critical Hermeneutics after Gadamer and Foucault.* Trans. Paul Hendrickson. Cambridge, Mass.: MIT Press, 1996.

Krajewski, Bruce. *Traveling with Hermes: Hermeneutics and Rhetoric.* Amherst: Univ. of Massachusetts Press, 1992.

Kuhn, Thomas S. *The Structure of Scientific Revolutions.* 2d enlarged ed. Chicago: Univ. of Chicago Press, 1970.

LaRue, Lewis H. *Constitutional Law as Fiction: Narrative in the Rhetoric of Authority.* University Park: Pennsylvania State Univ. Press, 1995.

Lessenberry, Jack. "Death Becomes Him." *Vanity Fair* July 1994.

Levit, Nancy. "Practically Unreasonable: A Critique of Practical Reason." *Northwestern Univ. L. Rev.* 85.2 (1991): 494–518.

Lipkin, David, M.D. "A Troubling Death." *Chicago Tribune* 7 Sept. 1996: 23.

Llewellyn, Karl. "On Our Case-Law of Contract: Offer and Acceptance." *Yale L. J.* 40.48 (1938): 1–36.

———. "On Philosophy in American Law." *Univ. of Pennsylvania L. Rev.* 82.3 (1934): 205–12.

Loven, Jennifer. "Kevorkian Jurors Describe Prayers, Tears." The Associated Press. 2 May 1994. 1994 WL 10141733 (Westlaw database).

Madison, G. B. *The Hermeneutics of Postmodernity: Figures and Themes.* Bloomington: Indiana Univ. Press, 1988.

Mailloux, Steven. Introduction: "Sophistry and Rhetorical Pragmatism." In Mailloux, *Rhetoric, Sophistry, Pragmatism.* 1–31.

———. *Rhetorical Power.* Ithaca: Cornell Univ. Press, 1989.

———, ed. *Rhetoric, Sophistry, Pragmatism,* Cambridge: Cambridge Univ. Press, 1995.

Maneli, Mieczyslaw. *Perelman's New Rhetoric as Philosophy and Methodology for the Next Century.* Dordrecht, Holland: Kluwer, 1994.

Mansfield, Cathy Lesser. "Deconstructive Reconstructive Poverty Law: Practice-Based Critique of the Storytelling Aspects of the Theoretics of Practice Movement." *Brooklyn L. Rev.* 61.3 (1995): 889–929.

Margolis, Joseph. "Philosophy in the 'New' Rhetoric, Rhetoric in the 'New' Philosophy." In Mailloux, *Rhetoric, Sophistry, Pragmatism.* 109–38.

Marker, Rita, and Kathi Hamlon. "Prisoner Number 284797." *Human Life Review* 25.3 (1999).

McBride, William L. "Professor Perelman and Authority." *Northern Kentucky L. Rev.* 12.3 (1985): 511–18.

McCloskey, Deirdre N. *If You're So Smart: The Narrative of Economic Expertise.* Chicago: Univ. of Chicago Press, 1990.

———. *The Rhetoric of Economics.* 2d ed. Madison: Univ. of Wisconsin Press, 1998.

McCloskey, Donald N. "The Rhetoric of Economic Expertise." In Roberts and Good, *The Recovery of Rhetoric: Persuasive Discourse and Disciplinarity in the Human Sciences.* 137–47.

McGee, Michael. "The 'Ideograph': A Link between Rhetoric and Ideology." *Quarterly J. of Speech* 66.1 (1980): 1–16.

McKerrow, Raymie E. "Critical Rhetoric and the Possibility of the Subject." *The Critical Turn: Rhetoric and Philosophy in Postmodern Discourse.* Ed. Ian Angus and Lenore Langsdorf. Carbondale: Southern Illinois Univ. Press, 1993. 51–67.

Meyer, Michel. *Rhetoric, Language, and Reason.* University Park: Pennsylvania State Univ. Press, 1994.

Mootz III, Francis J. "Desperately Seeking Science." *Washington Univ. L. Quarterly.* 73.3 (1995): 1009–23.

———. "A Future Foretold: Neo-Aristotelian Praise of Postmodern Legal Theory." *Brooklyn L. Rev.* 68.3 (2003): 683–719.

———. "Is the Rule of Law Possible in a Postmodern World?" *Washington L. Rev.* 68.2 (1993): 249–305.

———. "Law in Flux: Philosophical Hermeneutics, Legal Argumentation, and the Natural Law Tradition." *Yale J. of Law and the Humanities* 11.2 (1999): 311–82.

———. "Legal Classics: After Deconstructing the Legal Canon." *North Carolina L. Rev.* 72.4 (1994): 977–1038.

———. "The New Legal Hermeneutics." *Vanderbilt L. Rev.* 47.1 (1994): 115–43.

———. "Nietzschean Critique and Philosophical Hermeneutics." *Cardozo L. Rev.* 24.3 (2003): 967–1042.

———. "The Ontological Basis of Legal Hermeneutics: A Proposed Model of Inquiry Based on the Work of Gadamer, Habermas, and Ricoeur." *Boston Univ. L. Rev.* 68.3 (1988): 523–617.

———. "Postmodern Constitutionalism as Materialism." *Michigan L. Rev.* 91.3 (1992): 515–25.

———. "Psychotherapeutic Practice as a Model for Postmodern Legal Theory." *Yale J. of Law and the Humanities* 12.2 (2000): 299–395.

———. "The Quest to Reprogram Cultural Software: A Hermeneutical Response to Jack Balkin's Theory of Ideology and Critique." *Chicago-Kent L. Rev.* 76.2 (2000): 945–89.

———. "Rethinking the Rule of Law: A Demonstration That the Obvious Is Plausible." *Tennessee L. Rev.* 61.1 (1993): 69–195.

———. "Rhetorical Knowledge in Legal Practice and Theory." *Southern California Interdisciplinary L. J.* 6.3 (1998): 491–610.

Neel, Jasper. "The Degradation of Rhetoric; or, Dressing Like a Gentleman, Speaking Like a Scholar." In Mailloux, *Rhetoric, Sophistry, Pragmatism.* 61–81.

Nietzsche, Friedrich Wilhelm. "The Antichrist." *The Portable Nietzsche.* Ed. and trans. Walter Kaufmann. New York: Viking Press, 1954. 565–656.

———. *Beyond Good and Evil.* Trans. Walter Kaufmann. New York: Random House, 1966.

———. *Ecce Homo: How One Becomes What One Is.* Trans. R. J. Hollingdale. New York: Penguin Books, 1992.

———. *Friedrich Nietzsche on Rhetoric and Language.* Ed. and trans. Sander L. Gilman, Carole Blair, and David J. Parent. Oxford: Oxford Univ. Press, 1989.

———. *The Gay Science.* Trans. Walter Kaufmann. New York: Random House, 1974.

———. *On the Genealogy of Morals: A Polemic.* Trans. Douglas Smith. Oxford: Oxford Univ. Press, 1996.

———. "Twilight of the Idols." *The Portable Nietzsche.* Ed. and trans. Walter Kaufmann. New York: Viking Press, 1954. 463–563.

Orentlicher, David. "Learning Lessons of Life and Death from Kevorkian." *Chicago Tribune* 21 May 1996: A17.

Pavcnik, Marijan. "Legal Decisionmaking as a Responsible Intellectual Activity: A Continental Point of View." *Washington L. Rev.* 72.2 (1997): 481–504.

Perelman, Chaim. *Justice, Law, and Argument: Essays on Moral and Legal Reasoning.* Trans. William Kluback et al. Dordrecht, Holland: D. Reidel Publishing Company, 1980.

———. *The New Rhetoric and the Humanities: Essays on Rhetoric and Its Applications.* Trans. William Kluback et al. Dordrecht, Holland: D. Reidel Publishing Company, 1979.

———. "The New Rhetoric and the Rhetoricians: Remembrances and Comments." *Quarterly J. of Speech* 70.2 (1984): 191–96.

Perelman, Chaim, and Lucie Olbrechts-Tyteca. *The New Rhetoric: A Treatise on Argumentation.* Trans. John Wilkinson and Purcell Weaver. Notre Dame: Univ. of Notre Dame Press, 1969.

Posner, Richard A. *Overcoming Law.* Cambridge, Mass.: Harvard Univ. Press, 1995.

Poulakos, John. *Sophistical Rhetoric in Classical Greece.* Columbia: Univ. of South Carolina Press, 1995.

Poulakos, Takis. "Isocrates' Civic Education and the Question of *Doxa.*" In Poulakos and Depew, *Isocrates and Civic Education.* 44–65.

Poulakos, Takis, and David Depew, eds. *Isocrates and Civic Education.* Austin: Univ. of Texas Press, 2004.

Ramsey, Ramsey Eric. "Listening to Heidegger on Rhetoric." *Philosophy and Rhetoric* 26.4 (1993): 266–76.

Rickman, H. P. "Rhetoric and Hermeneutics." *Philosophy and Rhetoric* 14.2 (1981): 100–11.

Roberts, Richard H., and J. M. M. Good. Introduction: "Persuasive Discourse in and between Disciplines in the Human Sciences." In Roberts and Good, *The Recovery of Rhetoric: Persuasive Discourse and Disciplinarity in the Human Sciences.* 1–21.

———, eds. *The Recovery of Rhetoric: Persuasive Discourse and Disciplinarity in the Human Sciences.* Charlottesville: Univ. Press of Virginia, 1993.

Rubin, Edward L. "The New Legal Process, the Synthesis of Discourse, and the Microanalysis of Institutions." *Harvard L. Rev.* 109 (1996): 1393–1438.

Sandmann, Warren. "The Argumentative Creation of Individual Liberty." *Hastings Constitutional L. Quarterly* 23 (1996): 637–57.

Scallen, Eileen. "Classical Rhetoric, Practical Reasoning, and the Law of Evidence." *American Univ. L. Rev.* 44 (1995):1717–1816.

———. "Evidence Law as Pragmatic Legal Rhetoric: Reconnecting Legal Scholarship, Teaching and Ethics." *Quinnipiac L. Rev.* 21.4 (2003): 813–91.

Schaeffer, John D. *Sensus Communis: Vico, Rhetoric, and the Limits of Relativism.* Durham: Duke Univ. Press, 1990.

Schiappa, Edward. *Protagoras and Logos: A Study in Greek Philosophy and Rhetoric.* Columbia: Univ. of South Carolina Press, 1991.

Schrag, Calvin O. *Communicative Praxis and the Space of Subjectivity.* Bloomington: Indiana Univ. Press, 1986.

———. *The Resources of Rationality: A Response to the Postmodern Challenge.* Bloomington: Indiana Univ. Press, 1992.

Schütz, Anton. "Nietzsche between Jews and Jurists: A Note on the Christian Filiation of *The Anti-Christ.*" *Cardozo L. Rev.* 24.2 (Jan. 2003): 497–534.

Scott, Robert L. "On Viewing Rhetoric as Epistemic: Ten Years Later." *Central States Speech J.* 27 (1977): 258–66.

Sherwin, Richard K. "Law's Beatitude: A Post-Nietzschean Account of Legitimacy." *Cardozo L. Rev.* 24.2 (Jan. 2003): 683–703.

Simons, Herbert W. Introduction: "The Rhetoric of Inquiry as an Intellectual Movement." *The Rhetorical Turn: Invention and Persuasion in the Conduct of Inquiry.* Ed. Herbert W. Simons. Chicago: Univ. of Chicago Press, 1990. 1–31.

———. Preface. *The Rhetorical Turn: Invention and Persuasion in the Conduct of Inquiry.* Ed. Herbert W. Simons. Chicago: Univ. of Chicago Press, 1990. vii–xii.

Snyder, Jon R. Translator's Introduction. *The End of Modernity: Nihilism and Hermeneutics in Postmodern Culture.* By Gianni Vattimo. Baltimore: Johns Hopkins Univ. Press, 1991. vi–lviii.

Stamatis, Costas M. "Justice without Law: A Postmodern Paradox." *Law and Critique* 5.2 (1994): 265–84.

Stegner, Wallace. *All the Little Live Things.* New York: Viking Press, 1967.

Stone, I. F. *The Trial of Socrates.* Boston: Little, Brown, 1988.

Swickard, Joe. "Fieger: Crusader Now Seeks Martyr's Robe." *Detroit Free Press* 25 Nov. 1998.

"Tape of Suicidal Man Brings Tears to Eyes of Kevorkian Jury." *Seattle Post-Intelligencer* 22 Apr. 1994: A3.

Taylor, George H. "Racism as 'The Nation's Crucial Sin': Theology and Derrick Bell." *Michigan J. of Race and Law* 9.3 (2004): 269–322.

Thomas, Douglas. *Reading Nietzsche Rhetorically.* New York: Guilford Press, 1999.

Tushnet, Mark V. *The NAACP's Legal Strategy against Segregated Education, 1925–1950.* Chapel Hill: Univ. of North Carolina Press, 1987.

Unger, Roberto M. "The Critical Legal Studies Movement." *Harvard L. Rev.* 96.3 (1984): 561–675.

Valauri, John T. "Confused Notions and Constitutional Theory." *Northern Kentucky L. Rev.* 12.3 (1985): 567–93.

Vattimo, Gianni. *After Christianity.* Trans. Luca D'Isanto. New York: Columbia Univ. Press, 2002.

———. *Belief.* Trans. Luca D'Isanto and David Webb. Cambridge: Polity Press, 1999.

———. *Beyond Interpretation: The Meaning of Hermeneutics for Philosophy.* Trans. David Webb. Cambridge: Polity Press, 1997.

———. *The End of Modernity: Nihilism and Hermeneutics in Postmodern Culture.* Trans. Jon R. Snyder. Baltimore: Johns Hopkins Univ. Press, 1991.

———. *Nietzsche: An Introduction.* Trans. Nicholas Martin. London: Athlone, 2002.

———. "Philosophy, Metaphysics, Democracy." Trans. Paul Kottman. *Qui Parle* 10.2 (1997): 1–9.

———. "The Trace of the Trace." *Religion.* Ed. Jacques Derrida and Gianni Vattimo. Stanford: Stanford Univ. Press, 1998. 79–94.

———. *The Transparent Society.* Trans. David Webb. Baltimore: Johns Hopkins Univ. Press, 1992.

Verene, Donald Phillip. "Gadamer and Vico on *Sensus Communis* and the Tradition of Humane Knowledge." *The Philosophy of Hans-Georg Gadamer.* Ed. Lewis Edwin Hahn. Chicago: Open Court, 1997. 137–53.

Walsh, Edward. "Jury Acquits Kevorkian in Two Suicides." *Washington Post* 9 Mar. 1996: A1.

Walton, Douglas N. *Argumentation Schemes for Presumptive Reasoning.* Mahwah, N.J.: L. Erlbaum Associates, 1996.

Wangerin, Paul. "A Multidisciplinary Analysis of the Structure of Persuasive Arguments." *Harvard J. of Law and Public Policy* 16.1 (1993): 195–239.

Warnke, Georgia. *Gadamer: Hermeneutics, Tradition and Reason.* Stanford: Stanford Univ. Press, 1987.

———. *Justice and Interpretation.* Cambridge, Mass.: MIT Press, 1992.

Weinreb, Lloyd L. "The Case for Natural Law Reexamined—1993." *American J. of Jurisprudence* 38 (1993): 1–13.

———. "The Moral Point of View." *Natural Law, Liberalism, and Morality: Contemporary Essays.* Ed. Robert P. George. Oxford: Clarendon Press, 1996. 195–212.

———. *Natural Law and Justice.* Cambridge, Mass.: Harvard Univ. Press, 1987.

———. "Natural Law and Rights." *Natural Law Theory: Contemporary Essays.* Ed. Robert P. George. Oxford: Clarendon Press, 1992. 278–305.

———. *Oedipus at Fenway Park: What Rights Are and Why There Are Any.* Cambridge, Mass.: Harvard Univ. Press, 1994.

Weisberg, Richard H. "Nietzsche's Hermeneutics: Good and Bad Interpreters of Texts." *Property Law in Renaissance Literature.* Ed. Daniela Carpi. Frankfurt am Main: Peter Lang, 2005. 3–4.

Wetlaufer, Gerald B. "Rhetoric and Its Denial in Legal Discourse." *Virginia L. Rev.* 76.8 (1990): 1545–97.

White, Lucie E. "Subordination, Rhetorical Survival Skills, and Sunday Shoes: Notes on the Hearing of Mrs. G." *Buffalo L. Rev.* 38.1 (1990): 1–58.

Witteveen, Willem J. "After Rhetoric and before the Law." *Dutch J. for Legal Philosophy and Legal Theory (R&R)* 23.3 (1994): 208–20.

Yovel, Jonathan. "Gay Science as Law: An Outline for a Nietzschean Jurisprudence." *Cardozo L. Rev.* 24.2 (2003): 635–62.

Zoeller, Guenter. "Is the Life in the Law Worth Living?: Some Critical Remarks on Plato's *Gorgias.*" *Iowa L. Rev.* 74.4 (1989): 815–17.

Legal Materials

Cases

Bleidner v. Searles, 19 Conn. App. 76 (1989).

Bowers v. Hardwick, 478 U.S. 186 (1986).

Boy Scouts of America v. Dale, 530 U.S. 640 (2000).

Callins v. Collins, 510 U.S. 1141 (1994).

Compassion in Dying v. State of Washington, 79 F.3d 790 (en banc 9th Cir. 1996).

Cruzan v. Director, Mo. Dept. of Health, 497 U.S. 261 (1990).

Gratz v. Bollinger, 123 S. Ct. 2411 (2003).

Grutter v. Bollinger, 123 S. Ct. 2325 (2003).

Hopwood v. Texas, 78 F.3d 932 (5th Cir. 1996).

Hurley v. Irish-American Gay, Lesbian and Bisexual Group of Boston, 515 U.S. 557 (1995).

Kevorkian v. American Medical Ass'n, 602 N.W.2d 233 (Mich. App. 1999).

Kevorkian v. Thompson, 947 F. Supp. 1152 (E.D. Mich. 1997).

Lawrence v. Texas, 123 S. Ct. 2472 (2003).

Michael H. v. Gerald D., 491 U.S. 110 (1989).
People v. Kevorkian, 517 N.W.2d 293 (Mich. App. 1994).
People v. Kevorkian, 527 N.W.2d 714 (Mich. 1994).
People v. Kevorkian, 534 N.W.2d 172 (Mich. App. 1995).
People v. Kevorkian, 639 N.W.2d 291 (Mich. App. 2001).
Quill v. Vacco, 80 F.3d 716 (2d Cir. 1996), rev'd. by *Vacco v. Quill,* 521 U.S. 793 (1997).
Regents of Univ. of Cal. v. Bakke, 438 U.S. 265 (1978).
Romer v. Evans, 517 U.S. 620 (1996).
Smith v. University of Washington, Law School, 233 F.3d 1188 (9th Cir. 2000).
U.S. v. Shonubi, 895 F. Supp. 460 (E.D.N.Y. 1995), vacated by *U.S. v. Shonubi,* 103 F.3d 1085 (2d Cir. 1997).
U.S. v. Virginia, 518 U.S. 515 (1996).
Vacco v. Quill, 521 U.S. 793 (1997).
Washington v. Glucksberg, 521 U.S. 702 (1997).

Statutes

Cal. Fam. Code §§ 7540, 7541 (West 1994).
Conn. Gen. Stat. § 46b-172(b) (Supp. 1998).

Other Materials

Consolidated Brief of Lt. Gen. Julius W. Becton Jr., et al., as Amici Curiae in Support of Respondents (filed 21 Feb. 2003; available on Westlaw database at 2003 WL 1787554).

Index